PRAISE FOR THE WHERE THE HEART LIVES SERIES

"A wonderful, 19th-century-Idaho spin on the story of the prodigal son, *Beloved* has everything a great novel needs: genuine conflict, heartfelt emotion, characters you'll love rooting for, surprising twists and turns, and a breathless pace that will keep you reading late into the night. Above all, a powerful message of redemption rings through each chapter. You will love *Beloved*!"

—Liz Curtis Higgs, *New York Times*
best-selling author of *Mine Is the Night*

"Hatcher is a consistent 'must read' author. Her books are always engaging, and *Betrayal* is no different . . . You'll feel a warm, satisfying glow after turning the final page of this touching novel."

—*Romantic Times*, TOP PICK! 4½ stars

"Tender, evocative, and beautifully written, *Belonging* is a journey about love after loss, and about two hearts destined to become one—despite their stubbornness! *Belonging* is Robin Lee Hatcher at her best!"

—Tamera Alexander, best-selling author of
Within My Heart and *The Inheritance*

"Featuring an eye for detail and a strong female heroine, this wholesome romance marks a good start to this new inspirational historical series . . ."

—*Library Journal* starred review of *Belonging*

"Robin Lee Hatcher has created a memorable historic romance . . . she weaves in just enough historic fact and setting to transport the reader to the time and place without getting in the way of the story."

—*Idaho Senior Independent* review of *Belonging*

beloved

ALSO BY ROBIN LEE HATCHER

WHERE THE HEART LIVES SERIES

Belonging
Betrayal
Beloved

THE SISTERS OF BETHLEHEM SPRINGS SERIES

A Vote of Confidence
Fit to Be Tied
A Matter of Character

THE COMING TO AMERICA SERIES

Dear Lady
Patterns of Love
In His Arms
Promised to Me

OTHER BOOKS

A novella in *A Bride for All Seasons*
Heart of Gold
When Love Blooms
A Carol for Christmas
Return to Me
Loving Libby
Wagered Heart
The Perfect Life
Home to Hart's Crossing
The Victory Club
Beyond the Shadows
Catching Katie
The Forgiving Hour
Whispers from Yesterday
The Shepherd's Voice
Ribbon of Years
Firstborn

Robin Lee HATCHER

beloved

WHERE THE HEART LIVES

ZONDERVAN®

ZONDERVAN.com/
AUTHORTRACKER
follow your favorite authors

We want to hear from you. Please send your comments about this book to us in care of zreview@zondervan.com. Thank you.

ZONDERVAN

Beloved
Copyright © 2013 by Robin Lee Hatcher

This title is also available as a Zondervan ebook. Visit www.zondervan.com/ebooks.

This title is also available in a Zondervan audio edition. Visit www.zondervan.fm.

Requests for information should be addressed to:

Zondervan, Grand Rapids, Michigan 49530

Library of Congress Cataloging-in-Publication Data

Hatcher, Robin Lee.
    Beloved / Robin Lee Hatcher.
        p. cm. -- (Where the heart lives ; 3)
    ISBN 978-0-310-25777-6
    I. Title.
PS3558.A73574B45 2013
813'.54—dc23   201300827

Interior design: Walter Petrie

Printed in the United States of America

---

13 14 15 16 17 18 /QVS/ 20 19 18 17 16 15 14 13 12 11 10 9 8 7 6 5 4 3 2 1

Beloved, if God so loved us, we also ought to love one another.

1 John 4:11 NASB

PROLOGUE

Spring 1881

A lump formed in Diana Brennan's throat and tears pooled in her eyes. She missed her ma. She missed their tenement flat in Chicago. She missed Hugh. She missed her da, though she couldn't remember much about him. Not even what he looked like. She wanted things to be like they used to be. She wanted to go home. She didn't like it here.

Diana—at six years old the youngest of the children on the stage of the grange hall—sat in a chair, her feet dangling a good ten inches off the floor. The large room was full of adults, milling about and talking to one another. Fear made her cold. It didn't matter that similar scenes had played out in recent days as the children from Dr. Cray's Asylum for Little Wanderers traveled west, looking for people who were willing to take them in and give them new homes. She was still afraid.

Her older sister, Felicia, leaned toward Diana. "It's okay, Di. I'm right here. Nothing bad's gonna happen."

Diana wanted to believe Felicia, but she couldn't. Not anymore. Not since their big brother, Hugh, had been taken off the

1

train without them. Deep down inside, she knew nobody was going to take two girls home with them. Little as she was, she knew it was true.

"Hello, there." A man with a beard stopped in front of her chair and leaned down so he could look straight into her eyes. "What's your name, child?"

She blinked back the tears.

"Her name's Diana," Felicia answered for her. "She's six. I'm her sister, Felicia. I'm ten."

"Hello, Diana." The man had a nice smile. "A pleasure to meet you, Felicia. My name is Mr. Fisher."

Diana nodded, still unable to make herself talk.

He motioned with his right hand, and a woman joined him. "This is my wife. Gloria, this is Diana. She's six."

Mrs. Fisher had a nice smile too. "It's a pleasure to meet you, Diana. My, but you have beautiful hair."

"Thank you," Diana whispered at last, remembering her manners. She wanted to add that her red hair was just like her ma's, but the thought made her want to cry again.

"What do you think, my dear?" Mr. Fisher asked his wife.

"Yes, darling," she answered. "Oh, yes."

ONE

May 1900

To say the least, it was inconsiderate of Diana's almost-dead husband to show up at her engagement party.

Conversations around the dinner table in the Calhoun dining room fell silent as guests began to notice the tall, dashing stranger standing in the doorway, his gaze fixed on Diana Applegate. He wore formal evening attire, as if he too had been invited to the festivities. But this was no guest.

Brook Calhoun, Diana's soon-to-be fiancé, leaned toward her. "Who is he? Do you know him?"

"Yes," she answered, disbelieving the word as it came out of her mouth. "It's Tyson."

"Tyson . . . *Applegate?*"

"Yes."

"Great Scott!"

Tyson smiled at her from across the room, but there was nothing friendly about the expression. An odd humming started in Diana's ears, and she felt as though she was observing the moment

3

from a distance. Was any of it real? Was *he* real? This couldn't be happening. It couldn't be.

Get up. Get up and go talk to him. Make him leave. Get him out of sight. But her body refused to obey her mind's demands. *Do something. You must do something. Now. Now!*

She heard the ticking of the clock on the mantle, even though time itself seemed to stand still. Someone cleared his throat. Ice tinkled against crystal. A chair leg scraped the hardwood floor. Then something in Tyson's gaze told Diana he was tired of waiting for her to go to him. He was about to come to her. This at last spurred her to action.

To Brook she whispered, "I'll speak with him." She pushed back her chair from the table and, as she rose, said to their guests, "Please, everyone. Go on with your dinner. I won't be but a moment." Somehow she managed to sound normal, unconcerned. What a lie!

She hurried toward the entrance, avoiding eye contact with her mother. Her heart raced and skipped, and her thoughts scattered in a hundred directions at once.

"It's good to see you, Diana," Tyson said when she reached him.

She felt everyone's gazes on her back. Watching her. Watching the two of them. They were wondering who he was, how she knew him, what business he had with her. A chill shuddered through her.

"We need to talk," he added in a low voice.

This was no mirage. He was real. She felt his body heat upon the skin of her arms.

"Not here. Co—" Her voice broke. "Come into the library." She moved past Tyson and hurried down the hallway, trusting he would follow her to the room at the far end.

He did—and closed the door.

Moving across the room, Diana stared into the fireplace, still unable to calm the tangle of her thoughts. How could this be happening? Tyson Applegate was supposed to be dead. Missing on the battlefields of Cuba, his body never found. The court was scheduled to declare his death a fact tomorrow morning. But now, on the eve of her expected freedom from the husband who'd abandoned her, he'd returned.

Very much alive.

Not injured. Not frail. Not sickly.

She turned around. "You . . . you're supposed to be dead." The words came out a whisper—and she hated herself for sounding weak.

"I know. Sorry to disappoint you." Tyson gave his head a slow shake, and his expression seemed to say he regretted his flippancy. "When I learned that you were about to publicly announce your engagement to Mr. Calhoun, I realized it was important that I stop you."

The words didn't quite make sense to her. They should but they didn't. She turned her back to him again and covered her face with her hands. This was a nightmare. Surely it was a nightmare and she would wake up at any moment to find Tyson Applegate gone once more. Dead, the way everyone—including her and his father—had thought of him for the past two years.

"You deserve an explanation, Diana, but perhaps here and now isn't the time or place for it. I imagine you and Mr. Calhoun will have a few things to talk over."

A few things to talk over. She wanted to laugh at the understatement.

"Diana." Tyson's voice was low and near. Too near. "I'm sorry. I don't mean to be unkind. This wasn't the best way for you to find out that I'm still among the living. But when I learned the reason for this dinner party, I felt I had no choice but to come at once."

If he touched her, she wasn't sure what she would do. Scream. Cry. Faint. Perhaps all three.

"Here, Diana. This is where you'll find me."

She looked over her shoulder. He held a calling card for her to take.

"Please come and see me in the morning. There is much we must sort out."

Another understatement. She took the card.

"Until tomorrow." He turned and left the library.

Suddenly weak in the knees, Diana sank onto the nearby sofa. The shaking started deep within and worked its way out to her fingertips and toes. She hugged herself lest she shatter.

Tyson was alive. He was alive and he'd returned. But for what purpose? To save himself from embarrassment. It certainly couldn't be because he wanted her. He'd never wanted her.

"Never," she whispered to the empty room.

The door to the library opened again. This time it was Brook who entered. Wordlessly he sat beside her, but he didn't touch her. Didn't put a hand in the small of her back or an arm around her shoulders. Didn't offer any sort of comfort. Just sat there in stiff silence.

It was a few moments before she had the strength to look at him. "Brook, I . . . I thought he was dead. His father thought he was dead. All this time without a word from him."

"What did he say to you?"

She drew in a shaky breath. "He wants me to see him in the morning." She held up the calling card. "At this address."

"And?"

"He said there is much we must sort out."

"Ah."

That wasn't the response she wanted. She wanted him to hop to his feet and swear he would never let her go. She wanted him to promise to fight a duel rather than let her return to the man who had forsaken her so cruelly. Love might not have a place in her relationship with Brook, on either side, but there was a shared affection. They'd made plans for the future. Their future. She wanted him to demand that she divorce Tyson so they could marry. She wouldn't be the wealthy widow he'd proposed to, but everything else about her would be the same. Surely that would be enough.

She looked down at the card she held in her right hand. "I have no choice but to meet with him." *Say you'll go with me. Please, Brook. Say you want to go with me.*

"Yes, you must." He stood. "I think it best if I make your excuses to our guests. The less said now, the better. Don't you agree?"

"Yes," she whispered, fighting the lump rising in her throat.

A short while ago, she'd been seated at a table surrounded with well-wishing friends. But there would be no congratulations tonight. There would be no champagne toasts to Brook and his fiancée. Not now. Brook was ending their engagement before it officially began. What else could he do? She wasn't free to marry. Not him. Not any man. The only way she would be free was if she obtained a divorce. And few, if any, men of good society were willing to marry a divorcée.

That included Brook Calhoun.

"I am sorry, Diana. About . . . everything."

She continued to stare at the card in her hand. "I know."

"I envisioned this evening much differently."

Me too.

"Would you like me to send your mother to you?"

"Please." She drew in a ragged breath.

"Good night, Diana."

"Good night, Brook."

After the door closed, she covered her face with her hands and wept.

Tonight, Tyson Applegate had ruined her life for the second time.

Tyson leaned back in the carriage and closed his eyes, picturing Diana as she'd stood before him in a gown of shimmering gold. He hadn't expected that she would be even more beautiful now than she was on their wedding day. But she was. Stunningly beautiful with her pale, flawless skin and her fiery red hair and eyes the same green as the forests of deepest Africa.

Beautiful and hurt. Hurt by his actions.

Again.

He groaned, shame washing over him.

He'd used Diana Fisher abominably. That hadn't been his intention, of course. At first he'd simply been a young man attracted to a sweet, beautiful girl who adored him. But then his father had objected, had forbidden Tyson to ever see her again. She was a nobody. An orphan. Not the kind of girl suitable to become the wife of Jeremiah Applegate's only son. Not a proper wife for a future congressman or senator.

His father's disapproval had been what sealed their fates, his and Diana's.

Lord help him. The things he'd done out of defiance to his father. It was painful to remember. Remembering heaped guilt and mortification on his shoulders until the weight threatened to break him.

He drew a deep breath and opened his eyes. He was a different man today than the spoiled, rebellious, angry one who'd left home and family years ago. He'd come back to Idaho to prove it—to his wife, to his father, to himself.

The carriage drew to a halt in front of the house Tyson had purchased, sight unseen, before coming to Boise. He'd hoped Diana would be willing to furnish it, to purchase those things they would need to set up not just housekeeping but entertaining. He'd hoped she would be willing to give him another chance to be a good husband to her. He'd hoped she would want to help him in the new life he'd planned for himself. Why hadn't it occurred to him that she would have moved on with hers? What had he expected?

The truth was until earlier this year he'd given little thought to the wife he'd left behind. And even when he had, he'd thought she would still be waiting for him. One more example of the selfish man he'd been—and could yet be if he wasn't careful.

He didn't wait for the driver to dismount and open the carriage door. No need for that. It wasn't as if he didn't know how to take care of himself. He'd had no valet, butler, or footman tending to him when he climbed mountains in Asia or went on safari in Africa or when he fought beneath the relentless sun in Cuba. In fact, he still had no valet, butler, or footman to wait on him. Not yet. But if all went as planned, within a week he should have a full staff hired for home, grounds, and stables.

He entered the house through the front door and made his way in the dark up to the largest of the six bedchambers on the second floor. Once there, he lit a lamp, then slipped off his suspenders and removed his necktie and stiff collar before sitting in a wing-backed chair near the cold fireplace. Though there was a chill in the spring night air, he didn't bother to set a fire.

Memories from his adventurous past, both good and not so good, paraded through his mind. Those weeks in Cuba with Roosevelt and his Rough Riders were among the latter kind.

Tyson had learned many things in war. He'd learned he was a good soldier. He could follow orders, ride fast, shoot straight, and get by on lousy grub and little sleep. He'd also come to believe that war wasn't the better answer, even if sometimes it was the necessary one. Now he wanted to use those lessons he'd learned for the benefit of others.

Which was why he, at last, had returned to Idaho.

Amusing, in an odd sort of way, that the very thing his father had wanted most for him was what he now sought for himself.

August 1885

As he had done many times for as far back as he could remember, Tyson stood before his father's massive desk in the library, awaiting the lecture he knew would come. He was eighteen. A man. But his father always made him feel like a small boy.

"We will *not* have this conversation again," his father said, cold steel in his words. "You *will* study the law. Knowledge of the law will give you an advantage when the time comes for you to run for public office."

Tyson had no intention of running for public office. He had no intention of living the life his father had planned for him since birth. But he didn't waste his breath saying so. Not again. Jeremiah Applegate didn't tolerate disobedience. Not from his wife. Not from his son. Not from his employees. Not from anyone. But the day would come when Tyson would tell him to—

"Go see your mother. She is waiting to tell you good-bye." His father looked down at some papers on his desk. "I'll expect good reports of your progress at Harvard."

The assumed reply stuck in his throat for several heartbeats before he managed to force the words out. "Yes, sir."

Someday . . .

TWO

Diana's mother set her coffee cup in the matching saucer and looked at her daughter seated opposite her. "I could accompany you, dear."

"No, Mother." Diana shook her head. "I think it's better that I see him alone."

"I don't like it. I don't like it at all."

Diana didn't like it either, but it couldn't be helped. She had to face Tyson. She had to know what he wanted. Why he had returned after so long.

"What will we do if he casts you aside?" her mother asked.

Would he cast her aside? She wanted to be free of Tyson. But divorce? Divorced and penniless. No way to provide for herself and her mother. Would he do that to her? She couldn't know. Despite the years they'd been married, he was a stranger to her.

She pushed away the plate with her half-eaten breakfast on it. "I'd best go." She rose. "I will return as soon as possible. Try not to worry."

Her mother wouldn't obey, of course. She would do nothing *but* worry until Diana was home again. Worrying had become second nature to Gloria Fisher since the death of her husband. Diana's adoptive father, Byron Fisher, hadn't meant to leave his wife financially insecure, though that was exactly what happened. At one time, the Fisher family had been well-to-do. But her father had invested heavily in stocks and when the market tumbled five years before his passing, he'd lost almost everything. Perhaps that had been the reason for his heart failure at the age of fifty-five.

Tyson Applegate, on the other hand, had seen the fortune he inherited from his maternal grandmother grow and grow. And if he'd been declared dead, that money would have come to Diana, his widow. With it she could have taken care of her mother, allowing them both to live in comfort for the rest of their lives. Without it—

She felt a sting of shame. She didn't truly wish Tyson dead. Not even for his money. Oh, there'd been many moments when she'd *thought* she wished him dead—perhaps death coming to him in some horrible fashion. Eaten by cannibals on the Dark Continent or tortured by pirates in the Indian Ocean.

Diana gave her head a slow shake. She didn't want to be the sort of person who wished such things on another human being. Not even on the husband who'd abandoned her. Which didn't mean she'd forgiven him. She hadn't. She couldn't.

She made her way out of the house and down to the corner of their quiet street, where she hailed a hansom cab. The journey from the modest neighborhood where she and her mother rented a small house to the affluent boulevard listed on Tyson's calling card was not a long one, but they seemed worlds apart. It surprised her a little, to find him living in such a place. It was much more his father's style than Tyson's.

He must have been watching for her arrival because he came to the street and personally opened the cab's door. When he held out his hand, she stared at it, not knowing what to do. Take it? Don't take it? Let him help her? Refuse to touch him? The air around her crackled with tension.

If Tyson knew the turmoil swirling inside of her, his expression didn't reveal it. He waited with apparent patience until Diana, at last, placed her hand in his. After helping her to the ground, he paid the driver. She was grateful for that, of course. Her circumstances had changed drastically from yesterday morning to this. Could she even afford the cab fare home? Much depended upon what Tyson had to say during the course of this meeting.

"Thank you for coming, Diana."

The hansom cab moved away from the curb.

What choice did you leave me? She pressed her lips together. Better to let him do the talking for now.

"Come inside." He motioned toward the front door.

She moved up the brick walk, Tyson following behind her. Feeling his gaze on her back was disconcerting, although she couldn't say why. Most men watched her. Most found her beautiful. But this was different. This was Tyson. This was the man who'd broken her heart and taught her to guard it well in the future.

Keep your wits about you, Diana. He mustn't get what he wants unless you get what you want. But what exactly was it she wanted? What kind of future remained for her?

Another surprise awaited her inside the house. It was nearly empty of furnishings. On her right no books or desk in the library and no table, chairs, or sideboards in the dining room. Only two upholstered chairs and a small, round table with a lamp on it in the spacious parlor to her left. Her footsteps echoed off the bare hardwood floors, making the house seem cold and unwelcoming.

"Whose house is this?" she asked.

"Mine. I purchased it through a broker before I came to Boise. Haven't had time to furnish it." Tyson motioned toward the chairs in the parlor. "You must have lots of questions."

She did, but she hadn't any idea where to start. Wordlessly she entered the parlor and sat on the edge of the nearest chair, back stiff, hands folded in her lap. Her gaze roamed the room, looking anywhere but at Tyson.

"Why don't I start?" He took the other chair. She heard him draw in a slow, deep breath—and hoped that meant he was as uncomfortable as she was.

"First, I'll say again that I'm sorry about last night. It wasn't the best way for you to learn I'm not dead. But I thought it better to arrive unannounced than to have your engagement in the newspaper and then learn I'm alive."

She gave a reluctant nod.

"I won't ask you to forgive me, Diana. I don't deserve it. Not yet anyway."

Not yet? Her resolve to hold her tongue failed her. "I will never forgive you, Tyson. Never. Why would I?"

"Because you cared for me once."

"I was a foolish schoolgirl." *You crushed me. You used me. I learned to hate you a long time ago. Can't you see that? Can't you see what you did to me?* If she broke down and cried in front of him, it would be herself she hated, not him.

Tyson rose from the chair and walked to the large window facing the boulevard, his hands clasped behind him. When he turned toward her again, his expression was solemn. "Diana, I would like you to come and live with me."

"What?"

"We are legally man and wife. We should live together." He made a sweeping gesture with his arm. "Here in this house."

She stood. "Marriage wasn't reason enough for you to be with me for the last seven years. Why is it reason enough for us to live together now?"

"I had my reasons for leaving." He raked the fingers of one

hand through his hair. "Poor ones, as it turned out, but at the time they seemed good. I freely admit that I made mistakes and treated you shabbily. I was selfish and angry and thoughtless. Now I . . . I want to make it up to you."

It was tempting to slap him and to scream obscenities. He thought he could waltz back to Idaho, crook his finger, and make her come running? The audacity of the man! Selfish didn't begin to describe him. Shabby didn't begin to describe how he'd treated her.

"I will make it up to you, if you'll give me the chance." He took a step forward. "Believe it or not, I need you."

Tyson watched the different emotions play across Diana's face and wished he knew what she was thinking.

"You *need* me?" she said at last.

"Yes."

"Why?"

It seemed they stood on the edge of a great canyon. One misstep and they could plummet to the bottom. One wrong word and he could destroy all hope of reconciliation, all hope of making his life count for something.

"Why, Tyson? What has changed after all this time?"

He drew a deep breath. "I've changed."

Her eyebrows arched. "Have you?"

In an instant he knew what he must say. He must be honest with her. Completely honest with her. Perhaps for the first time ever.

"Well?"

He took a step toward her. "Diana, for you to believe I've changed, you'd have to see it. You'd have to see me day by day. Live with me. You wouldn't believe me if all I did was tell you what's different. Would you?"

"No. You're right. I wouldn't believe you."

He kept going as if she hadn't responded. "Here's what I can tell you now. I'm going to run in the upcoming election for the seat in the United States Senate, and time is of the essence."

She looked at him now as if he'd sprouted a second head.

"I'm already at a disadvantage as the parties have selected their candidates. I'll be running as a write-in."

"What has any of that to do with me?"

"Being separated from my wife would put me at an additional disadvantage. Voters like their candidates to be married. If possible, happily so. If I'm to have a chance in this election, I'll need you by my side."

The silence in the room became thick, heavy. A feeling of panic tightened his chest. There was so much more than that to say, more important reasons for them to be together, but he sensed she wasn't ready to hear them.

"I could never convincingly pretend that I loved you, Tyson. No one would be fooled. I'm not an actress."

"Couldn't you at least try?"

A look of defiance filled her eyes. "No. And if this is all you want, I believe I shall leave."

"Wait, Diana. Please. Perhaps we could find some way to make it worth your while."

This time her eyes narrowed. Moments dragged as she studied him. Then, after a long silence, she turned and walked to the entry hall. She looked to her right and then to her left before facing him again. "Doesn't it bother you that I had plans to marry another man?" Her voice was as cool as ice.

"As a matter of fact, it does."

A small smile curved the corners of her mouth.

"Do you love him, Diana?"

The smile vanished. "I don't believe my feelings for Mr. Calhoun are any of your business."

What about me? Do you love me? But that was something he didn't dare ask. He knew she'd loved him once. She'd loved him, and he'd thrown it back in her face. Whatever she thought of him now, he deserved it. Worse, probably. But that didn't mean he was going to give up on his plans. That didn't mean he would let her go before he had a chance to change her mind about him and about their marriage.

"Would you like to see the rest of the house?" he asked.

She weighed his question for a long while before she answered by turning and making her way across the entry hall to the library, then into the dining room, and finally past the butler's pantry into the kitchen.

Tyson followed her, letting her move at her own pace. He didn't say a word until she glanced into the downstairs bedroom. "I thought your mother might like this room."

Diana didn't look at him, but he sensed her agreement. It gave him a spark of hope.

They climbed the wide front staircase to the second story. One by one, she looked into each of the six bedrooms. When she reached the last bedroom—*his* bedroom and the only one with any furniture in it—she stopped and turned toward him. "What if I don't want anything to do with this? Or with you." She drew a quick breath. "What if I want a divorce?"

"I couldn't agree to a divorce."

"Why? Our marriage never meant anything to you. You told me so yourself before you left me. Why pretend it matters to you now?"

"I'm not pretending. It does mean something to me. More than something. I've come to believe marriage is sacred."

A laugh escaped her. Disbelief sharpened her features.

He was losing her. He felt the chance to make things right slipping away from him. He had to act fast. "Do you want to go on struggling to make ends meet? You and your mother could live in plenty here. And what if my father cuts off that stipend Mother requested for you? He could, you know. He isn't legally bound to do it."

The color drained from her face.

Good. It meant he'd found a vulnerability. Although he might dislike himself for using it—and any others he discovered—against her, he would still use it. This was a battle he couldn't afford to lose.

He moved a step closer. "Let's make a bargain, Diana. You and your mother move in here with me. You manage my home, furnish it, hire and oversee the servants, serve as hostess when I entertain, and stand beside me when I make campaign appearances. To the world we will exhibit a united front, a happy couple, glad to be together again. And when the election is over, whether I win or lose, you may leave if it is still your desire to do so."

"You would give me a divorce then?"

He shook his head. "No, I still wouldn't agree to a divorce. However, if you want to separate at that time, I will buy you a home and provide you with a generous allowance. Enough to keep you and your mother in comfort for the rest of your lives."

"You would do that?"

"Yes. I give you my word."

She frowned. "I would insist upon having my own room."

"Of course, but—"

She drew herself up a little taller. Her chin—never more stubborn in appearance than it looked right now—punctured the air. "I want the larger one in the front."

Relief flooded through Tyson. She'd acquiesced. He'd won—or at least given himself a chance to win.

"Let us be clear with each other, Tyson. I won't share your bed. Don't think that I will, no matter what you say or do."

Once again he was aware of the depth of her wounds, the wounds he was responsible for. The guilt weighed upon his shoulders, but he could not let her see it. Not yet. Not now. "As you wish. But I have a condition as well."

Silence reigned for a few moments before she asked, "What is it?"

"You must give me the chance to change your mind. About me and about our marriage."

"You won't be able to change my mind."

"Perhaps not. But you must at least let me try."

More silence, then, "You may try if you wish, but it won't do you any good."

July 1890

Tyson stood at the window of the small, airless, third-story office in downtown St. Louis, Missouri, where he worked as an apprentice attorney. Work he despised. A job his father had obtained for him—calling in a favor—before Tyson had earned his degree from Harvard University.

He hated himself almost as much as he hated the job. Where was his resolve? Where was his courage? Why hadn't he refused the job? Why hadn't he refused to go into law and instead done something that interested him?

The answer was simple—and embarrassing: because if he didn't do what his father said, he would be cut off without a penny, and that prospect was less than inviting.

Tyson was the first to admit that the Applegate name and fortune opened doors for him wherever he went, whatever he did. Beautiful young women wanted to be seen clinging to his arm.

Other young men wanted to be his friends. He dined in the best restaurants and rode the finest horses. He was surrounded by comfort wherever he was. And even resentment toward his father wasn't enough to make him willing to give up all that wealth allowed.

He swore softly and turned back to his desk.

THREE

Four days after her meeting with Tyson in his home, Diana stood in the bedroom of the small rental she'd shared with her mother for the past two years. The bed was stripped free of sheets and blankets. No paintings remained on the walls. All of their belongings were now in trunks and boxes, ready for the movers.

From the doorway, her mother said, "At least Tyson didn't leave us without income as I feared he might. That is some comfort."

"Very little."

"I wish there was something more I could do to help in your time of need. You were so quick to come to me when your father fell ill."

"I wanted to come. You know that."

"At least your agreement is only for six months. A woman can bear just about anything for that length of time. November will be here before we know it."

Diana nodded. *I've survived worse, I suppose.* "Let's go, then. There's no point lingering here any longer." She took her mother by the arm, and together they walked outside to the carriage that awaited them. Tyson's carriage, provided for this particular errand. It would carry Diana and her mother to his home where their trunks, boxes, and few furnishings would soon be delivered.

She hadn't seen Tyson since last Friday morning. They had communicated daily via notes delivered back and forth by a stable boy in Tyson's employ. Perhaps not seeing her husband was what had made it easy to pretend this day wouldn't come. That it was all a bad dream from which she would soon awaken. But it wasn't a bad dream, and she couldn't pretend any longer.

As the carriage carried the two women closer to Tyson's home on the east side of the city, nerves warred in Diana's stomach like a couple of alley cats on the midnight prowl. *I never should have agreed to this. Mother and I could have found another way to manage.*

Only she knew better. She'd had no other choice. Tyson had the money and the power. He even had the law on his side, just because he'd been born male. She had to go along with him if she hoped to have a decent life in the future. How else could she provide for her mother if neither Tyson nor his father gave her some sort of allowance? She had little schooling and no special skills. The one thing she had was her looks, but they would serve her little purpose as long as she already had a husband.

The carriage rolled to a stop at the curb, and moments later Diana disembarked, facing Tyson's home once again. *Her* home— perhaps her prison—for the next six months.

Her mother stepped to her side. "Gracious me. It's more than I expected."

Diana didn't reply as she drew herself up, holding her head high, assuming an air of confidence she didn't feel, and walked toward the front door. It was opened for them by a man she didn't know.

"Mrs. Applegate." He gave a slight bow.

She wondered how he could be so certain who she was. "Yes, I'm Mrs. Applegate." Perhaps Tyson had shown him a photograph or told him she had red hair. "And you are?"

"Upchurch, madam. William Upchurch. I'm the new butler. Mr. Applegate hired me yesterday. I have been expecting your arrival."

"It's a pleasure to meet you, Upchurch. This is my mother, Mrs. Fisher."

"Madam." Another slight bow.

"Is Mr. Applegate at home?" Diana asked.

"No, madam. He was called out but said to inform you he would return within the hour."

Strange. She'd dreaded seeing Tyson again, and now she felt slighted by his absence.

"Mother, let me show you where your room is."

"I'd like that, dear." Her mother peeked into the parlor. "It's so empty it echoes."

"I know. Tomorrow morning we'll go shopping for furnishings. We can't continue to sit on two chairs. Goodness knows where Tyson has been eating since there is no dining room table."

Upchurch cleared his throat. "Excuse me, Mrs. Applegate. It's been arranged for you to interview several women in the morning for the position of housekeeper."

"Oh, yes. Tyson mentioned that—" *In one of his notes.* "—but I'd forgotten. Mother, we'll go shopping in the afternoon."

"Whatever you wish, dear. I'm a guest in your home."

Diana led the way down the hall toward the back of the house and opened the door to the main-floor bedroom. "I hope you'll be comfortable here."

"Why, Diana, this is a wonderful room. Very spacious. And look, two closets. Have you ever seen the like? One on either side of the fireplace. Such luxury." Her mother walked to the west-facing window to look outside. "What beautiful lawn and gardens." She turned toward Diana again. "I shall be very comfortable here. How could I not be?"

Six months, Mother. Don't get too used to it. Remember it's only for six months.

"Will you show me the rest of the house before Tyson returns?"

Her mother's question made the nerves start fighting in her stomach again. "Of course. Until we hire more servants and acquire enough furniture, we shall have to make do for ourselves, so you had best know where things are."

Diana was glad for a reason to look over the house again, more slowly this time than the last. She would hate to be in the midst of interviewing housekeepers and have to admit she had no idea where the pantry was or that the laundry was in the basement or how many servant rooms were on the third floor.

The two women went downstairs and upstairs and looked into every cupboard and corner they found. When they returned to the main floor at last, they made their way to the parlor and sat on the two chairs.

Gloria waved a hand before her face. "Mercy, I'm worn out. Such a large house for just the two of you."

"There are three of us, Mother. This is your home too."

"Tyson must be planning for a large family, with all those bedrooms upstairs."

Diana sucked in a quick breath and whispered, "Mother!" The idea shocked her. Shocked her because it brought memories of sweet intimacies she'd once shared with her husband. And the idea hurt her too. Because there had been a time when she'd dreamed of having children with Tyson. But that dream was gone forever.

"Well, didn't you say he wants to convince you to stay with him? If he's successful in his mission, I should imagine he'll want children with you."

Diana began to regret telling her mother every detail of her meeting with Tyson.

"Your father always wanted a large family." Her mother's expression turned instantly sorrowful.

Diana leaned forward and squeezed her hand. "Tyson isn't anything like my father."

Her mother swallowed, shook her head, and shrugged in quick succession.

As if summoned by her words, Tyson appeared in the parlor doorway. "You're here." He smiled at Diana, then removed his hat and handed it to Upchurch, who waited just out of sight. As he strode into the parlor, Tyson shifted his gaze to Diana's mother. "Mrs. Fisher, it's a pleasure to see you again. I was very sorry to learn of your husband's passing. You have my deepest sympathies."

He already sounds like a politician.

"I'm told the movers will be here no later than three o'clock," he continued. "Enough time so both of you shall have beds to sleep in tonight."

"I should hope so." Gloria released the hand he'd offered her.

"And I thought we would dine out this evening. Then, with any luck, Diana—" He looked at her again. "—will approve of one of the women she interviews tomorrow morning. With both a butler and a housekeeper, things should function properly in the Applegate home from then on."

Diana's head throbbed. She would rather lie down and pretend none of this was happening than go out to dine and pretend to be a happy couple. And what did she know about hiring household staff? She supposed she'd learned a few things while living with her mother- and father-in-law, but it was very little. The Applegate mansion up north was four or five times the size of this house, and she had no idea how many servants had been needed to keep it running smoothly. She'd certainly paid no attention to their individual duties.

But this was the bargain she'd struck with Tyson. She would have to make the best of it.

There had been moments during the last four days when Tyson almost convinced himself his wife would be glad to move into this house with him. Perhaps because he hadn't seen her face, only her words on the notes she'd sent him in reply to his own. But now he could see her face, and the expression she wore dispelled any illusions that she might be glad about her present circumstances. She disliked him. Despised him. Perhaps hated him. And she certainly didn't want to be with him.

Can I blame her? Not if he was honest with himself.

The silence stretching between them began to feel uncomfortable.

Once again Tyson looked at his mother-in-law. "Have you seen the rest of the house, Mrs. Fisher?"

"Yes. Diana gave me a tour."

"Good." He nodded. "I hope you'll be comfortable."

"I'm sure I will be."

"Did you have a chance to go out to see the gardens?"

"No. But I have a good view of them from my bedroom window. It's all quite beautiful, Tyson. Another month and the colors will be even more glorious than they are now."

He returned his gaze to Diana. "May I show you and your mother the stables? I assume you haven't been out there yet. I've purchased some fine horses you might want to see. I remember how fond you are of riding."

This at last brought a spark of interest to his wife's eyes. He'd been counting on that. A love of horses was something they had in common.

He held out his hand toward her. "Please. Let's have a look at them."

She placed her fingers in his and allowed him to draw her up from the chair. He would have liked to keep holding her hand, but she withdrew it as soon as she was upright.

He pretended not to notice. "Mrs. Fisher, will you join us?"

"No," the older woman said. "You two young folks go along. I'll just sit right here and close my eyes for a short rest. I'm feeling the weariness in my bones."

Tyson wondered what his mother-in-law thought of him. Had Diana told her about their six-month bargain? Did Mrs. Fisher hope Diana would leave or stay? The woman had liked him once. Back when he'd come courting her daughter and had been all smiles and charm. Back before he'd hurt Diana, back before he'd proven himself the worst kind of scoundrel. If Gloria Fisher disliked him, he'd given her plenty of reasons for it.

He didn't have to wonder how Diana felt about him, and he knew better than to offer her his arm. Instead he indicated they should head out of the parlor. Together they made their way down the hall, passed the main staircase, and out onto the rear porch.

It was a beautiful day, the sky a cloudless blue, the air smelling of spring. Diana seemed a perfect fit for her surroundings—fresh, sweet, vibrant. She wore a dress of pale green that flattered her coloring. Although he supposed when a woman was as beautiful as his wife, even a flour sack would be made lovely on her.

The walkway ended at the back fence that separated the lawn from the pathway to the stables, arena, and paddocks. The wealthy merchant who'd built the home a decade before had raised Thoroughbreds for his four daughters. While Tyson hadn't purchased the property because of the large, modern stables, he was glad for it all the same. It pleased him because he knew it would please Diana.

They stopped in the wide doorway to the airy building. A row of closed stalls lined the eastern and western walls, and as if in welcome, horses thrust their heads over the gates. Diana made a soft sound of delight.

"That's a fine mare there." He pointed to the first stall to their right where a sleek bay bobbed her head and nickered.

Diana moved toward the horse, but Tyson stayed where he was, watching as she stopped outside the stall and stroked the mare's head, speaking to her, staring into her eyes. After a few minutes, Diana opened the gate and stepped inside.

In those first weeks after Tyson and Diana's wedding, they'd ridden together often. They'd both been happiest away from the Applegate mansion, riding through the forests that surrounded it. He supposed she'd liked spending time with her new husband, but his reasons had been less admirable. He'd wanted to avoid seeing or talking to his father. If that meant taking Diana along with him . . .

Regret stung his conscience. She'd loved him once. Perhaps it had been the immature, untested love of a teenage girl with her head in the clouds, but it could have become something more if he'd been a man of integrity. If he'd stuck around to nurture it. If he'd treated his wife with the care and tenderness she deserved. But he hadn't stayed.

He wanted to make it up to her. Would she let him?

"She's beautiful, Tyson. Exquisite lines. She must ride like a dream." Diana looked over the stall door at him.

"Glad you like her. She's yours."

"Mine?"

It felt good, giving something to her for no other reason than to bring her pleasure. "Yours." He moved to stand outside the stall.

He'd known the Arabian mare—with the faint white star on

her forehead and the short white stocking on her right hind leg—
would appeal to Diana. That much had been easy to foretell. But
he hoped he would learn many more things that appealed to her in
the coming weeks. If he could, he would give those to her as well.

As she returned his gaze, her expression changed from happy
to wary. "Why?"

"Why what?"

"Why are you giving her to me?"

"Do I need a reason to give my wife a horse?"

"It won't change anything between us, Tyson." Suspicion narrowed her eyes. Her chin lifted. "My affections cannot be bought
so easily. Not this time."

"I'm not trying to buy your affections. I'm just . . . It isn't . . . I
only thought . . ." His own sputtering response left him irritated and
made his voice gruff when he continued. "You'll need a horse, Diana,
and now you have one. Just say thank you and let it go at that."

She glared at him. "Thank you." The two words seemed to
freeze the air around them.

Females! Maybe this was the real reason he'd spent so many
years climbing mountains and tramping through forests with other
men. Men were easy to understand. At least for another man.

But women? Heaven help him.

"What?" Jeremiah Applegate shot up from his desk chair. "What
did you say?"

His clerk could hardly look him in the eye. "Your son was not
declared dead, sir." The man cleared his throat. "Your son is alive,
Mr. Applegate."

Jeremiah felt his eyes widen and his heart quicken. Tyson was
alive? Impossible! Alive? How could that be? But if it was . . . If it

was true . . . Overwhelming emotions surged through him—including fear that his hopes would be raised only to be dashed again.

Sounding doubtful, his clerk continued, "Your son is in Boise. With his wife."

"Tyson's in Boise City? With Diana? For how long?"

"I don't know, sir. Not long or I'm sure you would have heard of it before now."

Jeremiah turned toward the window. He'd spent a great deal of time and money keeping tabs on his son in the early years after he got his inheritance. He'd known what countries the boy visited and whom he kept company with. He'd known most everything of importance right up to the time Tyson went to Cuba to fight in the blasted war. And then had come word that his son was presumed dead.

It was like the sun had been extinguished from the sky.

Tyson's body had never been recovered, but other soldiers had reported him killed on the battlefield in a massive explosion. Everyone believed that to be true. Jeremiah's grief had been compounded by the inability to lay his son to rest beside Tyson's mother and grandmother. He'd lived with that grief for almost two years. Grief and regret.

Was it true? Was Tyson alive? And if so, how had he kept his father from hearing of it? How had he kept it from his wife? Jeremiah hadn't been looking for him, of course, but still . . .

The clerk cleared his throat again. "There's more, sir."

"Well? Speak up, man. What is it?"

"Tyson is planning a run for the Senate."

"In a few years."

"No, sir. In this election. I'm told he will announce his write-in candidacy soon."

"Write-in? Why would he do anything that foolish?" Waving

away the clerk, Jeremiah sank onto his chair, his thoughts a blur. From the moment Tyson was born, Jeremiah had had big plans for him. College. A law practice. Election to public office. Maybe even one day becoming president. But Tyson had struggled against his father's wishes from an early age. There had been many battles of will between father and son before Jeremiah saw Tyson graduate from college and become a lawyer.

But then the boy's grandmother had left him a fortune, and Tyson had married that Fisher girl. An Irish orphan from Chicago. No kind of wife for a politician, in Jeremiah's mind. Oh, she was pretty enough and not without the proper social graces. But if a man wanted to get ahead in this world, he needed to marry into a family of both influence and affluence. The Fishers had been nei-ther, and, to his shame—a feeling he despised but had felt all too often of late—Jeremiah hadn't let Diana forget what he thought of her.

He swiveled toward the window that overlooked one of the Applegate silver mines.

In one of their last arguments, Tyson had sworn he would never run for any political office. What had changed the boy's mind? Why had he kept his whereabouts a secret? Hadn't he known he was presumed dead? And what had made him return to the wife he'd left so long ago?

"I'd best get down there and see for myself." He stood again and strode out of his office.

August 1892

Diana hated to admit it, but she was homesick. She was almost eighteen—too old to feel that way. But she was homesick all the same. Her parents' friends, Mr. and Mrs. Stewart, and their daughters, Jane and Ophelia, had been kind to her throughout her stay at their northern Idaho home. But she was eager for her parents to return from New York so she could go back to Montana with them. She felt so out of place here, especially tonight.

Standing near a tall pine tree on the edge of the yard, Diana fought tears of loneliness as she watched the festivities. Torches burned all around, bathing the grounds in flickering golden light. The party guests of the two Stewart girls stood in small groups visiting and laughing, sharing the kind of stories that only longtime friends with common pasts could tell. The young women wore pretty pastel frocks in the latest designs. The young men wore light-colored summer suits.

"Why are you hiding, Miss Fisher?"

Diana sucked in a breath, surprised by the deep, male voice that came out of the shadows behind her.

He stepped into the light, and she recognized him. Tyson Applegate. Ophelia had pointed him out earlier in the evening, providing every detail she could think of. He was an attorney, recently returned to Idaho from Missouri. At twenty-five, he was older than most of the other guests. The only son of a mining tycoon, his family was the wealthiest and most important in the entire Silver Valley. Perhaps in the entire Northwest. According to Ophelia, every girl from sixteen to twenty-five and from Seattle to Missoula had set her cap for him. Understandable. He was handsome beyond description, self-assured, and very, very rich.

And he'd called Diana by name. He knew who she was too.

She lifted her chin in a show of confidence and hoped he hadn't seen how sorry she'd been feeling for herself. "I'm not hiding." A bald-faced lie.

"No?" He grinned. "Well, I am."

"You are?"

"Absolutely. I was on my way down to the dock. Care to go with me? We can take off our shoes and dip our feet in the lake."

"I-I . . ." She shouldn't go, of course. Alone, in the dark, with a man who was a stranger. But she found she couldn't refuse. "All right."

Tyson took her hand and led her down the path.

By the evening's end, he'd led her heart down a path straight to love.

FOUR

Brook Calhoun poured himself another brandy before settling into his favorite chair in the library, his thoughts as dark and cold as the fireless hearth.

Five days. Five days had passed since the night of the disastrous dinner party. Five days since Diana's husband's return had destroyed his carefully laid plans. Curse Tyson Applegate! Brook had done everything right. He'd befriended Diana soon after she moved from Nampa to Boise with her mother. He'd been kind and consoling. He'd been the soul of discretion these many months. He'd never let her see how desperate he was to get his hands on the great wealth she would inherit once her missing husband was declared dead.

He lifted the brandy snifter and threw the liquid to the back of his throat, enjoying the burn on the way down.

Diana was supposed to have been his. Her money was supposed to have been his. He'd had plans for it. Diana and her wealth would have been his ticket into the upper echelons of Boise society—and beyond Boise too. He wasn't meant to remain one of the middle class. He was born for greater things.

And now?

He'd had no choice but to call off their unofficial engagement.

To do otherwise would have been to endanger his reputation. And since he'd been living beyond his means while courting the lovely Mrs. Applegate, he couldn't afford to offend his more affluent and influential friends.

Anger surged inside him, and he swore as he slammed the snifter onto the side table, so hard he snapped its stem. He cursed again. He cursed God. He cursed Diana. And above all, he cursed Tyson Applegate.

Heads turned as Diana and Tyson followed the maître d' to their table. Tyson couldn't blame the men for craning their necks for a better look at his wife. She seemed to grow more beautiful by the hour. One would not believe she'd moved to a new home this very day, with scarcely enough time to unpack her trunks, and had prepared for this evening without benefit of a maid.

The gown she wore was the color of the sea off a tropical island he'd spent a number of months on early in his adventures. Although he suspected it wasn't the latest fashion—due to his father's miserly control over her income—she made it look new. Not to mention that the design accented her curves in the way it was supposed to. The square décolleté revealed the pale skin across her breastbone and the long stretch of her neck. Her hair was done up on her head with fiery ringlets curling at her nape. The music from a string ensemble—playing somewhere out of his view—kept time to the sway of her hips. Mesmerizing. Too bad they weren't attending a ball somewhere. Dancing would have allowed him to take her into his arms, hold her close, breathe in that earthy cologne she favored.

The maître d' held out a chair for her, and with a practiced sweep of one arm, she held the train of her skirt out of the way as she settled onto the seat. Tyson sat across from her.

"I've never dined in this restaurant before." Diana looked around the room with its high ceilings and sumptuous decor.

Tyson wondered why Brook Calhoun hadn't brought her here. From what he'd been able to learn about the man in a short period of time, Calhoun was all about moving in the right circles. Chez Les Bois was just the sort of place in which that man would want to be seen with a beautiful woman. But he already knew the answer to his own question: Brook Calhoun, it had been reported to Tyson, was short on income and had probably failed to pay his bill at Chez Les Bois one time too many.

Hadn't Diana ever suspected her erstwhile fiancé wanted to marry a *wealthy* widow? Or had she been so in love with Calhoun she hadn't cared about his motives?

Loathing rose in Tyson's throat. He disliked the idea that Diana might love Brook Calhoun. Loathed it more than he cared to admit.

"Is something wrong, Tyson?"

He met her gaze. "No. Why?"

"You were frowning at me."

"Must be the dim lighting."

She gave him a little smile that said she didn't believe him.

Thankfully, the waiter arrived at that moment. Dinner was ordered and an appropriate wine selected, and soon they were alone at the table once again.

"About tomorrow," Diana said.

"Yes?"

"Do you have a budget for me to keep within when I'm buying furnishings for your house?"

"*Our* house."

There was that arched eyebrow again, the look she gave him cool and aloof.

"And the answer is no, Diana. Spend what needs to be spent to furnish and decorate it appropriately."

If he'd expected her to show pleasure at the idea of shopping without limits, he was sorely mistaken. She was all business. "Would you like a desk in the library?"

"Yes. And lots of books on the shelves too."

"Do you want beds and dressers and wardrobes in the unused chambers upstairs?"

"Yes."

"Paintings and sculptures?"

He felt himself growing impatient. "Whatever you wish."

A smile tweaked the corners of her mouth, and he could see it pleased her that she'd gotten under his skin.

"I might be the ruin of you, Tyson. I've never managed a large household or had an unlimited amount of money to spend. I've never bought sofas and chairs or draperies or paintings for a home like yours."

"Ours."

She ignored his assertion a second time. "You may be making a very poor bargain, asking me to do all of this."

"A worse bargain than Mr. Calhoun would have made?" He was sorry the instant the words left his mouth, yet he said more. "Wouldn't he have wanted you to decorate and manage his home as well?"

How was it that green eyes could make him think of ice? The look she gave him now made him want to shiver.

"As I said, Diana, it is *our* house—"

"For the next six months. Only for the next six months."

He released a breath, determined not to let her rile him. "As you wish. But for those six months, please remember it is your home as well as mine. You should furnish it accordingly. Decorate it to please yourself. If you know nothing about such matters, I know even less. I've spent a great deal of time in recent years living in a tent, often without any civilized company to be found."

"My goodness. It's surprising you knew enough to put on shoes or wear a tie tonight."

Tyson leaned back in his chair. He didn't remember her having a gift for sarcasm. Was it an acquired trait or had he ignored it years ago? To his shame, he couldn't say for sure.

Looking at her husband, Diana felt a small catch in her chest as memories filled her mind. Memories of the Idaho lake party where she and Tyson first met. Memories of their whirlwind courtship in Montana. Memories of their wedding day. It seemed she could taste them on her tongue. Sweet . . . and then sour. Bitter. So bitter. She must remember the bitter. It was the only thing that would protect her from getting hurt again.

She narrowed her eyes. "Don't you think it's time you tell me where you were and what you were doing?"

"If you wish. I got the feeling you didn't want to know. You never asked."

He could be right. She might not *want* to know. But she still *needed* to know. "At least tell me why you allowed me to think you were dead. And explain how you managed to keep it a secret that you were alive. Especially from your father."

"I'm not sure I can explain any of it well."

"Try."

"All right." He nodded. "I'll try."

The appetizer—oysters, béchamel style—arrived. Diana half expected Tyson to use the interruption to change the course of their conversation. But he didn't. After the server left the table, Tyson took a sip from his wine glass and then began.

"You already know I was in Cuba with the Rough Riders. There was an explosion on the battlefield. The last thing I remember was running up a hill, yelling and firing my rifle. Suddenly I was airborne and then everything went dark. Doctors told me later that I suffered a traumatic concussion. I didn't come around for a number of days, and when I did, I had no memory and was unable to speak. Because of the brain injury, the doctors say. By then I'd been separated from my men and my identification had been lost. That's how I came to be presumed dead."

Could she believe him? Had he been badly injured, so much so that he'd lost his memory for a time?

"I was eventually sent to a hospital in Washington, DC. That's where I was when I began to remember."

"So why wasn't I notified once you were identified?"

Tyson set down his fork and leaned back in his chair. "Because I didn't tell them who I was. I pretended I still had no memory. I . . . I didn't want Father to learn I was alive." He shook his head slowly. "It's a poor excuse, but at the time I thought it was my chance to escape the past, once and for all. I could start a new life as someone else. As someone better than the person I'd been for too many years."

"You hated us that much? That you would let us think you dead."

"I didn't hate you, Diana."

"No?"

"No. And I didn't hate Father either. Not really. I hated the way he tried to control me and force me to his will. I resented the power he wielded over me, even after I was an adult. And I hated what I'd allowed him to make me."

An unexpected and unwelcome sea of emotions welled up inside of Diana, and she wished she'd never asked him to tell her why and how. What did it matter anyway? Knowing wouldn't change the past. Or her future.

"Ah, here comes our waiter." Tyson gave her a small smile. "Perhaps we should continue this discussion later and enjoy our dinner now."

She couldn't help but appreciate how artfully he steered the conversation away from anything unpleasant for the remainder of the meal. As they dined—the entrée was Bouchée Columbia with French peas and potato salad, the dessert a fancy ice called Argentine Glacé—they spoke of horses and the new businesses springing up in the capital city and articles that had made the front page of the newspaper in recent weeks and even some of the new fashions. Before Diana realized it, almost two hours had passed.

"Mother will wonder what's happened to us," she said when she realized the time.

Tyson stood and eased back her chair from the table. "It was a long and exhausting day. I suspect she is already sound asleep in her bed." He offered his hand to help her rise.

"You are probably right."

He motioned for her to lead the way toward the front door. Tables that had been filled with people earlier in the evening were now empty, the snow-white linens swept clean of crumbs. But there were still enough late diners to create a soft hum of conversation around them as they left.

Diana was grateful she didn't see anyone she knew. It would have been too exhausting to answer questions or pretend she was happy about her husband's return to the living. She would have to do both of those things soon enough. It was, after all, part of the bargain. But thankfully, not tonight.

Outside Chez Les Bois, the air was crisp, making her wish

she'd brought a wrap. But she didn't own one nice enough to wear with this gown. Hopefully, their carriage would arrive soon.

"Tyson Applegate!" a deep male voice exclaimed.

Tyson and Diana looked behind them.

The man—a distinguished-looking fellow with a close-cropped gray beard—stuck out his right hand. "So you're here at last."

"Justice Waverley." Tyson shook the man's hand. "It's good to see you again."

"Indeed." Mr. Waverley's gaze flicked to Diana and back again.

Tyson took hold of her arm above the elbow and gently drew her one step closer. "Justice Waverley, may I introduce my wife, Diana Applegate. Diana, this is Samuel Waverley. He sits on our state's supreme court."

"Mrs. Applegate." The judge bowed. "What a very great pleasure to meet you at last."

"Thank you, sir."

"It was my privilege to spend a good deal of time with your husband when I was in Washington last year. He has a fine mind and a good moral compass. One does not often find that in a younger man."

A fine moral compass? Those were not words she would use to describe Tyson. Such a man wouldn't desert his wife and traipse around the world with little thought for the family he'd left behind.

The judge returned his attention to Tyson, and when he spoke his voice was much lower. "I understand an announcement of your candidacy will be forthcoming. Very soon, I hope."

"Yes, soon."

"Good. Good. Our country needs men like you. Well, I imagine this is your carriage, so I won't keep you. I'll ask my wife to arrange a dinner party for you and Mrs. Applegate. I have a number of friends you should meet."

"That would be appreciated, sir."

"Good night, Tyson. Mrs. Applegate." The judge turned and walked away.

But Diana's thoughts were on the man standing at her side. She could tell herself all she wanted that she didn't care what Tyson had done or where he'd been or how he'd managed to hide these past two years, but the truth was her curiosity had been piqued again. After all, Justice Waverley was a man of no small influence in this state. She hadn't met him before tonight, but she knew his name. Everyone did. Now she'd learned he was a friend of her husband. That he admired Tyson. That he thought him a man of integrity.

The swirling confusion was giving her a headache, and she was thankful when Tyson helped her into the carriage so they could start for their home.

No. For *his* home. Not theirs, no matter what he said to the contrary. Never hers. No matter how confused she got, she mustn't forget that.

February 1893

They buried Tyson's maternal grandmother in the family plot on a Monday. Three days later Tyson was summoned to his father's study. When he entered the room, his father looked up from papers on the desk and motioned to a chair opposite him. "Sit down, boy. We have matters to discuss."

Boy. How he hated the way his father used that word. Tyson had celebrated his twenty-sixth birthday last month, but he still wasn't a man in the eyes of Jeremiah Applegate. Might never be a man in his eyes, no matter what Tyson did, no matter what he accomplished.

His father leaned back in his chair. "How long has it been since you returned from Missouri?"

"Six months."

"Your legal work on behalf of the mines is more than satisfactory."

It wasn't a question, so Tyson said nothing.

"Other mine owners have taken note of you, as well. It's time we widen your circle of acquaintances. I believe you and I should make a trip down to the capital later this spring."

Resentment rose like bile in his throat. Tyson understood the reason for this proposed trip. To realize his father's ambitions for him. Would he ever get out from under his father's control? Would he ever be allowed to live his own life instead of the one Jeremiah had chosen for him?

As if in answer to Tyson's silent questions, his father said, "But that isn't why I sent for you. It seems your grandmother has left you the bulk of her estate in her will."

Excitement thrummed in Tyson's brain—his maternal grandmother had been as rich as his father—and it took every fiber of resolve not to let the elation show in his expression.

Clearly disapproving of the inheritance, his father continued, "You won't receive the money immediately."

Tyson cleared his throat. "What are the conditions?" He tried to sound like a serious attorney and not an eager beneficiary.

"Her estate will come to you on your thirtieth birthday or upon your marriage. Whichever comes first."

Thirty. A month shy of four years from now. It seemed an eternity. Could he wait that long?

FIVE

The following week passed in a flurry of activity. Diana hired a head housekeeper, Edith Brown by name. A stern, no-nonsense kind of woman. Mrs. Brown went on to help Diana hire the cook, a house maid who would also serve as lady's maid to the two women of the house, and a kitchen maid.

Diana and her mother spent a great deal of time buying furniture and oil paintings, draperies, and carpets. They purchased china and table service and glassware, but they left it to the cook, Madge Cuddy, to buy the necessaries for the kitchen. Mrs. Brown was assigned the task of furnishing the servants' rooms on the third floor. Following Tyson's instructions, Diana and her mother also ordered a number of new gowns, for both casual and formal occasions. Diana had a new riding habit made too. Reluctant though she was to admit it, she was delighted by the update of her wardrobe.

Tyson kept busy preparing for the announcement of his candidacy for the Senate seat from the great state of Idaho. At least, that was Diana's assumption. He was absent from the house for many hours every day. Perhaps he needed to escape the chaos of the household as deliverymen and workmen came and went. It did seem that everything was at sixes and sevens from dawn to dusk.

Oddly enough, Diana was sorry to spend so little time with him during those hectic first days of what she'd come to think of as "the arrangement." And although they dined together in the evenings—the dining room table and chairs being among the first items delivered to the Applegate home—their conversations never turned toward the personal, perhaps because of her mother's presence.

Or perhaps he'd decided he wanted nothing more from her than a distant relationship after all.

Which suited her fine.

Tyson stood before the mirror and scraped the last trace of soap and stubble from his jaw with the razor. For the first time in a solid week, he didn't have a morning appointment. In fact, he had no appointments at all. The day was completely his, and he was determined to spend it with Diana. Alone. Without his mother-in-law.

He wasn't sure yet what Gloria Fisher thought of him. Perhaps a little grudging respect at this point in time, but surely no real affection. That would take some doing. He'd injured her daughter's feelings, and he suspected he would win Diana's forgiveness before he earned it from her mother.

But today was not about changing Gloria Fisher's mind about him. It was about wooing his wife. Something he knew little about. Oh, he knew plenty about how to seduce a woman. He was well acquainted with the type of gifts and the type of compliments the fair sex appreciated. But he was an amateur when it came to showing real affection to whom it mattered most—his wife. He hoped he wouldn't stumble too often over his own ignorance.

A rap on the door announced the arrival of Robert Sinclair, Tyson's newly hired valet. Mr. Sinclair was a dozen years Tyson's senior and limped from an injury received during England's First Boer War. About ten years ago, he'd immigrated to America and eventually arrived in Idaho.

"I'm sorry, sir," the valet said. "I haven't laid out your clothes. Was there a particular suit you wanted?"

"No need, Mr. Sinclair. I am taking my ease today."

"Very good, sir."

Tyson wiped his face with a towel as he turned toward the valet. "Do you know if Mrs. Applegate is up? Is she having breakfast in her room or going down?"

"I don't know, sir, but I can inquire of her maid."

"Yes. Please do."

Mr. Sinclair gave a brief bow and left the bedchamber. By the time Tyson finished dressing unaided, the valet had returned. "Liz reports that Mrs. Applegate is awake and eating breakfast in her room."

"Thank you, Mr. Sinclair. I believe I shall join her there."

A flicker of surprise crossed the valet's face, but he hid it quickly. "Shall I bring you a tray, sir?"

"No, thank you. I'll be down to eat after while."

Again he received a bow before the man departed.

"I hope I know what I'm doing," Tyson said aloud. Then he, too, left his bedchamber.

He followed the hallway to his wife's room. He hadn't entered it since before her furnishings arrived a week ago. He wondered how much she would mind him being there. Not at all? Far too much?

He knocked.

"Yes."

"It's Tyson. May I come in?"

Silence. Then, "Yes. Come in."

He opened the door.

She was still abed, her back resting against the headboard and several pillows, a breakfast tray over her lap. She wore a frothy-looking bed jacket of some sort, the same exact color as her eyes, and her hair fell over her shoulders in soft waves.

Beautiful. Enchanting. Mesmerizing. She was his wife, and the desire to join her in that bed hit him hard. Some men might have claimed the right to do so. He was not one of them. No matter that they were legally married. He'd given up the right to intimate relations years ago when he deserted her.

He cleared his throat, hoping she wouldn't guess the thoughts whirling in his head. "Do you have plans for the day, Diana?"

"No."

"Then I wondered if we might go for a horseback ride in the foothills."

"You aren't going out?"

"No." He smiled—and again hoped she couldn't guess how much he desired her, certain she would send him away if she guessed the truth.

Another lengthy silence filled the room before she said, "I should like to go riding, Tyson."

"Wonderful. Shall we say ten o'clock? I'll ask the cook to prepare sandwiches to take with us in case we grow hungry."

"I shall be ready at ten."

Tempting as it was to linger in her chamber, he withdrew, discretion being the better part of valor—or so Shakespeare said.

Diana released a breath as the door to her room clicked closed. She couldn't believe how much smaller her bedchamber had felt with Tyson standing in it. For that matter, she couldn't believe how underdressed she'd felt, despite the layers of bedclothes she wore and the blankets covering her hips and legs.

Disturbing. Most disturbing.

But she wouldn't think about that now. He'd invited her to go riding, and nothing could have kept her from accepting. She'd been dying to ride her new mare. Today she would finally have the chance to do so.

She set aside the breakfast tray and got out of bed. Her morning toilet was completed in haste, then she rang for the maid to help her dress. Not that she couldn't have managed on her own, but she suspected Liz's feelings would be hurt. The girl's confidence was not great. Asking for help would, no doubt, give the maid a boost and let her know she was needed.

A short while later, Diana inspected her reflection in the mirror. The tailored jacket and flowing skirt of her new riding habit were made of a forest-green wool. Beneath the jacket she wore a crisp white chemisette. The outfit was finished with a wide-brimmed bowler.

"I've never seen anyone so lovely as you, missus," the maid said.

"Thank you, Liz."

She wondered if Tyson would think the same.

Trying not to appear impatient, Tyson read the morning paper at the large desk in the library. There was plenty of political news. Earlier in the month, the Populist National Convention had nominated William Jennings Bryan for president and the so-called "middle-of-the-road" Populists had nominated Wharton Barker. The Republican National Convention wasn't until mid-June, but it was a foregone conclusion they would nominate President McKinley to run for reelection. Tyson hoped the party could convince Governor Theodore Roosevelt to run for the vice presidency. After serving with Teddy in Cuba, Tyson had nothing but respect for the man's leadership abilities.

Also in the paper was a story about some of the athletes representing the United States in the Olympic Games in Paris. Tyson smiled to himself as he read the article, remembering the month he'd spent in that romantic city. Someday he'd like to take Diana to see it.

Assuming, of course, that he could convince her to stay with him after the election.

"Oh. Tyson. I'm sorry. I didn't know you were in here."

He lowered the newspaper to look at his mother-in-law.

"I thought you'd gone out on business again," Gloria said. "I wouldn't have dreamed of disturbing you in your library."

"You haven't disturbed me, Mrs. Fisher. I'm simply passing the time while I wait for Diana. We're going riding."

"Riding? The two of you?"

"Yes."

She took a step closer to the desk, her expression serious. "Are you being fair, Tyson?"

"Fair?"

"Don't toy with my daughter's heart."

He folded the paper and set it aside. "I'm not toying with her heart, Mrs. Fisher. I assure you I'm not."

"When you left, you hurt her more than you know."

How could he respond to that? He was guilty as charged.

She continued, "I suppose all mothers want the same thing for their daughters. That they will find contentment and fulfillment wherever life takes them. When Diana introduced you to us, Mr. Fisher and I thought you a fine young man with much to recommend you. Your family. Your education. Your profession.

Your courteous nature. I suppose I knew that your feelings for my daughter were not as strong as hers were for you, but I was confident they would grow. Otherwise we never would have agreed to the match."

Again he didn't know what to say.

"Our approval was never about your wealth, you know."

"Yes. I know that."

She looked at her hands, folded before her waist. "I have never had a strong will like my daughter has. I believe she inherited that from the woman who gave birth to her. I was timid as a child, and as a woman I was content to agree with my husband's opinions and decisions. I liked my quiet role in marriage. But it did not leave me well prepared for life as a widow without any source of income." She drew a breath and let it out on a long sigh.

Before coming to Boise City, Tyson had made it his business to learn what had transpired in Diana's life—and therefore, in her parents' lives—in the years he was away. He'd discovered his father-in-law had lost most everything in the financial panic of 1893, although the man had managed to keep it a secret from his newlywed daughter at the time. Tyson also knew Diana had asked her father-in-law for help once the truth was known and that Jeremiah Applegate had refused to lift a finger to help her parents.

Tyson clenched his jaw. He would have to work a little harder at forgiving his father. He obviously hadn't achieved it yet.

"Tyson."

He returned his attention to his mother-in-law. "Yes?"

"If you break Diana's heart again, I don't believe I will remain timid. I will hurt you in whatever way I can. So help me, I will."

Tyson rose from his chair. He wished he could round the desk and give his mother-in-law a tight hug. Instead, he said, "I give you my word, Mrs. Fisher. I won't hurt Diana. At least not intentionally, and hopefully not by accident either. I want to prove myself a changed man and a good husband."

Whatever Gloria Fisher might have replied to him was interrupted by her daughter's voice, speaking to the housekeeper in the hall. A few moments later, Diana appeared in the library doorway. Tyson could tell she wondered what mother- and son-in-law had been saying to each other. Would she be surprised to know her mother had threatened to harm him if he broke her heart a second time?

"Are you ready?" he asked her, deciding it wise not to linger.

"Yes, I'm ready."

Gloria said, "You have a beautiful day for your ride. I hope you both enjoy it." She crossed the room and placed a kiss on Diana's cheek. "As for me, I plan to sit in the shade of the porch and knit. I shall enjoy the peace and quiet."

Tyson waited until his mother-in-law disappeared through the doorway before circumventing his desk and approaching his wife. "You look stunning in that riding outfit. And I love the hat. Is it new as well?"

"I'm glad you like it." She lifted her chin, tartness in her voice. "You paid for it."

He had the feeling she wanted to goad him into saying something he shouldn't. It didn't work. "Money well spent." He grinned as he motioned toward the back of the house. "Shall we? The horses await."

Nothing, absolutely nothing, was as wonderful as sitting atop a horse, breathing in the sweet air of morning, seeing the sunlight caress the greenish-brown hillsides. Diana hadn't known how much she'd missed riding until now.

Sitting astride a dapple-gray gelding, Tyson led the way on a track that followed a shallow stream. The flowing water created a soft melody that seemed in keeping with the beauty of the day.

They'd ridden for a good half hour when Tyson reined in and glanced over his shoulder at her. "Look. Up there on the ridge." He pointed.

She followed the direction of his arm. For a moment she saw nothing of interest. Just grass and sagebrush and rock. But then something moved. A red fox, watching them as intently as they watched it.

Diana whispered, "It's beautiful." Then she saw more movement in the grass near the fox. "She's got pups."

"Four of them, I think."

"I wish we were closer so we could see them better."

"Next time we ride up here we'll bring binoculars."

She liked the sound of *next time*—although she shouldn't. Not if she wanted to keep a proper distance between them.

Tired of the humans' attention, the fox darted away, her pups on her heels. Surprisingly fast, even the babies.

They rode on, and when the trail widened, Tyson fell back beside Diana. "Your mare seems calm."

"Yes. I thought she might be more difficult when we started out."

"I've had the groom exercise her every day."

"Well, that explains it." She reached down and stroked the bay's neck. "But I think we'd both like to canter a bit. How much longer will we follow this path?"

"I was told that when we reach that knoll"—he pointed—"the trail opens onto more level ground. We can give the horses their heads when we get there."

Diana was ready the instant they crested the hill. Without a word to Tyson, she kicked the mare. The horse shot forward as if propelled from a canon. Laughter burbled up in Diana's throat and trailed behind her. She didn't know where Tyson was, if he followed or sat still. It mattered not to her. All she cared about was the wind on her face, the pounding of hooves on hard ground, and the thrill of sitting atop such a magnificent horse. *Her* horse. It made her feel free and abundantly alive. Troubles, doubts, and fears didn't exist at this moment.

Tyson's gelding caught up with them. The two riders exchanged smiles, understanding what the other felt without the use of words. Eventually, of course, they had to slow their mounts, first to a gentle canter and then to a walk.

"That was grand!" Diana was breathless, as if she'd been the one running.

"Yes, it was." He was silent for a few minutes, then added, "Remember the last time we rode together?"

Something pinched her heart. Regret? Nostalgia? Hope? "Yes."

"Very different terrain up north. The trees and the underbrush. Not as desertlike as it is here."

"But this has a beauty of its own."

"You're right. It does. That's something I discovered in my travels. I can't say I liked every place I went, but each had its own kind of beauty. As a creator, God isn't repetitious. He likes variety."

She turned a narrowed gaze in his direction, uncertain what to think of that comment. The man she'd married had scorned religion. On the other hand, Tyson *had* attended church services with her and her mother this past Sunday. Much to her surprise. Perhaps he'd wanted to be seen there for political purposes. Or maybe . . .

"A penny for your thoughts, Diana."

She didn't plan her response. The question seemed to form and spill from her lips of its own volition. "After so long, Tyson, what made you decide to come back?"

March 1893

Diana stood in an aisle of the general store, a copy of *Pride and Prejudice* open in her hands. It had taken Miss Austen only a few paragraphs to make Diana forget she was supposed to watch for her mother's arrival.

"Miss Fisher? Is that you?"

Pulled from the world of the Bennets and Mr. Bingley, Diana glanced up. Her own world seemed to stop spinning when she recognized Tyson Applegate, standing in the aisle a few feet away. "Mr. Applegate." Her voice broke over his name.

He grinned. "What a surprise to find you here."

"I live here."

"In this store?" His eyes sparkled with mirth as his smile broadened.

It was if she'd last seen him only yesterday instead of seven months ago. Unable to resist his teasing, she returned his smile. "Not in the store, silly. I live in Dillon."

"That's right. You told me so when we met last summer. I'd forgotten."

But he hadn't forgotten her name. That pleased her beyond words—because she remembered every tiny detail about him. How kind he'd been to her. How handsome he was. How tall he was. The deep blue of his eyes. The thickness of his dark hair. A smile that could cause her heart to go pitty-pat. The laugh that rose from deep in his chest.

"I have business in Dillon and Virginia City and will be staying at the hotel across the street for a few weeks. Perhaps I might call upon you and your parents one evening, if that would be all right."

Her pulse galloped and her whole body tingled with pleasure.

"We would like that very much. Could you come for supper tonight?" Oh, heavens. She sounded too eager. She was eighteen years old, an adult, but she sounded like a schoolgirl.

"That's kind of you, Miss Fisher. I would like that. Restaurant food gets tiresome when eaten day in and day out. But you should ask your parents first. They might not want company on such short notice."

"They won't mind." Oh, dear. She'd gone from eager to desperate.

"Well . . . if you're sure."

"I'm positive."

SIX

"After so long, Tyson, what made you decide to come back?"

Diana's question was an important one and needed more than a quick answer. Tyson wanted to tell her something that would satisfy her—or at the very least help her understand him a little better.

He reined in.

She did the same.

He lifted his gaze toward the mountain peaks. "I was in Europe when the *Maine* blew up. I knew it meant war between America and Spain, so I came home on the first ship available. Then I learned Wood and Roosevelt were heading up the First United States Volunteer Cavalry."

"The Rough Riders?"

"Yes, that's what people called them."

Faces of some of the men he'd served with drifted through his memory. Although there'd been a small number of Rough Riders who were in their thirties—Tyson among them—and forties, the majority of the regiment had been young. Very young—eighteen, nineteen, twenty. Many had come from the West where they'd hunted with Theodore Roosevelt. A hale and hardy group of men, to be sure. Whether a private or an officer, every man in the First

Volunteer Cavalry had to be in perfect health, be able to ride and to shoot, and be able to do his duty and obey his superiors without fail. There had been some who could do far more than merely ride and shoot well. A few had known how to bronco bust the wildest of steeds. Others had been master marksmen, able to shoot their targets from the saddles of galloping horses.

Stirred by the memories of war, Tyson continued. "Did you know, after all of our training for the cavalry, only the officers had mounts while in Cuba? There weren't enough transports to carry all the horses there so they were left behind in Florida. When we got to Santiago, the horses were pushed overboard so they could swim to shore. Roosevelt had two mounts onboard, but one of them drowned."

"How awful."

"The heat was brutal in Cuba, and when we weren't broiling beneath the sun, we were drowning in the rainfall. 'Hell on earth' describes it best."

She made another sympathetic sound in her throat.

"I made a lot of friends among the men in my regiment and then I saw too many of them die from illness and lack of food and supplies. Ninety percent of the deaths in the war were due to disease, and too many of those casualties were because of poor planning on the part of the War Department." Tyson combed his fingers through his hair. "I have a lot of respect for Roosevelt. He took care of the men under his command the best he could, often using his own money to buy food and supplies. He and I talked more than once about the importance of public service. I suppose the seed for my run for the Senate was planted then. It grew after Roosevelt became governor of New York." He looked at his wife, hoping she would hear him. *Truly* hear him and then believe him. "But it was God who finally got through to me."

Skepticism filled her eyes. He feared for a moment she might ride away, refusing to listen to another word.

"I never gave much thought to God as a young man," he added quickly. "My parents always attended church, but I knew my father went only because society expected it. Religion was all about earning the respect of people in our community, not for any sort of relationship with a Savior. My father would never admit to needing anyone for any reason. Not even God. And yet he pretended to believe. I hated the hypocrisy. I had no desire to be a hypocrite too." Tyson wondered what he should he say next. He'd never talked much about his faith.

"He stopped going to church after your mother died," Diana said.

Tyson nodded, not surprised. "It was a young fellow in the cavalry who shared the Person of Jesus with me, not long before I was wounded. Once my memory returned and I could think clearly again, that soldier's words took root in my heart. And once they did, I began to change." He drew another deep breath. "I hope you can see that I've changed."

Yes, he seemed different to Diana. And she wasn't entirely pleased by the changes either. Not because they weren't good ones, but because they demanded she see him in a different light—and *that* she didn't want to do.

He's a politician now. He'll say whatever he needs to say to get votes. Any fool knows that.

She'd been a fool for too long. She mustn't continue to be one. She mustn't let his words confuse her. She mustn't let his polite attentions win her forgiveness. Certainly she wouldn't let him convince her that he'd found God while he was away.

Politician, indeed.

She turned the mare's head with the reins and started back toward the house. Tyson caught up with her in a few seconds.

"Mrs. Cuddy made us some sandwiches," he said. "We could find some shade and eat."

"No, I think it's better we go back."

"I'd hoped we could spend the day together." He sounded disappointed.

She almost relented.

Almost.

She kept the mare moving toward the house.

For some reason, she thought of Brook. Had Brook manipulated her emotions the way Tyson did? No. Never. But that was because he was completely different from Tyson. Solid and dependable. Steady in word and deed. She'd known what to expect from Brook Calhoun. Being with him hadn't confused her in the least.

Did I love him? Even a little?

No. Not even a little. She was fond of Brook, but she hadn't loved him. Hadn't wanted to love him. At least, not that wild, abandoned love she'd felt for Tyson. She would never feel so again, and thank goodness for that. No, it had been enough that she'd respected Brook. They'd been comfortable together. She would have made him a good wife and she believed he would have been a good husband.

But that was over. Even if Tyson ended their marriage after the election—which he'd said he wouldn't—Brook would not marry a divorcée. Would any man of the proper social standing? Unlikely. Then again, as long as Tyson took care of her expenses as he'd promised, perhaps she would be happier without a husband. Being married but living apart didn't hold the social stigma of divorce. She knew that from personal experience.

A wave of loneliness washed over her, an all too familiar feeling.

She'd been so friendless while living with her in-laws after Tyson left. And even once she came to Boise and met Brook, her only friends had been his friends. None of them would come calling while she was with Tyson.

"I've upset you, my dear."

She glanced toward Tyson, surprised to find him still beside her.

"What did I say?"

"Nothing. It's nothing." She shook her head. "I've just ridden long enough for one day. That's all."

His expression said he didn't believe her.

Well, she didn't care if he believed her or not.

May 1893

Standing together in the shadowed parlor of the Fisher home, Tyson gazed down into Diana's eyes. They revealed her devotion, her innocence, her goodness. He'd won her heart while in Montana on business, and she hadn't the guile to try to hide that truth from him.

Of course he'd won the hearts of other young women through the years. It wasn't a hard thing to do when he had the wealth of the Applegates behind him. He was considered a great catch by unmarried females and their ambitious mothers.

But Diana Fisher was different. She cared for him and not his money. He knew that was true. She was pretty and smart and without the irritating affectations of so many women of his acquaintance. She was good natured and laughed easily. He could honestly say he enjoyed her company.

There was one more thing about Diana that appealed to him, perhaps above everything else: his father was adamantly opposed to her. That Jeremiah Applegate had never met Diana didn't matter.

In his mind, the middle-class Fishers weren't worthy of a close alliance with the Applegates. Worse still in his father's opinion, Diana wasn't the Fishers' natural child. She was an orphan from the tenements of Chicago.

"Marry me, Diana," he whispered.

Her eyes widened as she sucked in a breath.

"Marry me tomorrow."

"Tomorrow? But I—"

"I don't want to return to Idaho alone. I want you to go there with me. As my wife. These past few weeks with you have been so special."

"Oh, Tyson."

He kissed her, not giving her a chance to list any reasons why marrying so quickly might not be the best idea. There were so many more reasons why it was. First and foremost, it wouldn't give Jeremiah Applegate a chance to interfere. Second, bringing Diana home as his bride would infuriate the old man. And, of course, there was the inheritance that would come to Tyson upon his marriage. A fortune that would free him from his father's control at last. Better now than wait until he turned thirty.

It was all too perfect.

"Marry me, Diana," he whispered again, his lips still close to hers. "I won't let you refuse. You mustn't refuse. Please."

SEVEN

There was a significant crowd gathered on the capitol lawn the following Friday morning. The news that Tyson Applegate, son of silver baron Jeremiah Applegate, was declaring his candidacy for the Senate had been leaked to the press the day before.

Although Tyson would run as a write-in candidate, it was no secret he enjoyed the support of influential members in the Idaho Republican party whose official candidate had been in office since 1890. The general consensus was that the unpopular senator would lose the election to the Silver Republican candidate come November. Many believed Tyson Applegate was the party's best hope to hang onto the Senate seat.

After an introduction where his participation in the Rough Riders was played up for all it was worth, Tyson gave a brief speech, enumerating the key things he hoped to accomplish if elected. It was a speech he'd written and rewritten many times over the past couple of weeks, and he still wasn't convinced he'd gotten it right.

Time would tell.

As he stepped back from the podium and placed an arm around Diana's back, he wondered what his father would have thought of it. No doubt Tyson would know soon enough. With the help of powerful friends, he'd managed to keep his status and identity a secret for longer than he'd dared hope. The task had been made easier because everyone who cared had believed him dead so no one had looked for him. That was no longer the case. If his father didn't know he was alive right now, he would know by tonight.

Tyson should have sent a telegram this morning. He and his father had many differences, but Jeremiah Applegate was still his father. A strong supporter of the Silver Republican candidate, without a doubt.

Just one of many areas where Tyson disagreed with the man who'd sired him.

With determination, he returned his focus to the here and now, waving to the crowd with his free arm. Then he glanced at Diana. "It's begun."

"It's begun," she whispered back.

He couldn't tell what she thought. Her expression was pleasant enough to fool people who didn't know her, to make them think she was happy with her husband's candidacy. But it wasn't pleasant enough to fool him.

Earlier in the week, he'd hoped he and his wife had taken a few steps closer to each other. Instead Diana had chosen to widen the distance between them. It felt to Tyson as if the problems in their marriage were becoming as wide as the Grand Canyon. How was he to change that?

"Thank you for standing with me," he said.

She didn't respond with words, but if he read the look in her eyes correctly, she believed he'd given her no other choice. He couldn't argue on that score, but he'd done it for a good purpose. In the end, she wouldn't regret it. He swore she wouldn't.

His new assistant, Herbert Eastman—a rail-thin fellow who tried to hide his youthful years behind a generous mustache—appeared at his side. "Mr. Applegate, Justice Waverley would like a moment of your time. He's with some men who work with him."

Tyson wondered at the wisdom of Samuel Waverley being here for this announcement, let alone introducing Tyson to other men in government. A judge should not appear to favor one party over any other. But Justice Waverley apparently wasn't concerned his presence would appear in a negative light.

Tyson motioned for Diana to follow his assistant, but she shook her head.

"Would you mind terribly if I excused myself?" she asked softly. "I'm afraid I've developed a headache."

Come to think of it, she did look somewhat peaked. "Shall I call for the carriage to take you home?"

"No. I can wait until you are through. But I would like to sit down somewhere away from all these people."

Tyson looked toward the entrance to the capitol. "Go inside. I'm sure you'll find a quiet spot somewhere. Try the basement. It'll be cooler down there. I'll come looking for you as soon as I can."

"Thank you. And please apologize to Justice Waverley for me."

Tyson watched for a few moments as Diana made her way toward the steps. Then he turned and followed his assistant.

Diana had told the truth. Her head was splitting. She was beyond grateful to find a cool, poorly lit corner with a bench against one wall where she could sit and close her eyes.

However would she survive the next six months? How many times would she have to stand on some platform and stare into the sun and listen to speeches and smile until it seemed her cheeks would crack from the effort? She hadn't expected it to be this difficult. It was the pretense, she supposed, that made it so hard. But perhaps with time she would get used to pretending.

Six months. I can stand anything for six months.

The words were becoming her mantra.

"Hello, Diana."

Her eyes opened in time for her to see Brook doff his hat. Surprise caused her to sit straighter. What else should she feel, seeing him for the first time since the night of the dinner party? Pleasure? Gladness? Knowledge that she'd missed his company? She felt none of those things. Only a kind of confusion. Almost a sense that being with him in this deserted hallway, away from the sight of others, was somehow wrong.

"You're looking lovely." He motioned to the bench. "May I join you?"

"Yes."

He sat. "I take it that announcement is why your husband returned to Idaho."

"Yes."

"And to you."

"Yes."

"Rather cruel of him to use you in this way." Brook turned his gaze down the hallway. "I've missed seeing you, my dear. The past two weeks have been much too quiet without you."

His words surprised her. He'd seemed so coldly formal when they'd parted company. She'd thought—

"We both know we can never marry, even if you were free of him."

Those words were more what she'd expected of him.

"Not unless he was to die after all," Brook added.

A shiver coursed through Diana. Something about his tone of voice—

He looked at her again. "But I do hope we can remain friends."

"Of course we can."

"Your husband wouldn't object?"

"He would have no right to." She tilted her chin. "I'm allowed to choose my own friends."

Brook chuckled. "I forgot you have a habit of speaking your mind when I least expect it."

"Do I?"

"Yes." His smile faded. "I hope you will be honest with me now. Do you *want* to reconcile with your husband?"

There was so much she would like to say in answer to that question. She wanted to let years of hurt and anger spill forth. But the words lodged in her throat.

"Are you happy? That he's returned."

"No." She shook her head. "Well, yes. I mean, I'm glad he wasn't killed in Cuba. But I never thought Tyson would want me to live with him."

Brook drew in a deep breath and released it, then stood. "Perhaps we could meet for lunch. Next week or the week after."

Awareness of the pounding in her temples returned. "Yes. I would like that, Brook."

"Then I shall be in touch." He tipped his hat, turned on his heel, and strode away.

She closed her eyes a second time and tried to ignore the guilty sensations that swirled in her stomach. Why should she feel guilty? She'd done nothing wrong. It wasn't as if Tyson's supporters or his opponents wouldn't know she had been seeing Brook Calhoun when everyone—well, most everyone—had thought her husband dead in Cuba.

But he wasn't dead. He was alive. Very much alive. And she knew, deep in her heart, that he wouldn't want her meeting

Brook for lunch or sitting beside him on a bench in the capitol building.

All the more reason she would go if Brook extended an invitation again. She must prove her independence. To herself as well as to Tyson.

Tyson drew back against a wall and watched Brook Calhoun hurry up the stairs from the basement. A few moments later, the man disappeared through the capitol entrance, no doubt headed to his offices on Bannock Street. Tyson had seen Brook in the crowd earlier, but he hadn't thought much of it at the time. Many prominent Boise businessmen had been present for his announcement. But seeing the man come up from the basement of the capitol was another matter altogether. Because Diana was down there.

Had the two of them planned to meet today? Was that the reason for her claiming she had a headache? So she could go inside and meet with her former fiancé?

He pushed off the wall and went down the stairs. It wasn't long before he found her, seated on a bench, eyes closed. He stopped and simply took pleasure in looking at her. Tendrils of red hair curled on her nape. Her dress was both simple and elegant—how was that possible?—the color not quite blue, not quite green. Her mouth was—

He swallowed hard, then cleared his throat.

Her eyes flew open.

"How are you feeling?"

She hesitated a moment. "Better, I think."

"Are you ready to go home?"

"If you are." She stood.

He offered his arm.

She hesitated again before taking it.

They followed the corridor around to the staircase and were halfway to the top before Tyson said, "I thought I saw Mr. Calhoun in the crowd while I was speaking."

"Brook?"

He waited for her to say she'd seen him too. That they had met inside the capitol building and spoken to each other. But she said nothing—and her silence was the same as a lie.

"Yes," he said after a lengthy pause. "Of course, I only saw him the once in his home, but I'm fairly certain it was him."

They reached the main doors and he opened one for her to pass through. She seemed to think that an excuse for her continued silence.

Irritation tightened his jaw. Why did Diana have to make reconciliation so difficult? Couldn't she see he earnestly wanted to make their marriage work?

Once again he offered his arm. She placed her gloved fingertips in the crook, and they descended the steps of the capitol. The crowd of supporters, newspaper reporters, and curious bystanders had dispersed, and they were able to walk to their carriage undisturbed.

Undisturbed on the outside, at least.

Tyson could not say the same for his thoughts.

Bitterness burned Brook's tongue, but he'd learned through the years to disguise his true feelings. No person he met as he followed the sidewalk along Bannock Street would have guessed anything disturbed him.

But the anger was there, all the same. He'd been so close to marrying a fortune. There wasn't anything he couldn't have done with Diana's money once it was his to control. He could have expanded his business concerns. He could have purchased a larger home and hired more servants. He could have moved in ever more powerful circles.

But Tyson Applegate had returned, destroying all of Brook's plans.

He wanted to make the man pay. He *would* make him pay. And although she didn't know it, Diana was going to help him.

May 1893

Nerves twirled and tumbled in Diana's stomach as Tyson helped her disembark from the carriage. Her trepidation increased tenfold when she lifted her gaze and took in the splendor of the Applegate mansion.

"This is where you grew up?" She'd known Tyson's family had money, but she'd had no idea—

"No. Father had this monstrosity built after I was sent to boarding school. When I was a small boy, we lived in a house about a mile from here."

Diana and Tyson had been married only four days, but already she'd learned to avoid asking her new husband about his father. What sort of ogre was Jeremiah Applegate to earn so much animosity from his son?

It seemed she was about to find out.

Tyson took her arm and guided her up the steps to the front door. It opened before them, and the manservant who stood just inside bowed slightly when he saw Tyson.

"Are my parents at home, Billingsly?"

"They are, sir. In the family parlor."

"Thank you." Tyson glanced at Diana. "Ready?"

She nodded, even though she felt anything but ready to meet Jeremiah and Nora Applegate. Her dress that had seemed handsome and stylish in Montana now felt dowdy. Why hadn't Tyson told her what to expect? Why hadn't he warned her?

The sound of their footsteps accompanied them down a long, high-ceilinged entry hall. A hallway that seemed without end. But at last Tyson turned toward an open doorway and they stopped.

Diana moistened her lips and tried to push back the rising fear.

"Mother," Tyson said. "Father."

Nora Applegate looked up from her needlepoint. "Tyson!" She rose from the settee and hurried toward them, smiling broadly. "I didn't know you were expected back this evening." She kissed his cheek before looking toward Diana.

"Mother, I would like you to meet Diana . . . my wife."

Jeremiah Applegate shot to his feet, the book he'd held dropping to the floor. "What?" It was more roar than word.

"My wife, Father. Diana and I were married on Wednesday."

"Have you gone mad?" Jeremiah demanded. "You knew my feelings."

Diana was young and inexperienced in the ways of the world, but she still understood her father-in-law's meaning. He didn't approve of her. He'd told Tyson he didn't approve of her even though they'd never met. Whatever the reason for this disapproval, she longed for the floor to open and swallow her whole.

Ignoring her husband, Nora embraced Diana. "Welcome, my dear." She took a step back, her smile genuine and tender. "I wish I'd known you two were coming today. We would have been better prepared to welcome the bride and groom. You must be tired after your journey. Let me show you to . . . to the bedroom next to Tyson's so you can freshen up."

Diana glanced at Tyson, half afraid to leave his side.

"Go on, Diana. I'll be up after I've had a chance to talk with Father."

Nora put her arm around Diana's shoulders, turned, and steered her into the hallway and toward the sweeping staircase.

"Were you so desperate to get control of your inheritance that you were willing to marry anything in a skirt?" Jeremiah's booming voice reached Diana before the parlor door swung closed.

She wanted to cry. She wanted to run away. But from someplace within, she found the strength to keep climbing the stairs, her tears caught in her throat.

EIGHT

Morning sunlight spilled through the dining room windows, illuminating the polished tabletop and causing the glassware to sparkle.

Diana and her mother were alone in the room. Tyson had eaten and left the house before Diana arose. Upchurch had gone into the kitchen moments before, no doubt to replenish a dish that needed no replenishment.

"I shall get fat," she said, looking at the breakfast before her. There was a half-eaten bowl of wheat germ with sugar and cream. On her plate were the remains of a small beefsteak and some fried potatoes, but she'd eaten every last bite of the cakes with maple syrup, a favorite of hers. Lifting her gaze to her mother, she added, "I'd forgotten how wasteful the very rich can be. There's enough food on the sideboard to feed an army."

Her mother swallowed a bite of food. "Perhaps a slight exaggeration, dear."

"Perhaps."

"If that's how you feel, speak to Mrs. Brown or to the cook. After all, you are mistress of this house."

True. She *was* mistress of the house. It was up to her to make these kinds of decisions. But decision-making was much easier when money was limited and there were only two women in the household.

Upchurch returned to the dining room. "Would you care for more coffee, Mrs. Applegate?" He set the dish he carried on the sideboard.

"No, thank you, Upchurch. I believe I've had enough of everything."

"Very good, madam."

"Please tell Mrs. Cuddy everything was delicious."

"Yes, madam. I will tell her." The butler turned and left the dining room.

Diana looked at her mother again. "I believe I'll walk down to the stables. I need some exercise after such a large breakfast. Would you like to come with me?"

"Thank you, dear, but I think not. I've never appreciated horses the way you do. You get that from your father." Sorrow caught in her mother's voice.

In response, tears filled Diana's eyes. After more than two years, she sometimes went days without remembering she would never see her father again. She could pretend miles rather than death parted them. But whenever her mother was sad, the truth came back.

"Mother, I'm so thankful you and Father chose me to be your daughter." Her own voice cracked with emotion. "I don't tell you often enough."

Her mother smiled, though it remained tinged by sadness. "And I don't tell you enough how much God blessed us by sending you all the way from Illinois for us to choose."

Not all children from the so-called orphan trains had stories such as Diana's. Perhaps most didn't. She'd been loved and adored. What about her brother and sister? She didn't have any idea if Hugh or Felicia had been raised in good homes, if they'd been well dressed and well fed. She didn't know where they lived today or if they were even alive. Was it too late to find out? Perhaps she should ask Tyson to help her. If he could fool the army into thinking he was dead, surely he could find out what had happened to her brother and sister.

"Gracious sakes alive!" Her mother stood. "Haven't we become sentimental this morning? You go for your walk, dear. I'm going to do some knitting."

Diana used the cloth napkin to dry her eyes before rising from her chair and walking out to the east-side veranda. The verdant lushness of late spring surrounded her, and the scent of new-mown lawn tickled her nose. The slightest of breezes caused leafy tree limbs to bob and dance. Flowers bloomed in an array of colors—pinks, purples, yellows, reds, oranges—and she imagined the gardens would be even more beautiful come August.

As Diana followed the pathway toward the stables, her thoughts returned to her childhood. The Fishers hadn't been rich, but she'd never wanted for anything she needed and rarely had she gone without those things she wanted. Even she had to admit she'd been spoiled as a child.

Diana had been six when her real mother died. Old enough that she could remember the poverty that surrounded her family and neighbors in their tenement flat in Chicago. Old enough to remember what it was like to have threadbare clothes and to go to bed hungry. How far she'd come from that life in the last nineteen years. She should thank God more often for all He'd done for her, all He'd given her. She certainly didn't deserve the blessings.

Is Tyson one of those blessings? A disturbing and unexpected question. One she didn't want to entertain. She shoved the thought away and moved on with quick, determined steps.

The stables were cool and quiet when she entered. Through the open doors at the far end of the building, she saw the groom working a horse in the closest paddock. Standing on the rail, watching, was the stable boy.

Diana paused long enough to give her bay mare a pat on the neck, then headed toward the doorway to observe the training session. She was about to step into the sunlight when a sound caught her attention. It sounded like a cat in distress. She turned a full circle but saw nothing. Perhaps it had been her imagination. No, there it was again. That was definitely a feline's protest.

She took several steps backward and turned in a slow circle, her gaze searching corners and shadows in the barn.

"Meooooow!"

Diana looked up. There, hanging from a narrow ledge by its front paws, was a skinny, matted creature. Its hind legs grasped at the air, its front paws scratched for something to hold onto. And then it fell.

Plop! It hit the ground, sending up a cloud of dirt and sawdust.

"Oh, dear." Diana knelt beside the kitten—for she could see now that it was still a young cat, perhaps six months old or so—and picked it up. "You poor thing. You're half starved." She stood, cradling the kitten against her chest, surprised that it remained docile. Perhaps the fall had knocked the wind out of it. "We must get you something to eat."

As he entered the house, Tyson heard a shriek of surprise come from the kitchen. He dropped his hat onto the table in the entry hall and strode quickly toward the back of the house.

"I'm sorry, Mrs. Applegate, but I'll not have fleas in my kitchen." That was Madge Cuddy, the cook.

Fleas?

"I don't think it has fleas," Diana replied.

Tyson looked into the kitchen. His wife stood near the icebox, holding a gray tabby cat against her chest.

"I just need to get it something to eat," she said.

"Well, take it outside where it belongs and I'll bring some milk and table scraps." Mrs. Cuddy pointed toward the door leading onto the veranda. "Please, ma'am, get it out of my kitchen before we're infested."

Diana's chin tipped upward. "It does *not* have fleas." Then she obeyed the cook.

After the door closed behind Diana, Tyson stepped into the kitchen. "Trouble, Mrs. Cuddy?"

The woman looked up, her eyes rounding. "Mr. Applegate. I didn't hear you come in, sir."

"No." He felt a strong urge to promise that he didn't have fleas either. Laughter rose in his throat, but he caught it before it escaped. "You were busy." He glanced toward the door opposite him. "I'll let you find that food for the cat while I join my wife."

The cook nodded.

He hurried across the kitchen and out onto the veranda, where he found Diana seated on the top step, crooning to the cat. "Poor kitty. You don't have fleas. Don't let Mrs. Cuddy scare you. It's all right."

Tyson cleared his throat.

Diana looked over her shoulder and frowned. "Oh. Tyson. It's you. I thought you were Mrs. Cuddy."

"Hmm. Not sure I care for that."

He'd hoped for a smile. He didn't get one.

"I didn't mean it that way," she answered.

"I'm relieved." He walked to the steps and sat beside her. "Where did *that* come from?" He motioned with his head toward the kitten.

"In the stables. I don't think it's been living there long. Surely someone would have found it before now if it had. Poor thing. It's nearly starved to death."

"*Does* it have fleas?"

Diana's back stiffened. "No."

"Are you sure? You'd better let me look. Trust me when I say you don't want any of those tiny bugs crawling on you."

Her expression turned comical—part insulted, part uncertain—as she passed the tabby into his waiting hands.

Diana was right about the kitten being nearly starved. She—his inspection told him it was female—wasn't much more than skin and bones. She meowed at him, but it wasn't much as complaints went. And he was thankful she didn't try to bite or scratch as he gave her coat a close inspection.

"You're in luck," he said at last. "She doesn't have fleas."

Diana whisked the kitten back into her arms, smiling at last—not for him but for the young feline. "I'm going to call her Tiger because of her stripes."

Too late Tyson realized what giving the kitten a name meant: a cat for a pet. A cat in the house and not in the stables where it belonged. He couldn't say he liked cats much anywhere, although he supposed they served a purpose when it came to keeping the rodent population under control.

He cleared his throat. "Maybe you shouldn't let yourself get too attached, Diana. She might die, being so skinny and all. She might be diseased. You can't tell."

"I won't let her die." There was that stubborn tilt of her chin again. "And she isn't diseased."

Well, if determination was all it took, Tiger still had nine lives to her credit.

Tyson heard the door open behind them.

78

"I've brought the food you wanted," the cook announced.

Diana rose quickly. "Thank you, Mrs. Cuddy. And you don't have to worry about fleas. Mr. Applegate gave her a thorough inspection."

The cook made a sound in her throat. Disbelief? Righteous indignation?

Tyson twisted on the top step to watch as his wife took the cat to where Mrs. Cuddy had set down a saucer and bowl. Before Diana could put Tiger on her feet, the feline leapt from her arms and began gobbling up the scraps of meat on the saucer. When every last tidbit of solid food had disappeared, the cat lapped up milk as fast as her tongue could go.

"You'll never be rid of it now," the cook said before going inside.

Exactly what I was thinking, Mrs. Cuddy.

Diana had a soft spot in her heart for the broken and the lost. As a child, she hadn't been able to do anything for the strays she'd found because being around dogs and cats made her adoptive father sneeze and sometimes his eyes would swell shut. But now she was an adult and mistress of her own home. She *would* keep Tiger, and not even Tyson would be allowed to tell her she couldn't.

She picked up the cat and turned toward her husband, prepared to do the necessary battle. But she found him standing, too, watching her. The tender look in his eyes touched something deep inside and stole the fight right out of her.

"I suppose you'll need a bed for her to sleep in," he said.

She nodded, surprised there would be no argument.

"You'll have to keep her away from Mrs. Cuddy's kitchen."

Another nod.

"Well, then . . ." He stepped toward her.

The breath caught in her chest, mirroring her uncertainty at what he planned. She almost thought he would embrace her. Perhaps even kiss her.

Instead he reached out and stroked the cat's head. "Welcome to the family, Tiger."

Standing at the dining room window, Gloria watched the scene on the veranda play out and felt her heart soften a little toward her son-in-law. Perhaps he'd changed for the better. Perhaps he did want to make Diana happy, as he claimed.

She meant what she'd said to Tyson earlier in the week. If he hurt her daughter again, Gloria would spend the rest of her life trying to make him pay for it. Not a very Christian way to think or act, she knew. But wasn't an eye for an eye also part of the Bible?

Guilt niggled at her conscience. Perhaps it would be better to spend her time praying that both of them would be able to forgive and learn to truly love each other. Love was such a precious and powerful emotion.

She closed her eyes and pictured Byron. She'd loved being married to him, and he'd cherished her, always treating her with such gentleness, as if she were a fine porcelain doll. Even her inability to give him a child of their union hadn't changed the way he'd felt about her. Oh, if only Diana could have married a man more like her father.

A smile came to her lips as she opened her eyes again.

Diana was made of sterner stuff than porcelain. She was stronger than her mother in so many ways. Tyson would have to prove himself her equal if there was any hope for their marriage.

August 1893

Diana watched moonlight and shadows dance across the ceiling of the bedchamber. Despite Tyson sleeping next to her, she felt alone and lonely. She longed for the respite of sleep, but in this wee hour of the night, escape from her troubled thoughts eluded her.

Tyson had come to her room earlier in the evening. He had come into her bed, and she had welcomed him there, as she always did, eager to please him, wanting him to know how much she loved him. Although it wasn't unusual for him to seek her out at night, it was rare for him to fall asleep in her bed.

He didn't love her. She knew that now. She should have known it from the start—he'd never said he did, not even when he proposed—only she'd been too blinded by her own love for him to realize it.

Tears trailed from the corners of her eyes, dampening the pillow beneath her head.

Some days she was able to pretend all was well. When she and Tyson went riding together through the forests that surrounded the Applegate mansion, for instance. He seemed happier then. Freer. Almost glad to be with her. But in the silence of the night, she was forced to see things as they were: Tyson had married in order to receive his inheritance before his thirtieth birthday, and he had chosen Diana to be his wife simply because his father didn't think her good enough.

Her husband shifted in the bed and sighed.

Diana squeezed her eyes closed. *Please, God, make him love me. Please. Please. Please.*

NINE

Tyson stood in the entrance hall, dressed in evening attire, waiting for Diana to come down the stairs. He felt a rare bit of nerves. Tonight they were guests of Justice Waverley and his wife—along with a few of the Waverleys' closest friends. It wasn't officially an endorsement, of course, but it was as good as one.

He checked his pocket watch. What was keeping Diana? If she didn't hurry, they would be late.

From behind him came his mother-in-law's voice. "This is a big night for you, isn't it?"

He turned. "Yes, I believe so."

She cocked an eyebrow.

He nodded. "It's definitely a big night. No question whatsoever."

"You surprised me, you know."

"How is that?"

"Letting Diana keep that cat."

"Mrs. Fisher, there isn't anything I would withhold from Diana if it's in my power to grant it. But to be honest, I'm not sure my *letting* had anything to do with it. Her mind was made up, and she didn't need nor want my permission."

His mother-in-law laughed softly. "You gained a measure of wisdom in your travels."

"I hope so, madam. I do hope so."

A sound drew Tyson's gaze toward the staircase, and his mouth went dry at the sight that met his eyes. Diana favored green in all its varied hues, but tonight she wore a gown that was the exact same shade of red as her hair. Gold threads ran through the fabric, making it shimmer as she moved.

If he could have his way, he would call off this evening at the Waverleys, sweep his wife into his arms, and carry her back up that staircase and straight into the bedroom. Only there was one problem. It was *his* bedroom and not *their* bedroom. His wife she might be, but for the present she was a wife in name only.

"Diana." He paused and cleared his throat. "Diana, you look stunning. Perhaps it is you who should be running for office. There isn't a man alive who wouldn't vote for you if he could see you in that gown." He waited for her to smile.

She didn't oblige. "I know you mean that as a compliment, Tyson, but I assure you, I would not want to get any man's vote simply because he thought me beautiful. I should want it for the same reason you want it—because he believed I could do a good job as a senator."

He inclined his head in silent agreement. She was right. He wanted to win this election because he had something of worth to offer the people of Idaho. And he admired Diana for speaking her mind. Had she always been so sure of her own opinion? He didn't think so. At least that wasn't how he remembered her.

"Mother," Diana said, "would you mind checking on Tiger before you retire for the night? I've shut her in my room." She cast a glance in Tyson's direction. "I wouldn't want her to trouble Mrs. Cuddy in the kitchen."

"Of course, dear. Don't you worry about the kitty. Just go and have a pleasant evening."

The Waverley home on Harrison Boulevard was spacious, elegant, and tastefully decorated, and Iris Waverley, a woman in her forties, had most certainly been blessed with the gift of hospitality. Diana had met her for the first time this evening, yet she'd been made to feel as if they were old friends.

As Diana looked around the dinner table—candlelight reflecting off china, crystal, and silver—she couldn't help thinking this might have been her life these past seven years—if only her husband had wanted her at his side.

She glanced across the table at Tyson. He was talking with Helen Graham, the much younger wife of a state representative. Diana knew Mrs. Graham by reputation, of course. The woman was a leader in Boise society and a strong supporter of the arts and woman's suffrage. Could Diana have become a hostess of the same renown had things turned out differently?

Kendall Michaels, editor for the *Idaho Daily Statesman*, leaned close at Diana's left side and asked, "Are you interested in politics, Mrs. Applegate?"

"I became interested when my husband decided to run for the Senate seat." She offered a smile that she hoped look genuine.

The editor laughed, making heads turn in their direction. "Thank you, Mrs. Applegate. It's refreshing to hear such honesty." He looked toward Tyson. "Your wife does you credit, Mr. Applegate."

Tyson's gaze met with Diana's. "She does, indeed."

The softly spoken words felt intimate, almost like a caress, and if she wasn't mistaken, her cheeks flushed in response. How maddening that she let him do that to her. Where was her pride? Where was her self-control? They were playacting, after all. This was not a real marriage. It was little more than a business agreement. She would help him get elected. He would provide her with a home and income of her own. Nothing more.

"How tragic that Mrs. Applegate thought herself a war widow for so long." Kendall Michaels' gaze remained on Tyson. "Think of the scandal it would have been if she'd married Mr. Calhoun only to discover her first husband still lived. You'd have made her a bigamist."

A small gasp escaped Diana's lips. All other conversations ceased, and the air became thick with tension.

"Yes." Tyson's voice was controlled, and if he minded the man's comments, it didn't show. "It would have been unfortunate, indeed. But since the belief that I died in Cuba was entirely my fault and not hers, her reputation would have remained untarnished. Just as it is now." He looked at Diana again, though his words seemed to be for everyone else around the table. "I regret any hurt I caused her. I regret it all deeply. I'm thankful she's given me the opportunity to redeem myself in her eyes."

Is that what she'd done? Given him an opportunity to redeem himself. Yes, she supposed it was, in a way. She'd agreed to let him try to change her mind about him—and she thought, perhaps, he was succeeding. At least a little.

"I pray I shall prove worthy," Tyson ended.

Justice Waverley cleared his throat. "You shall, my good man. You shall. I have every confidence in you."

"Thank you, sir."

"I predict you and your beautiful wife will take Washington by storm after you're elected."

"Samuel," Iris said to her husband, "you promised we would not speak of politics nor the law at the dinner table."

"So I did, my dear. I apologize. And look. Here comes our dessert."

Flaming cherries jubilee was just the right distraction to direct attention away from Diana and Tyson. The guests *oohed* and *ahhed*. Private conversations soon resumed. The elderly gentleman seated on Diana's right asked her how long she'd lived in Boise, and soon he was telling her interesting stories about his early years in Idaho prior to statehood.

Tyson seethed on the inside.

It wasn't unexpected that someone from the press would have questions about why his family had believed him dead. But he hadn't expected those questions to come up at *this* dinner party. Nor had he expected anyone to say them in such a way as to hurt or embarrass Diana. And judging by her reaction, that's exactly what Kendall Michaels had done.

When the gentlemen left the dinner table for the smoking room, Tyson made certain he was nowhere near Mr. Michaels. It was better he avoid the newspaperman until he managed to subdue his temper. He didn't want to ruin his chances of being elected because he socked one of the judge's guests in the nose. Especially so early in the race.

While the other men enjoyed their cigars and their glasses of port or whiskey, Tyson—who'd given up smoking and all but the occasional glass of wine—tried to visit with each one of them, answering their questions, sharing his opinions and positions on various subjects. But his thoughts throughout that hour were never far from Diana. How was she doing with the other ladies? Did she feel ostracized because of Michaels' thoughtless comments? How could he protect her in the future from similar remarks?

He wanted to win this election. There was no question about

that. He believed it was what God had called him to do. He also believed he had a better chance of winning the election if his wife was by his side. But getting elected was not the main reason he wanted to save his marriage to Diana. Even before he'd returned to Idaho, even before he'd seen and talked to her again and spent time with her, he'd wanted to prove himself a changed man, a better man.

"I wouldn't worry about her," Justice Waverley said in a low voice. "Your wife has courage and backbone."

Thankful it was just the two of them in this corner of the smoking room, Tyson nodded. "Yes, she does."

"Someday you'll have to explain to me why you spent so much time with continents and oceans between the two of you."

Selfishness, stubborn pride, and stupidity. That's how Tyson could have answered.

"Gentlemen," the judge said, taking a step away from Tyson, "shall we rejoin the ladies?"

Since he had neither a cigar to put out nor a drink glass to put down, Tyson was free to lead the way to the parlor. He paused long enough in the doorway to sweep the room with his gaze until he found Diana standing next to the grand piano, singing while Iris Waverley played.

His wife had a beautiful, clear voice. Something else he hadn't known about her.

Tyson strode across the spacious parlor, smiling when she looked his way. She quickly trained her eyes on the music again, but not before she stumbled over the lyrics. Color rose in her cheeks. Strange, how something as innocent as a blush could make him want to take her in his arms and kiss her until the ability to breathe left them both.

Lying beneath light bedcovers that night, Diana stared toward the ceiling, her thoughts in too much turmoil to allow her to fall asleep. The evening at the Waverley home had been difficult for her. Too often, with the exception of their host and hostess, she'd been made to feel like a bug under a microscope, inspected by men and women alike. People who were part of society's upper crust who knew she was not. There'd also been that despicable newspaperman, Mr. Michaels, and his comments meant to sting and embarrass. He'd succeeded, too, although she'd done her best not to show it.

As for Tyson, her feelings toward him confused her more each day. And no wonder. She wanted them to live peacefully together for six months while still holding onto her hurt. She supposed she couldn't have it both ways.

If only her life could go back to how it had been just a few short weeks ago.

"Why is this happening, God? I could have been happy with Brook. We were fond of each other, and he didn't confuse me. I knew what was expected with him. Why did Tyson have to come back and ruin everything?"

If God had an answer, He didn't share it with her.

September 1893

Years of bitter resentment exploded inside Tyson's chest as he glared at his father. "You had no right to attempt to meddle with my inheritance."

"I was looking out for your interests, boy."

"No, you were trying to control me. Like you've always done.

Like I've let you do because I didn't have the backbone to stand up to you. Because you held the purse strings. But you don't hold them anymore, and try as you might, you won't ever hold them again. I'm an attorney, thanks to you, and I know how to protect what is mine." He spun on his heel and headed for the door.

"Tyson, come back here. We're not finished."

He yanked open the study door. "Yes, we are. For good." He stepped through the opening and slammed the door closed.

He'd almost reached the grand staircase when he lost control of his temper. With a swing of his arm, he sent a vase and its contents flying across the hall. A gasp drew his gaze to the second-floor landing where Diana watched him with wide eyes. Frightened eyes. Sad eyes.

Guilt added to his fury.

He needed to get out of this house before he did or said something he'd truly regret.

TEN

It was the last Sunday in May, but soaring temperatures made it feel more like the heart of summer.

Finished with the midday meal, Diana's mother excused herself from the table and went to her room to lie down. Diana considered doing the same. A mostly sleepless night—coupled with a lengthy sermon at church that morning, a large meal, and the heat—had left her eyelids feeling heavy.

"Maybe you should lie down too," Tyson said, echoing her thoughts. "You look tired."

Agreeing with him would be like admitting thoughts about him had kept her awake in the night. She shook her head. "I believe I'll go sit in the garden and read."

"Would you like company?"

Hating the temptation she felt to capitulate to his charms, she shook her head a second time. "I shall enjoy my book more if I'm alone."

He looked disappointed, and his expression tugged at her heart a second time. She glanced down at her plate lest she change her mind.

After a lengthy silence, Tyson said, "I believe it's time we plan our first dinner party."

"So soon?" Her eyes darted up again. "Do you think we're ready? There is much still to be done. More furniture to buy. More linens and such."

"You've done wonders with the house, Diana, and you've hired a capable staff. Our guests are sure to be impressed."

Begrudgingly, she warmed beneath his praise.

"We'll make our first gathering an intimate one. Three or four couples. You could invite some of your own friends. We needn't start with my political supporters."

My own friends. Did she have any? Any true friends. Any close confidants besides her mother. Since no one of her acquaintance had come calling to see how she was getting along in her new home, she knew the answer was no.

An all-too-familiar sense of loneliness swept over her. "I'll think about who I might ask."

"Don't look so glum, Diana. I have great faith in you."

It was good someone did, for she had little in herself.

Half an hour later, she sat on a shaded bench on the east side of the house. Bees buzzed around flowers that grew nearby. Small birds chirped and bounced from limb to limb in the tree that grew behind her. A book of poetry lay open on her lap, but she had a hard time concentrating on the words on the page.

Why was it, she continued to wonder, that she had no close friends? She wasn't an unlikable person. At least she didn't think so. She wasn't vain . . . although she was partial to pretty clothes and jewelry. She wasn't dishonest . . . except for an occasional little white lie to save someone's feelings. She wasn't given to gossip. Well, she might enjoy listening to a juicy tidbit, but there was no one to tell it to later, so that didn't count.

She'd been a shy child, especially after she was separated from her brother and sister. But after going to live with the Fishers, after experiencing the love they'd showered upon her, she'd come out of her shell. She'd had lots of friends in Montana. She'd never wanted for anything, and she'd been happy.

All that changed after Tyson left her behind on his father's estate. She'd stayed with the Applegates at first because she was certain her husband would return, because she was waiting for his letters, because she loved him. She'd stayed because of her mother-in-law, whom she'd grown to care for deeply. She'd stayed because she was—

The snap of a twig yanked her attention toward the house in time to see a boy step onto a wooden crate and reach for something on the counter just inside the kitchen window. One of Mrs. Cuddy's pies, if Diana wasn't mistaken.

She stood. "Young man, what do you—"

A board in the crate snapped in two with a loud *crack*. The boy's foot fell through the hole and he tumbled backward, yelping in pain. A berry pie came with him, smacking him in the face as he hit the ground. He tried to get up before Diana could reach him, but his foot was stuck inside the crate.

"Don't move," she said as she knelt beside him. She put a hand on his shoulder to make certain he obeyed. A quick look revealed a bloody shin and calf above a dirty bare foot, and an ankle that was beginning to swell. "Mrs. Cuddy!"

The boy tried to jerk free of her hold.

"Be still or you'll be sorry." She tightened her grip.

The cook's face appeared at the window. "Good heavens! What's happened?"

"Could you send Mr. Applegate outside, please? I'm afraid this young man has injured himself."

"Young man? A thief more like."

"Please, Mrs. Cuddy."

The cook disappeared from view without another word.

"Let go o' me." The boy tried to wrench free again.

Beneath the berries staining his face, he was layered with a great deal of dirt. His clothes hadn't seen a wash pan in a month of Sundays. Diana guessed him to be nine or ten years old. He was much too thin, reminding her of Tiger, the starving kitten.

"What's your name, young man?"

"I don't gotta tell you nothin'."

Oh, dear. She drew a steadying breath. "Would you rather tell me your name or tell it to a policeman? Because we have a telephone in the front hall and I can call for an officer if that's what you wish."

The boy's eyes narrowed, and she had the distinct feeling he was assessing her, deciding if she'd made an idle threat or meant it. He must have decided upon the latter because he finally answered, "Ned."

"What's your last name, Ned?"

"Ain't got one."

"Everyone has a last name."

"Not me. Don't got a pa. Never did. You know what that makes me?" His eyes dared her to answer his question.

She knew what he meant but chose not to speak the word aloud, instead asking a question of her own. "What about your mother, then? She must have a last name."

"She's dead."

Emotion tightened Diana's throat.

"You gonna let go o' me? It was just a pie." He wiped some of the berries from his face with his dirty fingertips and stuck them into his mouth. "Ain't even that good."

"If not, it isn't the pie's fault."

The screen door to the kitchen slammed closed, then Tyson

called, "Diana? Mrs. Cuddy said you needed me." He appeared around the corner of the house, coming to a quick stop when he saw her and the street urchin on the lawn.

"Tyson, this is Ned. He's hurt himself. Will you carry him into the house?"

"What?" Her husband's eyes widened.

"We need to wash away the dirt and blood and see if he needs stitches. And I'm afraid he won't be walking on that ankle for a while. Hopefully it's sprained and not broken."

"Maybe we should deliver him to his home instead. I can call for the carriage."

"Ain't got no home."

"I can believe that," Tyson muttered.

"His mother is dead and he has no father." Diana rose from the ground but remained alert, in case Ned decided to attempt an escape a second time. Judging by his expression, the pain had worsened enough to keep him still. "Please, Tyson. Carry him inside."

Her husband stepped closer and lowered his voice. "Diana, that kid likely has the fleas or lice the cat didn't have."

"He has no place to go." Suspecting her husband was about to mention taking the boy to the children's home, she quickly added, "Didn't Jesus say to care for the widows and orphans?"

That was unfair, Tyson wanted to tell her. Instead he stepped past her and set about freeing the boy's foot from the wooden box. Ned glared at him, a ridiculous expression on a dirty face smeared with berry juice. Still, if looks could kill, Tyson would be dead on the ground this very moment.

"The lady wants you inside." He scooped the kid up from the ground. "So inside you're going."

"Take him to the white bedroom at the front of the house. The one that adjoins mine."

Tyson didn't know why it mattered where he carried the boy; Ned wouldn't be staying long. But he wasn't about to argue with Diana. Not when she had her jaw set like that. He carried the boy around to the entrance off the back hall, not wanting to go through Mrs. Cuddy's kitchen. No point riling the cook any more than they already had. Up the servants' staircase they went, Tyson with Ned in the lead, Diana following right behind. When he reached the bedroom, he set the boy on a chair rather than place him on the bed.

As he straightened, Tyson looked at Diana. "Better clean up that leg before putting him on the bed unless you want that new bedspread ruined."

"Stay with him while I get a few things."

Tyson nodded. After she left, he looked at the boy again. "Now, tell me where you live."

"Here and there."

"Exactly *where* is here and there?"

Ned shrugged. "Barns, sometimes. Back alleys, others. Don't much matter long as it's dry and out o' the wind."

"How long have you been living like that?"

"Since right after my ma died." His voice cracked, making him sound a little more like the child he was, but he didn't give in to tears. "Four years now, I reckon. I was at the orphanage awhile. Didn't like it."

Four years? The kid was young, ten years old at most, but there was a host of worldly experience in his voice and eyes. How had he managed to survive for so long? Maybe Diana was right. They would clean him up and fill his belly with good food, and then they could find him a place to live.

"Mister, I ain't goin' back to the orphanage. I hated it there, and I ain't gonna go back to it never."

"We can talk about that later. For now, there's one thing you need to know." He pointed a finger at the boy. "While you're in this house, you'll do whatever my wife tells you. Hear me? You hurt Mrs. Applegate's feelings, you disobey her, you cause her any grief, it'll be *me* you answer to. Understood?"

"Sure. But I ain't plannin' to stay, so it don't much matter."

Tyson opened his mouth to give Ned a piece of his mind, but sounds in the hallway made him press his lips together again. Moments later Diana bustled into the room with towels and a large bowl. She wore an apron, its large pockets bulging with bandages and other items. Behind her was Liz, carrying a kettle of warm water.

Tyson moved out of the way, standing with his back against the wall near the doorway. Diana knelt and set the large porcelain bowl before the chair; Ned's feet hung several inches above the floor. With the maid's help, Diana bathed not only his wounded leg, but the other one as well. Then she moistened a small towel with fresh water from the kettle and told him to wash his face with it. He obeyed, and from beneath the berry juice and grime emerged a spattering of freckles over his nose and cheeks.

Diana looked over her shoulder at Tyson. "I don't think he needs stitches, but the swelling is bad. Perhaps we should have a doctor look at it, to be sure it isn't broken."

The orphanage might have a physician on staff, but Tyson kept that thought to himself, knowing neither his wife nor the boy would welcome the suggestion. "I'll send for a doctor." He pushed off the wall and went downstairs. "Upchurch?"

The butler appeared as if he'd been waiting for his name to be called.

"Mrs. Applegate wants a doctor to look at the boy's ankle."

"I'll see to it at once, sir."

Throughout his lifetime, Jeremiah Applegate had seldom admitted he was wrong—even if he was. He'd believed it best to decide what one should do and then do it without apology. That's how he'd lived, in business and at home. But in the years since Tyson left, Jeremiah had had plenty of reasons to second-guess himself. His wife had tried to help him see the truth before she died. He should have admitted to her that he'd been mistaken as a father. He should have promised that he would try to change in the future. But change didn't come easily to someone like him. Men still feared him. Would his son still hate him?

He sighed, aware of the ache in his heart, the one he'd felt daily from the moment Tyson stormed out of the study and then out of his father's life. His son might never believe it, but Jeremiah loved him fiercely. Was it possible Jeremiah might learn to show it before it was too late?

October 1893

"Is it bad news, dear?"

Diana looked up from the letter in her hands and met her mother-in-law's watchful gaze from across the morning room. "I'm not sure. Mother writes that she and Father moved to Nampa, Idaho, last month. I had no idea they were even considering a move. It must have come up suddenly."

Nostalgia wrapped around her heart as memories from girlhood flooded her mind. She loved her parents' home in Montana. She'd thought she might go to live with them. Her marriage appeared to be over. There'd been no word from Tyson since the day he'd fought with his father, broken that vase, and then left the house.

Nora leaned forward on the settee. "My dear, are you aware that the railroad went bankrupt this last summer? It's possible your father had to move in order to have employment."

"Bankrupt?"

"The financial panic that began in the spring has impacted people all over the country. Few are as fortunate as we."

Diana closed her eyes and covered her mouth with the fingers of one hand. How ignorant she must appear to her mother-in-law. Since coming to stay under this roof, she'd been focused only on herself, her marriage, and her husband. Nothing else. No one else. Too selfish to even know what had happened in her parents' lives. Now that she knew the truth, should she go to them? Or would she be more burden than help if she did?

"Tyson will be back," Nora said softly.

She looked at her mother-in-law again.

"Don't give up on him, Diana. Be patient. And remember, it isn't your fault that he left."

Isn't it?

"We must learn to forgive so much in this life. Forgiveness may be the most important lesson we have to learn, above all else. I hope you'll be able to forgive Tyson when the time comes, my dear. Promise me you'll try."

Diana's throat tightened, and her reply came out in a whisper. "I'll try, Mrs. Applegate. I promise."

ELEVEN

Balancing a tray with her left hand, Diana rapped once with her right, then opened the bedroom door. Ned was sitting up in bed, his injured leg propped with several pillows.

"I brought you something to eat." She crossed the room, smiling.

The boy scowled back at her, as if he didn't want the food. She knew better. Over the past twenty-four hours, Ned had eaten every last crumb on his plate, no matter how much Mrs. Cuddy put on it.

"How is your ankle doing? Is it hurting less?"

"Same as it was last time you asked me. I could walk on it if I wanted. Don't need those crutches the doc left."

"Use them anyway. The more you rest, the quicker you'll heal." Diana set the tray over his lap and handed him a cloth napkin, then sank onto the edge of the bed to watch him eat.

Ned picked up the sandwich. "Why you being so nice to me?" He took a big bite and began to chew.

"I'm being nice because you were hurt and I wanted to help."

"I been hurt before and nobody helped."

"I'm very sorry to hear it."

"I ain't gonna stay, you know. No matter how nice you are to me."

He reminded her a little of Hugh. Her brother hadn't trusted people. Perhaps with good reason. Hugh had done his best, at thirteen years old, to keep his sisters with him, but Dr. Cray's Asylum for Little Wanderers hadn't paid him any heed. No one wanted to take in three half-grown children.

"I was six years old when my ma died," she said softly. "Same as you were."

"Yeah?"

"My brother and sister and I were sent to live with different families in the West." She wanted to add that she knew what it was like not to have anyone to look out for her, but that wouldn't be true. Her adoptive parents had loved and cared for her. She hadn't had to live in alleys or barns. Ned shouldn't have to live that way either.

The boy's eyes narrowed. "What's that sound? Been hearin' it all morning."

"Sound?" Diana listened, then smiled again. "That's my cat, Tiger, pawing at the adjoining door. I think she'd like to come meet you when you're finished eating. Would that be all right?"

"I guess. Long as she doesn't scratch me. Cats can be mean."

"Perhaps some cats are, but not Tiger. She's a dear."

"Well, she better behave. That's all I gotta say. If she don't, I'll hit her with one of them crutches."

Diana wanted to laugh at his tough talk but couldn't encourage cruelty. "Hitting her wouldn't be very kind, would it? She's much smaller than you are."

"I like dogs. There's one that used to follow me around out on this end o' town, but I haven't seen him in a week or two. Maybe a coyote got him."

"I hope not. What did you call him?"

"Dog. What else?"

What else, indeed.

They fell silent while Ned ate the remainder of his sandwich, a bowl of canned peaches, and a large slice of Mrs. Cuddy's berry pie—the one that had survived Ned's fall the previous day. When he was finished, Diana took the tray and set it in the hall before going to the door that adjoined her room to Ned's. She opened it. Tiger meowed loudly before rubbing up against her skirt, first one direction, then the other.

Diana picked up the kitten and carried her toward the bed, whispering near the cat's ear, "You two must become good friends. You have much in common."

As Tyson left the private men's club on Main, he saw Kendall Michaels come out of a restaurant across the street. Tyson paused and took a step back into the shadow of the awning. A reflex action, and one he was thankful for when he recognized the man with Michaels: Brook Calhoun.

Dislike for both men rose like bile in his throat.

This would explain the newspaperman's remarks at the judge's dinner party. If Calhoun and Michaels were friends, Michaels might have felt justified in attacking Tyson through Diana. But that might also imply Calhoun cared about her. Not a comforting thought.

Tyson had convinced himself that Brook Calhoun felt no true affection for Diana. That his interest had been in the fortune he would come into if he married Tyson's widow. Could he be wrong about that? Had the man's feelings for Diana been real? And if so, what about her feelings for him?

Intolerable questions, all of them. They complicated an already complicated situation.

He wondered if he'd done the right thing, telling Diana he

needed her by his side to win the election. Would it have been so terrible to leave that out? He could have simply said he wanted their marriage to work. But that wouldn't have been honest. He owed her honesty. After so many years of neglect and betrayal, that was the very least he owed her.

Tyson's carriage pulled to the curb, and he climbed in, his thoughts continuing to churn.

It amazed him how Diana had filled his home—his life—so completely and in such a short period of time. Sometimes he feared he thought about her when he should be thinking about the election, about matters of importance to the country, and not his own domestic happiness.

Happiness? A small smile curved his mouth as he looked out the carriage window. Yes. Except when he let jealousy creep in, it made him happy to think of her. To wonder what she did when he was away from the house. To watch her brush a loose tendril of hair back from her face as they sat at the supper table. To see her hold that scrawny stray cat. Even to observe her as she tended to the injured street urchin who'd taken up residence in one of the empty bedrooms.

Peculiar, wasn't it? He'd scarcely given Diana a thought while he traipsed around the world, climbing mountains, exploring islands, hunting big game, visiting famous cities, charming beautiful women, going to war. Now, thinking about her kept him awake at night.

As the carriage pulled into the driveway leading around to the back of the house, Tyson saw a black cab at the front curb and wondered who might have come visiting. He tapped the roof and called to the coachman, "Stop here, Gibson." As soon as the vehicle halted, Tyson opened the door and hopped to the ground.

He felt no foreboding. He had no reason to. His first clue of the trouble awaiting him inside wasn't until Upchurch didn't open the front door. Tyson opened it himself and stepped into the entry hall. He saw the butler at once, standing to one side of the parlor doorway, looking uncertain. A moment later he knew why.

"I should have been informed at once!" Seven years hadn't removed the thunder from his father's voice.

Now Tyson felt the foreboding.

"I'm sorry, Mr. Applegate," Diana replied in a softer tone. "It wasn't my place to do so."

Before his father could respond, Tyson moved to the parlor entrance. "She's right, Father. The fault is completely mine."

Jeremiah Applegate's voice might not have changed, but his appearance had. His hair had thinned. It and his beard were stone gray instead of black. He'd also put on a good thirty pounds. The years had not been kind to him.

Tyson crossed to Diana's side. "I planned to contact you soon, but I've been rather busy since my return to Idaho." He drew a quick breath and lied. "You're looking well."

"That's all you have to say to me? I look well?"

Tyson hated the defensiveness that welled inside of him. The Bible said he must honor his father. He should also remember that a soft answer turned away wrath.

He drew in a deeper breath this time. "You're right, Father. There is much more we need to say to each other. Perhaps we should go into the library where we can speak in private." He looked at Diana. "Would you ask Mrs. Brown to prepare a room for my father?" He hoped she saw the apology in his eyes. He never should have allowed his father's anger to fall upon her shoulders. Not again.

"Of course. I'll have his things taken to the green bedchamber."

Tyson gave her a nod, then looked at his father. "The library is across the hall." He led the way.

After closing both doors, Tyson rounded the desk and sat in his chair. Jeremiah took a seat opposite him. Ironic, wasn't it? After all the times they'd faced each other in his father's library with his father seated on this side of the desk.

"Do you hate me so much, Tyson?"

His father's question took him by surprise. He'd expected a dressing down. "I don't hate you."

"Don't you?"

"No."

"Then why did you let me believe you were dead?"

A fair question. "It took a long time for me to get over my anger. Maybe I did hate you for a time. At least I hated the way you tried to mold me into being like you. I resented the way you tried to control me, even after I was an adult."

"Not a single letter after your mother died. You didn't even write to your wife."

Guilt pressed upon Tyson's shoulders. "I was determined to keep you from interfering again. The only way I knew to do that was to stop writing completely and try to go where you couldn't find me." He shook his head. "But I was wrong to handle matters that way. It wasn't fair to you, and even more, it wasn't fair to Diana."

"And your mother. You broke her heart."

"I know." Emotion formed a knot in his throat, but he persisted. "Since it was too late to ask Mother for her forgiveness, I had to settle for God's alone. But I hope she knows how sorry I am."

His father's eyebrows rose.

"Thankfully, it isn't too late to ask for your forgiveness, Father."

The man in Tyson's memories had never been in want of words, but his father appeared speechless. If Tyson didn't know better, he might even believe his father was fighting tears.

At long last, Jeremiah rose from the chair. "Perhaps we could continue this conversation at another time. If you wouldn't mind showing me where I am to stay . . ."

"Of course." Tyson stood.

"Son?"

"Yes?"

"I have never been happier than at the moment I learned you were alive."

It was as close as his father had ever come to telling Tyson he loved him, and it was Tyson who now found himself speechless. He motioned with his hand and led his father from the library.

After talking to Mrs. Brown about a room for Jeremiah and then informing Mrs. Cuddy there would be one more for supper, Diana went outside. Her mother was seated on a stone bench in the shade of a gnarly tree, her knitting needles moving in a steady rhythm.

"Oh, Diana. Come sit with me, dear. I have been enjoying the gardens so much. Imagine how they shall look in another month."

"Yes, it is lovely here." Diana sank onto the bench. "We have a houseguest."

Her mother chuckled. "I hope it isn't another stray cat or another orphan."

"It isn't. It's Tyson's father."

"Mr. Applegate is here?" Gloria's smile faded. "Good heavens."

"I don't know how long he plans to stay."

"Was Tyson expecting him?"

"No. At least, he didn't tell me so." Diana glanced toward the house. "I believe he hoped to avoid this confrontation awhile longer."

"I should think that would be true of you too."

Jeremiah Applegate had never liked Diana. He'd thought her unworthy of marrying into his family, and he'd never tried to disguise those feelings from her. He'd blamed her for Tyson's absence as well as his continued silence as months stretched into years. Jeremiah's feelings and his words would have driven Diana away, if not for Nora.

"Are we to dress for supper now that your father-in-law has come?" Her mother's question intruded on Diana's thoughts.

Diana shook her head. "No, he is family. We will treat him as such."

"As you wish, dear." Her mother gathered her knitting items. "But I believe I had best go inside and freshen up before Mr. Applegate and I are reintroduced."

Diana stayed on the stone bench, wanting time to quiet her nerves. She'd tried not to let on—to either her father-in-law or Tyson—but the arrival of Jeremiah had shaken her. His raised voice had brought back a host of bad memories. In an instant, he'd made her feel like the young, naive, inexperienced wife who couldn't keep her husband from deserting her, like the bride whose groom didn't want her.

With a small sigh, she rose and walked toward the back porch, lifting her chin and straightening her shoulders as she went. She had made a bargain. Having her father-in-law in their home was, she supposed, an expected part of that bargain. She would get through this evening and through as many evenings as were necessary until she could leave this house—and Tyson.

She went upstairs, stopping to check on Ned first. He was asleep with Tiger curled on his chest. The boy's reddish-brown hair fell onto his forehead, almost touching his eyebrows. Whoever had cut it last had taken no care to keep it even. But despite that, he was a cute child.

Especially while he's sleeping.

She smiled as she backed out of the room and closed the door. Then she went into her own bedchamber to get ready for the evening. They might not dress formally for a family supper, but she wanted to look her best all the same. Jeremiah had always been able to make her feel inadequate with little more than a glance. She needed every tool at her disposal to keep that from happening now.

Her choice for the evening was a cream-and-gold gown with a high neck, pouter-pigeon front, and gored skirt with pleating in the back. The silk fabric was overlaid with appliqué lace squares and black velvet. The design of the gown, along with the corset beneath, provided the perfect S-curve silhouette every fashionable woman hoped to achieve.

Feeling like a soldier girding himself for battle, she rang for Liz.

As Tyson watched Diana enter the parlor that evening, he wondered if his father could see what an amazing woman she'd become. It was more than her beauty, for she'd always been beautiful. No, it was something more, something deeper. Something he couldn't yet name. Something that made him want to spend the rest of his life discovering the secret corners of her heart.

Was this love?

Diana paused and looked behind her. A moment later his mother-in-law appeared in the entrance.

"Ladies, you look lovely." Tyson moved toward them, stopping beside Diana, then turning to face his father. "You remember Mrs. Fisher, of course."

"Indeed." Jeremiah gave a slight bow. "A pleasure to see you again, Mrs. Fisher."

Gloria acknowledged his words with a nod but there was wariness in her eyes. The same wariness Tyson had seen more than once in her daughter's eyes. And who could blame either of them for distrusting the Applegate men? Tyson hoped he'd made a bit of progress toward changing their feelings about him, and with any luck, his father wouldn't make things worse during supper.

He offered his elbow to his wife. "Shall we go in?"

"Yes." She slipped her fingers into the crook of his arm.

He glanced toward his father, who—surprisingly—took the hint and offered his arm to Gloria.

So far, so good.

The pleasant mood continued until they were halfway through the evening meal. Then a thunderous crash from upstairs put an end to their conversation and drew all eyes toward the ceiling.

"What was that?" Jeremiah demanded of no one in particular.

Tyson exchanged a glance with Diana. "Ned."

"Who's Ned?"

He ignored his father and rose from the chair. "I'd better see what happened."

"I'll go with you," Diana said, also standing.

The two of them hurried out of the dining room and up the staircase. Tyson opened the door to the bedroom. Ned was on the floor next to the overturned straight-backed chair. Nearby, the chest of drawers lay on its front, the pitcher and bowl that had sat on it broken into several large pieces.

"Ned, what happened?" Diana knelt beside the boy.

"Stupid cat," was all he answered.

"Tiger?" Diana looked around the room. "Where is she?"

"I don't know. Under the bed, I think."

A kitten that weighed no more than five pounds hadn't knocked over the heavy bureau. Any fool would know that.

Diana glanced at Ned's injured leg. "Did you hurt yourself when you fell?"

"Nah."

"Why weren't you using your crutches?"

Ned gave her a sullen look.

"Tyson." She looked up at him. "Will you carry Ned to the bed?"

That got a response from the boy. "I don't need carryin'!"

"Sorry, Ned." Tyson moved forward and scooped him off the floor. "A gentleman doesn't argue with a lady." Three steps and he placed the boy on the bed, then looked over his shoulder at his wife.

"Tiger? Here, kitty, kitty." Diana placed her cheek close to the floor and peered under the bed. "You poor thing. Come here, Tiger. Here, kitty, kitty. Oh, Tyson. She's scared to death. Can you get her?"

Never argue with a lady, he reminded himself as he joined her on the floor, first on his hands and knees, at last on his belly. It took his eyes a few moments to locate the kitten, cowering in a shadowed corner beneath the bed. It took a few moments more to wriggle forward and clasp a hand around her middle. As he drew her out from her hiding place, she hissed and bit his hand while scratching his wrist with her back claws. He managed to hang on, even though his instinct was to hurl her back to the corner.

He wasn't sure he should give the kitten to Diana, lest she be bitten or scratched, too, but the decision wasn't left to him. His wife whisked Tiger away, cradling the feline to her chest and crooning to her. No hisses. No biting. No scratching. In Diana's arms, the wild creature became completely docile.

Lucky cat.

November 1893

Nora Applegate leaned across the distance that separated them and took Diana's hand in her own. "My dear child, don't you know what this means?"

Diana shook her head.

"You're with child. You're going to have Tyson's baby."

"His baby?" she whispered.

Nora moved to sit beside her on the settee. "This will bring him home."

Did she dare hope her mother-in-law was correct? Would this news bring Tyson home? But how could it, when they'd heard nothing from him since soon after he left? His single letter had given no forwarding address. He hadn't shared where he meant to go or whom he meant to go with.

As if understanding Diana's unspoken doubts, Nora said, "I will speak to Jeremiah at once. I will ask him to hire someone to find Tyson."

TWELVE

The next morning, Diana awakened with a song in her heart. Happy, that's what she was. Very unexpected considering the strange turns of her life over the past three weeks.

Last night, her father-in-law hadn't said a single untoward thing throughout their supper. Even his surprise over the injured orphan staying in the room next to his hadn't brought the expected harsh criticism.

But it was the memory of Tyson drawing Tiger from under the bed that made her smile now. He'd done it for her. He'd allowed the kitten to scratch and bite him without a word of complaint.

For me. He did it for me.

Tyson did seem different from the man who'd married and left her years earlier. Oh, he was still as charming as ever. Only the charm seemed more . . . genuine. Not a way to impress anyone or achieve some goal, but just him being himself. He seemed more at ease with the world, less likely to erupt in anger as he used to. Especially around his father.

Was it possible she could learn to trust him again? To care for him again? The questions caused her stomach to tumble, followed by an urgent need to see Tyson. A need to know if any of this was true.

She hastened to eat the breakfast the maid brought to her room, then washed and dressed in what seemed record time. Still, it was close to three-quarters of an hour before she descended the stairs. Her first stop was the library, but instead of Tyson sitting at his desk, she found her father-in-law, the newspaper open before him.

Swallowing a sound of disappointment, she said, "Good morning, Mr. Applegate."

He laid the paper on the desk. "Good morning, Diana."

"I trust you rested well."

"Well enough."

"Was the bed comfortable? I'm sure we could—"

"The bed was fine."

"I'm glad." She glanced over her shoulder toward the parlor.

"If you're looking for my son, he's gone out."

Diana noticed his choice of words. His son. Not her husband.

"You and I hardly had a chance to talk last night." Jeremiah motioned to a chair on the opposite side of the desk. "Please, join me."

She felt like a schoolchild about to get a scolding from the headmaster.

He studied her for what seemed a long time before he said, "You've changed, Diana, since I saw you last."

"Have I?"

"Yes. You've developed some backbone." There was a note of approval in his voice. "I was surprised to learn you were with Tyson. I'd heard you planned to marry a Mr. Calhoun."

It was no surprise that her father-in-law knew about Brook, even though there'd been no official announcement. Jeremiah made it his business to know as much as he could about everybody in his life.

"Why did you return to him?"

"I'm still his wife."

Jeremiah leaned forward. "Yes, you are. But aren't you afraid he might leave you once again?"

"No."

It wasn't a lie, really. She didn't fear Tyson leaving her again. What she feared was that she would want him to stay.

"Excuse me, madam." Upchurch cleared his throat behind her.

A welcome interruption. "Yes."

"This just arrived for you." He stepped closer and held out an envelope.

She took it. "Thank you, Upchurch."

He nodded and left the library.

Thankful for an excuse to end this uncomfortable conversation, Diana faced her father-in-law again. "Please excuse me, Mr. Applegate." She rose from the chair and went into the parlor. Only then did she look at the envelope. Brook's handwriting. She broke the seal and removed the notecard.

Dearest Diana,

Would you be so kind as to join me for luncheon today at my office? Unlike a restaurant, we shall be undisturbed there. Shall we say 1:00? I look forward to seeing you. I have missed our times together.

Your devoted friend,
Brook

A confusing wealth of emotions welled within her. Tears stung her eyes. She desperately needed a friend. She would join Brook for lunch.

From his second-story office window overlooking Bannock Street, Brook watched Diana alight from a hansom cab and grinned. She'd come. He'd been certain she would, even though the invitation had been very last minute.

He turned and went into an adjoining meeting room where an excellent luncheon had been laid out for two. They would serve themselves so they could be alone. Eventually, he would want others—especially Tyson Applegate—to know about this assignation, but not yet. Not until he knew how best he could use it to his advantage. If he was careless, he could harm his reputation in the community as well as Diana's. He didn't care about hers, but he cared a great deal about his own.

The door to his office opened and his secretary ushered Diana in.

"Thank you, Paulson," Brook said, dismissing the man. "Diana." He went forward to take her hand. "You look lovely, my dear."

She gave him a small smile.

It wouldn't have been hard to be married to Diana. She was a rare beauty, and she had just enough spirit and intelligence to make her interesting but not so much as to make her uncontrollable. She would have been an asset to him beyond the fortune he'd expected her to bring into marriage. But her husband's untimely return had spoiled all of that for Brook.

Hatred burned like hot coals in his gut. He would make Tyson Applegate *wish* he were dead before he was through.

"Come and sit down, Diana. We'll eat and you can tell me how you're getting along. You've been in my thoughts so often these past weeks."

Tyson only half listened to Owen Hanson, his recently hired campaign manager. His supporters assured him the fellow—a man in his fifties with salt-and-pepper hair and muttonchops—knew his business when it came to elections. But Tyson was having a hard time staying focused today. His thoughts kept straying to Diana . . . and to his father. Last night had gone better than he'd expected. What about today? Perhaps he shouldn't have left them alone this soon.

"Mr. Applegate," Owen said, drawing his attention to the present, "I believe it is important you speak to this group. Most of these gentlemen are dissatisfied with the current field of candidates. If you show them you are a man ready to lead and make sound decisions, they will support you wholeheartedly."

"Fine. Fine. Arrange it. When did you say I'd give the speech?"

"Next Tuesday evening, sir. A week from today."

"All right." He glanced at his pocket watch. It was only two o'clock, and there were a number of letters on his desk that he should address. Instead, he stood. "I believe I'll call it a day, Hanson. We can resume in the morning."

His manager looked displeased. "Very good, sir."

Rather than calling for his carriage, Tyson decided to walk home. It was less than two miles from his campaign office on Main Street to his home on the east side of town. The fresh air would do him good and the exercise might clear his mind. At least he hoped it would.

It surprised him, how distracted he'd become since Diana came to live with him. The campaign was important. He wanted to win this election as much as ever. And yet, changing Diana's mind, winning her affections, had become vital to him as well. It wasn't enough to save his marriage, to have her remain with him as his wife out of obedience to the Bible or out of obligation or because of what society would say. He wanted something deeper, something truer, something . . . more.

He wondered, not for the first time, if his father had loved his mother. Even a little. The union of Jeremiah and Nora Applegate had begun as a merger, not a love match. Two wealthy, industrialist families had come together through the marriage of their children in hopes of building a great dynasty. At least, that's how Tyson viewed it.

Perhaps Tyson's relationship with his father might have been different, better, if his mother had been able to have more children. But no more babies had come after Tyson was born, and so all of his father's plans for the future had been focused on his one and only son. And Tyson's mother had seemed to fade into the woodwork a little more with each passing year.

Thoughts of his mother brought a fresh pang of regret. She'd died in November of 1896, but Tyson hadn't learned of it until months later. It was too late to make up to her for all of his shortcomings, but he prayed it wasn't too late to mend bridges with his father. God would have to show him how best to do that.

When Tyson entered the house through the front door, Upchurch met him in the entrance hall wearing a surprised expression. "I didn't hear a carriage, Mr. Applegate. Forgive me for not meeting you at the door."

"I walked home, Upchurch. Beautiful day out." He glanced up the stairs. "Is Mrs. Applegate in her room?"

"No, sir. She went out."

"Where?"

"She didn't say, sir. She had me call for a hansom cab as she didn't want to engage the carriage, should you require it."

"And my father?"

"I believe he is in the garden with Mrs. Fisher."

It was Tyson's turn to wear a look of surprise. "Really?"

"Yes, sir. And the boy is with them."

"The boy? Do you mean Ned?"

"I do, sir. The boy said he could not stand to be shut up indoors any longer. They went outside right after the noon meal."

This Tyson needed to see for himself. "Thank you, Upchurch."

He left his hat with the butler and headed for the back door at the end of the hall. He found the threesome in what had quickly become his mother-in-law's favorite spot. His father and Gloria sat on the stone bench in the shade of the tree. Ned was on the ground, breaking twigs into tiny pieces and piling them, like a miniature stack of firewood.

"Tyson," his mother-in-law said. "We didn't expect you for hours. Is it that late?"

"No. I came home early. Upchurch told me Diana went out. Did she tell you where she was going?"

"To meet a friend for lunch, I think."

Tyson's disappointment was sharp.

His father rose from the bench. "Perhaps you and I might talk. As pleasant as Mrs. Fisher's company is—" He gave Gloria a brief smile. "—it's you I came to see."

"Of course. But if you don't mind, I want to go down to the stables first. I've got a mare that's ready to foal, and I want to see how she's doing." It was another delaying tactic; Ned's fall the previous evening had helped him avoid a private discussion with his father after supper. Now this.

"I don't mind. Why don't I walk with you? I haven't seen your stables yet." Jeremiah looked at Gloria again. "You'll excuse me, Mrs. Fisher."

"Of course, Mr. Applegate."

Jeremiah's gaze dropped to Ned. "Boy, can you manage the stairs on those crutches when you're ready to go in?"

"'Course I can." Ned didn't look up from the growing stack of broken twigs. "Got down here all right, didn't I?"

Tyson caught a sudden glimpse of himself when he wasn't much older than Ned—sullen, rebellious, resisting authority at every turn. And lonely too. Wishing his father could approve of him once in a while.

With a nod to his mother-in-law, Tyson turned and walked away, his father falling into step beside him.

Halfway to the barn, Jeremiah broke the silence. "Today was my first real opportunity to speak at any length with your wife's mother. She's a rather pleasant woman."

"Yes, she is." Tyson could have pointed out that the lack of opportunities to speak with Gloria Fisher was entirely Jeremiah's fault. He bit back the words. Especially since the same could be said of him.

A few more steps and his father said, "I guess there is no changing your mind about the election."

"No."

"I still believe it is foolhardy."

Tyson stopped in his tracks. "Father, why do you object? You always wanted me to run for public office, from the time I was a boy in short pants. That's what your choice of schools I attended was all about. That's what my studying the law was all about. It's even why you objected to my marriage." He felt old resentments rising inside him and swallowed hard to keep from giving voice to them.

"It isn't your candidacy I find foolhardy, Tyson. It's your rushing into it. It's this last-minute write-in candidacy of yours. You can't win without a better plan. You can't win without the power of a party behind you."

"Maybe I can. Maybe not. I'll leave that in God's hands."

His father stared at him in silence for what seemed a long while. "Do you think the Almighty cares whether or not you win an election?"

Tyson took an equally long time to answer the question. "I'm not sure. But I know God cares about changing my character, and whether or not I win this election, I'm sure the Lord will use the experience to mold and shape me for the better."

"Never thought I'd hear talk like that coming out of your mouth."

"Father, you need to understand something. I'm not the same angry young man who walked out all those years ago. I was wrong to have left my wife the way I did. I was wrong for not writing. To her or to Mother or even to you. I was wrong in more ways than I can count. I didn't honor my parents. To my shame, I didn't honor my marriage vows. I was thoughtless and reckless and selfish. But some good things came out of those years I was away. I grew up. I learned to take responsibility for my decisions. I learned to act rather than react. I learned that people matter more than possessions or money or power. And most important, I discovered that Christ is more than a good man who once walked this earth. He is divine and He died so I might live. With everything in me, I want to please Him first and foremost."

"Good lord," his father said.

"Yes." Tyson smiled without humor. "He is a good Lord."

A long silence stretched between them.

"Perhaps you'd better show me that mare now," Jeremiah said at last.

January 1894

Diana lay in the bed, curled on her side, her heart breaking. She'd lost the baby, and with everything in her, she wished she could die too. While she'd been pregnant with Tyson's child, she'd held out hope he might want to return to her. What hope could she cling to now?

Hearing the bedroom door open, she rolled to her other side, facing the wall.

"Diana?" As Nora spoke her name, she laid a hand on Diana's shoulder. "I'm so very sorry, my dear."

A sob escaped Diana's throat.

"But I believe in my heart you will still give me grandchildren. I have asked God for it, and I'm believing in His answer."

"Without a husband?" Diana whispered.

"You are not yet twenty, my dear. You are young and healthy, and when Tyson returns, there will be children of your union. I am sure of it."

Diana spoke the question that was never far from her thoughts. "What if he never returns?"

"He *will* return. He just needs a bit more time to find his way home." Nora leaned in and kissed her cheek before whispering, "We love him, you and I, and we must pray for him. No matter how long it takes, I know God will answer our prayers."

Diana wished she had the same strong faith as her mother-in-law, but she didn't have it and didn't think she ever would.

THIRTEEN

When Diana first met Brook Calhoun, she'd believed her husband dead. Everyone had believed it to be so. Nothing improper had passed between her and Brook. Not ever. He had conducted his courtship quietly, both of them aware the courts would have to take action before they could marry. During that time, he'd never given her cause to question her decision to become his wife. He'd been a gentleman and treated her with courtesy and respect. There hadn't been a great passion between them, but she'd been certain a kind of love would come with time.

Then why did being with him now feel so wrong?

She placed her fork on the plate next to her untouched dessert. "I should go."

"So soon?"

"I must. Mother will wonder where I am, and there is my father-in-law to consider. He is a guest in our home and I mustn't neglect him."

"You told me Mr. Applegate never showed you the slightest concern. Why should you care whether or not he feels neglected now?"

She glanced toward the window, Jeremiah's voice whispering in her head. *"But aren't you afraid he might leave you once again?"*

"I care about you, Diana," Brook said. "I worry about you. I think you've lost weight."

"Have I?"

He pointed at her plate. "You barely touched your food."

"I ate a late breakfast."

His expression was grave. "I can see you're unhappy. I wish it were in my power to do something to change that."

Was she unhappy? She'd awakened that morning with such lightness of heart . . . because of Tyson's rescue of her frightened cat. Not enough to prove him changed. Not enough to—

Brook reached across the table and took hold of her hand. "I will be here whenever you need me."

That sense of wrongness swept over her again. But why was she surprised by it? Her world had been turned upside down, beginning with Tyson's return from the dead. Everything was wrong, not just this moment with the man she'd thought to marry. Everything.

She slipped her hand from his grasp and rose from the chair. "I must go."

"We'll do this again." He stood too. "Remember, my dear, you can confide in me. No matter what the trouble is, I will listen and be of whatever assistance I may be."

Diana nodded.

"I'll have Paulson get you a cab."

"Thank you."

It seemed to Diana that air returned to the room after Brook left, but she had no time to analyze the feeling before he came to escort her down the flight of stairs and out to the sidewalk where a hansom cab awaited her. Brook gave the driver the address before assisting Diana into the cab.

"If ever you need me," he said softly as he closed the door. "Remember."

Had his father ever been this subdued before? Not in Tyson's memory.

Jeremiah commented occasionally about the horses and the barn and the paddocks as Tyson showed him around, but he didn't criticize or offer unsolicited opinions. When Tyson suggested they return to the house, Jeremiah said he was going to explore the foothills for a short while. The subject of Tyson's run for the Senate hadn't come up again, and now it seemed his father had forgotten it.

Impossible. Jeremiah Applegate never forgot anything. More likely he was waiting for a more opportune time to broach the matter.

After watching his father walk up the trail beyond the barn and paddocks, Tyson headed toward the house. He prayed silently as he went—for wisdom, for submission to authority, for clarity of action. And once again for the people he'd hurt.

Gloria and Ned had abandoned their place in the shade, so Tyson walked straight to the back door. He'd just closed it behind him when he heard Upchurch welcome Diana home again. Tyson hurried down the hall toward the front of the house.

When his wife saw him, her eyes widened with surprise. "Tyson. I didn't expect you home so early."

"I didn't expect it either. Your mother said you went to lunch with a friend."

Her gaze dropped to her hands as she tugged off her gloves. "Yes."

He knew immediately that she didn't want him to ask for the

name of her friend. It was meant to be a secret. But why? Before he could inquire, she asked a question of her own.

"Where is Mother?"

"Not sure. She was outside with my father and Ned when I got home, but no one's out there now."

Diana's eyes widened again. "Ned went outside? Did someone carry him down the stairs? What if he'd fallen again?"

"You can't keep him locked in that room upstairs. Fresh air will do him good."

"But—"

"It's only a sprain, Diana, and boys his age heal fast. He probably could get by now without those crutches."

With her lips pressed together like that, it was clear she wanted to argue with him. But she didn't.

He took a step toward her. "Maybe we should talk about where Ned's going to go when the doctor says he's okay."

"Must he go? I'd like him to stay. Tyson, he has no one. No family. No home. He hates the orphanage. He's said so. We have this huge house and all those empty bedrooms." She motioned with her hand toward the upstairs.

Had she forgotten he was running for the Senate? Now was not the best time to open his home to some street urchin. Especially not with his father and her mother also in the house. And yet he couldn't seem to tell her that, not when she looked at him with those beseeching eyes, not when he knew how much he needed to atone for in their marriage. If he had to make amends for his wrongs by allowing her to bring stray cats and stray boys into their home, then so be it.

"Please," she whispered, unaware the battle was already won.

"Ned can stay, Diana. As long as you wish it so, he can stay."

"Thank you."

The look in her eyes made him feel ten feet tall.

When Diana went upstairs, she stopped to look in on Ned. He was standing by the window, looking down at the boulevard. The crutches were leaned in a corner, apparently not needed, as Tyson had suggested.

"Hello, Ned."

He glanced over his shoulder. Bathed and dressed in the new clothes Diana had sent Liz to buy yesterday, he looked like any other well-cared-for boy his age.

If she hadn't lost her baby, her child would have been just about six years old. Would he have been anything like Ned? Perhaps the same freckles spattered across the nose.

She shoved the painful thought away. "I heard you went outside with Mrs. Fisher and Mr. Applegate. I'm glad you're doing better."

Ned shrugged. "I don't like bein' inside so much. Not used to it." He wriggled. "Makes me itchy."

Tyson had tried to tell her the same thing a short while before.

"Besides, somebody's gonna steal my stuff if I don't get back to it." He turned toward the window. "If they haven't taken everything already."

She wondered what possessions he could have. Certainly nothing of value to anyone but him. "We could send someone for your belongings."

"I'd better go myself. Can't stay here much longer anyway."

Diana took a couple of steps into the room. "But we want you to stay, Ned. This is your room for as long as you'd like."

He turned around, frowning at her. "Why're you bein' so nice to me? You ain't got no call to be this way. I tried to take that pie, ya know."

So much suspicion. So much bluster. Diana wished she could

take Ned in her arms and hold him close. She wished she could convince him he could trust her to care for him and to take care of him. But rather than say what he didn't want to hear, she changed the subject. "Would you like me to bring you some books to read? It would help pass the time while you rest your ankle."

He hesitated a moment before answering, "Ain't got much use for readin'."

As clear as if he'd said the words aloud, she realized he *couldn't* read. Which shouldn't surprise her, knowing his mother had died when he was only six and he'd spent most of the years since living by his wits on the streets. He hadn't had an opportunity to go to school, to learn reading, writing, and arithmetic. Equally as clear, Ned didn't want her to know he couldn't read. Even a young boy had his pride.

"Perhaps you've never read the right kind of book," she said. "I'll have to ask my husband what stories he enjoyed when he was your age."

"Won't make no difference."

"Perhaps not, but I'll ask Tyson anyway."

"Ask me what?"

Her pulse jumped at the sound of his voice—she hadn't expected Tyson to follow her upstairs—and a muddle of emotions swirled inside her. Guilt because of her secret lunch with Brook. Anxiety over Jeremiah's question that morning. Wishfulness for . . . for something that seemed out of reach. She did her best not to let her expression reveal any of those emotions when she turned toward him. "What was your favorite book when you were a boy?"

"That's easy." He grinned. "*Roughing It* by Mark Twain. It made me want to go all the places Twain went and see everything he'd seen. Did you know Mr. Twain planned to spend only three months in Nevada, and instead he spent seven years exploring the West? *Roughing It* tells about those adventures."

Is that what gave you wanderlust? Is that book one of the reasons you left me behind?

Tyson looked at Ned. "Bet you'd like *A Connecticut Yankee in King Arthur's Court.* I was in college by the time it was published, but I loved it."

Diana didn't have to look behind her to know the boy scowled, still refusing to admit he'd never learned to read.

"There are other good authors," her husband continued, "but Twain remains one of my personal favorites."

She decided to change the subject rather than let Ned's discomfort increase. "Tyson, Ned has some belongings he's worried might be stolen if he doesn't retrieve them soon. Could you take him to get them?"

"Of course." He met her gaze. "Do you want us to go now?"

She nodded.

"Will you come with us?"

Once again she remembered the way Tyson had looked as he drew Tiger from under Ned's bed. Once again she remembered the expression on his face that had seemed to say, *I did this for you.* And once again she wondered if she could learn to trust him, to care for him, perhaps even to—

No, that was impossible.

"I'll send for the carriage," he said at long last. "You and Ned can meet me in the front hall in ten minutes. All right?"

"All right."

From the parlor window, Gloria watched as Tyson helped first Ned and then her daughter into the Applegate carriage. They almost looked like a family, and it pleased her, although she believed it shouldn't.

Perhaps Tyson can make her happy this time.

Love was a wonderful thing. Gloria had been loved by her husband and had loved him in return. She wanted the same for her daughter—to be in love and to be loved. And she wanted her daughter to have the blessing of children too. She wanted—

"Excuse me, Mrs. Fisher."

She glanced over her shoulder as Jeremiah stepped into the parlor.

"I was looking for Tyson."

"He and Diana are just leaving. They shouldn't be gone long."

Jeremiah joined her at the window in time to see the carriage pull away from the curb. "Wish I knew what that boy is thinking."

Gloria was certain he spoke to himself and not her, but she answered anyway. "He isn't a boy, Mr. Applegate. He's a man, and I'm beginning to believe he may have become a fine one. Whatever else happened to him on his travels, he seems to have matured into a man of faith and integrity."

"Unlike his father."

"I didn't say that."

"You didn't have to say it, Mrs. Fisher. I'm becoming painfully aware of my own shortcomings."

She felt a sudden sorrow for this man who had great wealth and yet was so poor in the important things of life. In contrast, she had known a limitation of financial resources, and yet she had an abundance of the things that truly mattered.

Jeremiah met her gaze. "I was too hard on my son, and I was unkind to your daughter in the years she lived under my roof." He drew in a slow breath and let it out. "I believe I was unkind to her as recently as this morning."

"You were?"

"It was not my intent, but yes. I was."

Gloria frowned. "You never thought Diana worthy of your son, did you?"

He looked out the window again, not answering.

"You thought he should make a more politically advantageous match."

A pause, then, "I admit that was my hope."

"Mr. Applegate." She turned fully toward him, waiting to continue until he faced her as well. "Might I give you a word of advice?"

He cocked an eyebrow.

"Let these two young people live their own lives. Allow them the chance to make their own decisions and, when necessary, to make their own mistakes. Let them seek God's will without your interference. In doing so, you might enjoy a new and better relationship with your son."

For a few moments, his expression was grim. Then the slightest of smiles bowed the corners of his mouth. "You are a wise woman, Mrs. Fisher. I shall do my best to heed your advice."

February 1894

Tyson tossed the whiskey to the back of his throat and felt it burn its way down to his gut. With any luck, he'd soon be lost in a drunken haze.

"You're in a foul mood, Applegate," the man opposite him said.

Tyson couldn't remember the fellow's name. One of the "friends" he'd managed to pick up since arriving in—Funny. He couldn't remember where he was. No matter. He'd learned a man could have countless friends as long as he bought all the liquor to drink.

"Haven't you heard?" another man at the table said. "His father made another grab at his fortune. Trying to force sonny boy back to the wilds of Idaho."

Tyson ground his teeth. He must have done a little too much talking when he was in his cups last night. Even drunk, he should mind his words better. For all he knew, one of the men around this table could be in his father's employ, hired to keep tabs on him.

He cursed silently as he downed another shot of whiskey.

For months now, he'd been moving from state to state, city to city, and yet he never seemed to get out from under his father's thumb. The anger never left him for long. Multiple times he'd ended a night in a fistfight. Sometimes with an acquaintance. Sometimes with a complete stranger.

To make matters worse, when he sobered up each morning, guilt washed over him. He'd left Idaho to defy his father, to get even with the old man, but the person he'd hurt the most was his mother. And Diana. He'd hurt her too. She must hate him by this time. Maybe as much as he hated his father.

He might have gone back. He might have sucked in his pride and returned to Idaho if his father hadn't tried some legal maneuvering to wrest the inheritance from Tyson's control. That had been the last straw.

He needed to get away. He needed to get himself and his money beyond his father's reach. Far, far beyond. Europe, perhaps. The Far East. Africa. Wherever that place was, he would look until he found it. No matter how long it took.

FOURTEEN

Over the next few days, Jeremiah surprised himself time and again. Whenever he wanted to dole out a word of advice or speak a word of criticism, he heard Gloria Fisher's cautionary voice in his head, and somehow he managed to keep silent. Perhaps the adage about an old dog and new tricks wasn't always true.

Or perhaps it was because he saw ever more clearly the part he'd played in the troubles he'd had with his son and his culpability in the hurt caused his daughter-in-law. It wasn't easy to look unflinchingly into one's own soul, but that's what he tried to do. And the better he saw himself, the better he seemed to see others as well.

Diana, for instance. In the past, he'd accused her of marrying Tyson for the Applegate fortune. He'd considered her a social-climbing nobody, unsuitable for his son. Even when Diana had remained so devoted to her mother-in-law, caring for Nora as her health declined, Jeremiah had refused to acknowledge her kind actions, her steadfastness, her courage despite disappointments and heartaches. Never for a moment had he stopped blaming Diana for Tyson's absence.

But the fault had been his own.

Somehow, he would make it up to her. And somehow he

would make up for a lifetime of mistakes to his son too. He *would* find a way.

Hearing her father-in-law's voice coming from Ned's room, Diana paused at the top of the stairs to listen, but she couldn't make out the words. Intrigued, she moved toward the door that had been left ajar and looked inside. Surprise washed over her. Jeremiah sat on Ned's bed, a book open in his hands, reading aloud to the boy. And Ned seemed captivated by the story. She didn't think she'd seen him this still. Not even in sleep. The sight tugged at her heart.

Did she make a sound? She must have, for Jeremiah looked up and their gazes met.

"Diana!" He sounded pleased to see her. "Come and join us."

Caught eavesdropping, she pushed the door wide.

"I was reading a story to Ned. He said Tyson left the book here yesterday." He glanced at the novel's spine. "*A Connecticut Yankee in King Arthur's Court.* I believe we're about to enter another time."

Diana didn't know this man. He looked like Tyson's father, but he was a stranger to her. She tried to hide her surprise as she stepped into the room.

"Nora read to Tyson every night when he was a boy. He got his love of reading from her." His expression grew wistful. "I wish I'd joined them more often than I did." Jeremiah reached over and affectionately ruffled Ned's hair.

Was this what it felt like to go through the looking glass? Perhaps she had lost her mind. First she'd imagined Tyson as changed. Now Jeremiah. Was she gullible enough to believe it of either of them?

Her father-in-law motioned to the chair against the wall, then lifted the book from his lap and began to read. "'When I came to again, I was sitting under an oak tree, on the grass, with a whole beautiful and broad country landscape all to myself—nearly. Not entirely; for there was a fellow on a horse, looking down at me—a fellow fresh out of a picture-book.'"

Diana sank onto the chair.

"'He was in old-time iron armor from head to heel, with a helmet on his head the shape of a nail-keg with slits in it; and he had a shield, and a sword, and a prodigious spear; and his horse had armor on, too, and a steel horn projecting from his forehead, and gorgeous red and green silk trappings that hung down all around him like a bed quilt, nearly to the ground.'"

She imagined Tyson as a boy, lying on his belly on the bed, heels of his hands cupping his chin, listening to his mother read a story. Or maybe it wasn't Tyson. Maybe it was Tyson's son she imagined.

The baby she'd lost. The loss she tried not to remember.

Tears sprang to her eyes and pain stabbed her heart. "Excuse me," she whispered as she rose from the chair.

Keeping her eyes lowered, she hurried out of Ned's room and into her own. She leaned her back against the door as she fought to control her emotions. It had been a long, long time since she'd allowed thoughts of her miscarriage to rise to the surface. Remembering hurt too much.

He—she was convinced the child had been a boy—would have been learning to read by this time. She imagined him with dark brown hair and blue eyes. Like his father's. Even at only six, he would have been on his way to becoming a fine horseman. He would have—

Stop. She had to stop. She could not let in the memories or the wishful thinking that came with them. She could not soften toward Tyson. She must stay firm in her resolve. She would be a fool to believe he wouldn't betray her again if she gave him the chance.

God, help me.

Diana had withdrawn from Tyson again. He felt it the moment he saw her upon his return from the campaign office. The headway he'd made over the last few days, especially when the two of them were with Ned, had vanished. When Diana looked at him down the length of the supper table that evening, she didn't seem to see him.

Was it hopeless, his idea that they could learn to love each other in a new and lasting way, his desire for them to build a real marriage from a poor beginning? Perhaps . . . but he wasn't giving up. He had five months left to change her mind about him, to make her want to stay. Now all he needed was to figure out how to go about working that miracle.

The telephone in the entry hall rang just as the family finished their dessert. A few moments later, Upchurch appeared in the dining room doorway and announced that Tyson's father had a call. Jeremiah excused himself.

"I know it's early," Gloria said, "but I believe I shall retire for the evening." She glanced between her daughter and Tyson.

"Are you feeling ill, Mother?" Diana asked.

"No, dear. A bit tired is all."

Before Tyson could say something to stop her, Diana rose from her chair. "I believe I shall do the same. Good night, Tyson. Please bid your father a good evening for me."

Tyson sighed as he leaned back in the chair. He said a silent prayer for God's guidance. It was going to take divine intervention for him to break through the wall his wife had erected around her heart.

The sound of his father clearing his throat drew Tyson's gaze to the dining room doorway.

"Son, I must return north tomorrow. There are matters at the Number Two mine requiring my personal attention."

"Trouble?"

"No." Jeremiah shook his head. "But matters I cannot delegate. I'm sorry. I was looking forward to going with you for that speech you're giving in Twin Falls."

It surprised Tyson, the twinge of regret he felt at the news. He supposed he should take some comfort that his father's visit, although brief, had been without rancor. Pleasant, even.

"It's a nice evening," his father continued. "Care to step outside with me?"

"If you like."

Dusk had settled over the valley by this time, and the back-yard was bathed in shadows. The two men sat in chairs on the veranda.

Jeremiah lit a cigar. After puffing it to life, he looked at Tyson. "Mind if I make an observation?"

Tyson shrugged. Would he mind?

"I believe you'll make a good senator if you get elected. I'm proud of you."

He tried not to let the surprise show on his face. "Thank you."

"When I return, I'd like to be of help with your campaign."

There was no hiding his amazement now. "You don't have to do that, Father. I know you support the Silver Republican candidate. I wouldn't ask you to go against your conscience."

"Perhaps you've managed to change my mind."

"In a few days? I doubt that."

"Stranger things have happened." His father smiled before puffing on his cigar.

Another lengthy silence followed. A comfortable silence. It was his father, once again, who broke it.

"Diana didn't seem herself at supper."

"No, she didn't."

"I think it may have something to do with Ned."

"With Ned? Why?"

"Well, not with the boy specifically."

"I'm afraid I don't understand what you're getting at."

Jeremiah looked off into the gathering darkness. "She wrote to you, you know. Many times. I should have made certain her letters reached you. I could have, if I'd wanted to. I didn't want to." He returned his gaze to Tyson. "You need to ask her what happened a few months after you left home for the last time."

Uneasiness swirled in Tyson's gut.

His father tamped out his cigar. "I believe I shall follow the ladies' example and retire early." He rose. "Good night, Son."

"Good night, Father."

April 1896

Diana held Nora's right hand between both of her own. On the opposite side of the bed, Jeremiah stood, silent, watching, waiting.

"Diana." Her mother-in-law's voice was soft and raspy.

She leaned forward. "Yes?"

"Forgive him."

"Nora, I—"

"Forgive Tyson. I know he's hurt you. Deeply hurt you. But don't hold that hurt in your heart. You will be the one who pays for it if you do."

Tears filled Diana's eyes, blurring her vision. Knowing her mother-in-law hadn't long to live—hours at most—hurt more than she'd expected. Her lengthy illness was what had kept Diana in the Applegate home. That and a secret shred of hope that Tyson would finally tire of his travels on the opposite side of the world and come home. Home to his mother. Home to Diana.

It had been a foolish hope. One she must release as surely as she must let go of Nora as she moved from this life to the next.

Loneliness washed over Diana. She'd lost so much in her twenty-one years. Her father had deserted his family. Her mother had died when Diana was only six. Her brother and sister had been separated from her. Her husband had abandoned her after only a few months of marriage. Yes, she was loved by the parents who'd adopted and raised her, but even they had left the Montana home where so many of Diana's memories had been made. And now Nora was leaving her too.

As if reading Diana's thoughts, her mother-in-law said, "God is right beside you, my dear." Her eyes drifted closed. "He will never leave you nor forsake you. Keep that truth close to your heart."

FIFTEEN

On Saturday afternoon, while Tyson accompanied his father to the train depot, Diana sat at the desk in the library to write invitations to their first dinner party. It would be a small, semiformal affair, as Tyson had suggested. Naturally they would invite Samuel and Iris Waverley. They would also invite the Grahams, whom Diana had met at the Waverley's a week before. The other two couples were strangers to her, both of the husbands influential in political circles according to Tyson.

But what about her mother? It wouldn't do to have an uneven number at the table, and she would not hear of her mother having supper in her room. No, she would need a single gentleman to take the empty place. But who? She knew few unattached men, and Tyson knew even fewer, given the brief length of time he'd been in Boise.

Mentally, she ran through the short list, beginning with men at their church. There was Mr. Johnson, but he was as deaf as a post and when he talked he always shouted, unable to hear himself otherwise. Not the best of guests. There was Mr. Baker, but he struck her as never quite honest. Her mother disliked Mr. Nelson, although Diana didn't know why. Of course, there was Brook's uncle, Marcus Calhoun. He'd served as her mother's dinner companion more than once in the past year. But Marcus had left for a trip to Europe the day after the dinner party at Brook's home when—

Brook. Why hadn't she thought of it sooner? She could ask Brook. He'd said she could call on him if ever she had need, and her mother liked him well enough. And hadn't Tyson agreed Diana could choose her own friends? Brook was her friend. Inviting him could be her own small way of announcing her independence. Maybe not to all of Boise society but most surely to her husband.

She pushed doubt aside as she reached for another engraved card and began to write.

"Miss Diana?"

As she slid the card into its envelope, she glanced up. "What is it, Ned?"

The boy stood in the doorway to the library, a sheen of perspiration on his forehead, his hair in its usual disheveled condition. Though he still favored his bad ankle, he hadn't used the crutches in three days.

"'Member that dog I told you about, the one I said liked to follow me around?"

"Yes, I remember."

"He ain't dead like I feared, but he's ailin' real bad."

"How do you know?"

"Mr. Romano found him. Says Dog oughta be put out of his misery. You won't let him do that, will you? You won't let him shoot my dog."

Diana rose from the chair. "*Your* dog?"

The boy jutted his jaw defiantly. "As much mine as anybody's, I reckon. I fed him when I could, and he followed me around, like I told you."

"Where is he now? Your dog."

"Down at the barn."

"Then let's go have a look at him."

Relief sparked in Ned's eyes before he turned and hurried down the hall as fast as he was able. Diana followed right behind.

It wasn't even a week since she'd seen a dirty street urchin standing on a crate, trying to steal a pie from the Applegate kitchen. But already it was hard for her to imagine this house without Ned in it. She dreaded the day when he might decide to leave. He could at any time. He was sly and smart and used to fending for himself. How could she convince him to stay?

Why should he stay if I don't mean to do the same?

Ridiculous question. After the election, she wouldn't live in this house any longer, but surely she would have a place big enough to include Ned. Only she would have to think about that later.

Claude Romano and Fernando Diaz—the head groom and stable boy whom Tyson had hired soon after his arrival in Boise— were standing to one side of the barn entrance when Diana and Ned arrived. On the ground between them was a small dog lying on his side. His wiry coat was tan and grizzled, like an old man's beard. His square-shaped head was mostly black. He lay so still Diana wondered if he'd died already. But when Ned dropped to his knees, the dog slapped his tail against the boy's thigh a couple of times.

"You're gonna be okay, Dog," Ned said as he leaned close.

Diana looked at the head groom. "What seems to be the matter with him, Mr. Romano?"

"Not sure, ma'am. Could be he ate something spoiled. Could be he got into some poison. Could be diseased." He jerked his head toward the foothills. "I was working one of the colts up that draw when I found him. No telling how long he's been up there. I brought him back here and tried to give him some food. He doesn't seem to have the strength to lift his head long enough to eat, though I got some water down his throat." He lowered his voice almost to a whisper. "He should be put out of his misery, ma'am."

"No!" Ned cried. "You're not gonna shoot him. Miss Diana ain't gonna let you do that."

"Ned," she answered quickly, "we'll have to do what's best for the animal."

The boy's eyes narrowed. "You didn't shoot me when I was hurt."

"Of course not. It's not the same thing."

"Who says?"

"Ned—"

"I ain't gonna let you do it." The defiant look disappeared, replaced by tears in his eyes. "He's a good dog. Not his fault he's sick."

Diana drew a deep breath before looking at the groom again. "Send for the veterinary surgeon, Mr. Romano. And let's make the dog as comfortable as we can until he gets here."

"Yes, ma'am."

The stable boy was dispatched for the animal doctor, and Claude Romano moved the ailing canine into an empty stall, placing him on a bed of straw covered with a horse blanket. Ned didn't let anything or anyone keep him too far from the dog.

Lord, please don't let Dog die. Please let him live. I know there are greater problems in the world, but this matters so much to Ned.

"Diana?"

She turned at the sound of Tyson's voice, unreasonably glad he'd returned.

"Upchurch said there was some sort of problem down at the stables."

"Not a problem, really." She stepped out of the stall and drew her husband a short distance from the opening. "Ned's dog is sick. We've sent for the veterinary surgeon."

"Ned's dog?"

"Yes."

"I didn't know he had a dog."

A full explanation seemed too complicated now, so she shrugged as she looked toward the stall again.

"I suppose it's going to end up living in the house too," Tyson said under his breath.

She heard him . . . and couldn't keep from smiling.

A wife, Tyson had wanted. A widowed mother-in-law, he'd expected. But a cat, an orphan, and now a stray dog as well? What a menagerie! Exactly when had he lost control of his household?

The answer to that last question was easy: he'd lost it the moment he decided to reunite with his wife. He hadn't known it then, of course. He'd still thought he had a firm grip on the reins of his life.

He glanced heavenward and wondered if this was God's way of teaching him not to rely on human wisdom. Or perhaps he'd become prideful. Either way, he suspected the Lord was taking him down a notch or two.

He watched as Diana returned to the stall. She touched Ned's shoulder with her fingertips and spoke to him, something that caused the boy to look up and nod. She had a way with that kid. If not for her, the boy would have bolted as soon as he could walk without crutches.

Ned . . . What had Tyson's father said last night? Something about Diana not being herself because of Ned. It hadn't made sense then. It didn't make sense now. *You need to ask her what happened a few months after you left home for the last time.* That same uneasiness rolled in Tyson's stomach. He knew they needed to talk about the past, he and Diana, but he was afraid of that discussion all the same. He had so much to be forgiven for. Far more than he should expect of her.

When the veterinarian arrived, Tyson followed him into the stall and stood against a side wall next to Claude Romano. Meanwhile, Diana drew Ned with her to the opposite wall while the doctor examined the dog.

Speaking softly, the groom assured Tyson that Rutger Van Pelt was a qualified veterinarian with a degree from a college of veterinary medicine in Pennsylvania. Quacks abounded in animal husbandry, but Claude Romano would make certain no such person came near any of Tyson's horses or other animals.

After a thorough examination, Dr. Van Pelt stood and looked at Tyson. "I won't pretend your son's dog isn't very ill, Mr. Applegate, but I believe he'll recover."

"I'm not—" Ned began, but Tyson saw Diana stop the protest with a quick squeeze on the boy's shoulder.

"The dog's a stray," the groom said, no doubt insulted the veterinarian thought the Applegates would own a dog as sickly as this one.

"I see. Well, he's malnourished and dehydrated. He'll need to be fed and watered in frequent but small amounts until he gains strength. I'll leave you with a powder to administer twice a day. Small canines like this one are naturally active. You'll have to keep him closed up so he doesn't overexert himself as he begins to mend. Rest and good nutrition are what will aid his recovery."

"I can keep him with me," Ned interjected. "I'll make sure he's quiet. I'll take good care of him."

Just as Tyson had feared. The dog would be moved into the house. Because even if he could've refused Ned, he was helpless against the beseeching look Diana sent his way.

Tyson walked with Dr. Van Pelt to his buggy and got a few more tips on caring for the dog. By the time the veterinarian pulled away and Tyson turned around, he saw Claude carrying the dog toward the house, Diana and Ned right behind him.

He just knew that dog was going to be trouble.

July 1896

Bored and restless, Tyson laid his cards facedown on the table. "Gentlemen, I'm done for the night." He rose to his feet. "Hope your luck is better than mine."

He went outside. The night was hot and sticky, but at least there was a breeze on the stone patio. Light from a full moon frosted the elegant grounds of the Kingston villa.

"Beautiful, isn't it?" Pauline Kingston asked from the shadows.

Blast. He wouldn't have come outside if he'd known she was there. "Yes." He turned and watched her walk toward him. "It is."

She put her arms around his neck and leaned close. "You've been ignoring me all evening."

"Have I?"

"Yes."

"Sorry."

But he wasn't sorry. He was bored with Pauline as well as with the nightly round of parties and drinking and gambling. Right now, he couldn't remember the reason he'd followed Pauline and her brother Quentin from India to Italy. It wasn't because he'd taken her for a lover—although he had.

"What's wrong, *amore?*"

For some reason, her question stirred to life another woman's image. Diana's image. Sweet and beautiful. Innocent and naive. Diana . . . his wife. Pauline didn't seem to mind that he was a married man. At least he assumed he was still married. He wondered—

A yearning for home hit him hard. It happened a lot lately, but he wasn't about to give into it. If he gave in, he would find himself under his father's thumb once again.

And that he could not allow.

SIXTEEN

Tyson shared his opinion about the dog with Diana, and soon everyone in the household called the mutt Trouble. Even Ned.

One thing could be said about the boy—he kept his word. In the days that followed, while Trouble was too weak to go up and down the stairs on his own four legs, Ned carried him outside several times a day. The boy also coaxed food down him when no one else could and got him to drink water too. Ned rarely left the dog alone.

Not that Tyson saw much of that devotion firsthand. He heard about it from Diana over supper after long days of campaign work, days spent delivering speeches in Boise and other towns, days spent handling a multitude of details that would drive an accountant mad. He'd been so busy with the campaign, in fact, he forgot they were hosting a dinner party on Friday.

When he walked in the door—tired and wanting nothing more than a quiet few hours spent conversing with his wife—Upchurch informed him Robert had laid out Tyson's evening attire and was waiting upstairs to assist him.

"And Mrs. Applegate?"

"I believe she is dressing as well, sir."

"Thank you, Upchurch. When are our guests expected to arrive?"

"Within the hour."

He swallowed a sigh and headed up the stairs to his bedchamber. His valet was waiting in his room, as Upchurch had said.

"Good evening, sir," Robert greeted.

"Good evening." He removed his tie and loosened his collar. "I suppose the house has been in somewhat of an uproar today."

"Indeed, sir. But Mrs. Cuddy runs her kitchen like an army sergeant. She and Upchurch will make certain the evening goes off without a hitch."

"I believe it."

Tyson changed out of his business suit and into one suitable for a semiformal dinner in the home. It occurred to him as Robert finished with his tie that he probably should inquire about their guests. He knew the Waverleys were coming, but for the life of him, he couldn't recall who else was to be in attendance. He wasn't certain he'd asked Diana after providing her with a list of possibilities.

He would ask her now.

But as he left his bedroom, the doorbell rang, announcing the arrival of the first of their guests. And when he looked, he saw Diana had preceded him down the staircase and was moving into the center of the entry hall. He hurried after her so she wouldn't be alone when Upchurch opened the door.

Diana glanced at him as he stepped to her side. He knew her well enough to recognize her anxiety.

"You look beautiful," he said softly.

She gave him a nervous smile.

Upchurch announced, "Justice Samuel Waverley and Mrs. Waverley. Mr. Brook Calhoun."

Cold surprise shot through Tyson as his gaze darted to the front entrance. The two men removed their hats in unison, followed by their gloves, and handed the items to the butler.

Iris Waverley stepped up to Diana and the two women clasped hands.

"We're delighted you could come," Diana said.

"We wouldn't have missed it, my dear. My, what a lovely home."

Tyson found his voice. "Welcome, Iris. Samuel."

Upchurch announced the arrival of two more couples. Tyson's brain barely registered the names as he shook Brook Calhoun's hand and mumbled some sort of greeting. Did he sound earnest? He couldn't be sure.

Diana said, "Mother was glad you could come, Brook. Thank you for joining us."

"And where is my lovely dinner companion?"

"I don't know." Diana turned to look down the hallway just as her mother stepped into view. "Oh, good. Here she comes now."

Brook moved away from the host and hostess and greeted Gloria Fisher with a bow and a kiss on the back of her hand.

Tyson schooled his expression, not wanting his guests to see the anger that flared to life in his chest. His wife's betrayal was as sharp as a knife. He'd thought . . . He'd thought . . .

What had he thought? That a few weeks and some pleasant moments would heal the wounds in their marriage? Seven years of neglect couldn't be overcome as easily as that. Still, he hadn't expected this.

The knife twisted deeper into his heart.

Although Diana couldn't see it on her husband's face, she sensed his displeasure. Had sensed it the instant Brook stepped into the house. She'd been wrong to invite him, no matter how justified it seemed at the time. Sensible, too, to pair him with her mother. Or maybe it hadn't seemed sensible. Maybe she'd done it out of spite. Which was probably why she'd never found a moment to tell Tyson who would be present tonight.

Somehow Diana managed to smile and move among their guests, making them feel welcome, but the minutes dragged by. She avoided looking at her husband as much as possible, fearing what she might see in his eyes.

Dinner was announced, and the party moved to the dining room, Diana leading the women, Tyson and the men following behind. The gentlemen pulled out chairs for the ladies, then seated themselves. Samuel Waverley was assigned the chair on Diana's right. His wife sat on Tyson's right at the opposite end of the table. Gold-rimmed china and crystal glassware glittered in the lamplight. An elaborate centerpiece decorated the table. Almost in perfect unison, the party removed their napkins from the table and put them on their laps.

Tyson's valet had been drafted to serve at the table for this affair. Under Upchurch's watchful gaze, Robert brought in the soup course and first served Iris Waverley, then moved slowly and easily around the table until everyone had a bowl of bean soup before them.

Later, over asparagus polonaise, Tyson and Brook spoke briefly about horses without any show of animosity from either of them. Diana began to relax. Perhaps she hadn't made a dreadful mistake after all. Perhaps she'd misread Tyson's reaction when he saw Brook at the door. Perhaps—

A movement in the front hall caught Diana's eye, and she looked up in time to see Ned pass from sight. Where was he off to? The front door and the library were the only possible destinations. Since he couldn't read, he would have no reason to go to the library. But she could think of no reason for him to go out the front door either. She had explained they were entertaining guests this evening, making sure he understood he should use the servants' staircase when he took Trouble outside.

Should she go check on the boy? There must be a reason he'd come downstairs. Did he need her for something?

No, she answered herself. She couldn't leave the table in the middle of dinner. It would require an explanation, and what would she say about the orphan boy who was staying with them?

The door from the butler's pantry swung open, and Robert appeared again, carrying the main course of baked salmon. Diana's thoughts returned to her guests.

Perhaps Tyson should have considered the acting profession instead of politics. He'd pulled off the evening without alerting anyone, not even Brook Calhoun, of his true feelings. But by the time Tyson and Diana stood near the door to bid their departing guests a good night, he felt the facade grow thin.

"Thank you for including me," Brook—the last to leave—said to Diana, holding her hand longer than necessary. Then he looked at Tyson, his smile tight. "It was a pleasant evening, Mr. Applegate."

Temper on the rise, Tyson nodded rather than risk saying something he shouldn't.

Brook turned and walked toward his waiting carriage. A few moments later, Upchurch closed the door.

Diana went into the parlor and sank onto the first chair. She emitted a soft groan as she covered her face with both hands. Tyson followed her into the parlor, but he didn't sit down. Instead he walked to the window and stared out at the darkness.

"I thought it went rather well," Diana said. "Don't you? Mrs. Cuddy should be commended. Everyone thought the dinner delicious."

"Why did you do it?"

"Do what?" .

He turned to face her, anger increasing because of her response. Could she possibly *not* know what he meant? "Why did you bring Calhoun into our home?"

"Oh, that." She offered a slight smile. "I needed someone to balance out the table with Mother. I couldn't think of any suitable gentleman but Brook. Mother knows and likes him. It seemed a good solution. I . . . I didn't think you'd mind since he is . . . since he's a friend of mine and Mother's."

"You were all but engaged to marry him, Diana. Can you truly not see why I would mind?"

Her smile faded and her chin tilted in defiance.

"You are my wife and he was your . . . your paramour."

"He was no such thing. There was never anything improper between us." She rose to her feet, hands clasped at her waist. "When you say it that way, you make it sound scandalous."

"It could be construed that way, a married woman engaged to another man."

"Brook and I had a proper courtship. I was thought to be a widow by everyone, including me. Including your own father. It was only the paperwork declaring my husband dead that was unfinished."

"But I *wasn't* dead."

"How was I to know that? You didn't bother to contact me. At least not until you *needed* a wife for political reasons."

Tyson took a step toward her. "I've told you I'm sorry for that. How many times must I beg your forgiveness? I'm sorry." His voice rose. "I'm sorry!"

"Sorry doesn't change the past. Sorry doesn't change that you abandoned me. That you didn't want me. That you forgot I was even alive."

"I didn't forget you were alive."

"Didn't you? Well, you acted like it."

"We had a bargain, Diana. A bargain that you would be my wife for the six months of the campaign. Truly my wife in all ways except . . . except one."

Heat flared in her cheeks, showing she knew his meaning. "And I've kept the bargain in . . . in all ways except one. But I will choose my own friends."

The anger that had earlier seared him with heat turned suddenly cold. "Are you . . . Are you in love with Brook Calhoun?"

"Am I in—" Up went her chin again. "What I feel for Brook is none of your concern."

Tyson was across the parlor in a flash. He didn't consider his actions. He acted out of pure instinct as he wrapped her in his arms and did what he'd wanted to do for a solid month: he kissed her. There was more anger than passion in the press of his mouth against hers. He wanted to mark her as his. He wanted others to know she belonged to him. He wanted *her* to know she belonged to him. He wanted her to submit to him as a wife was supposed to submit to a husband.

Husbands, love your wives . . .

He hated the small voice of his conscience. He hated what the words implied. Would Tyson lay down his life for Diana? Like Christ for the church, would he do only what was best for her? Could she trust him completely, without hesitation or reservation? The answer to the first two questions was, he didn't know. The answer to the last question was a resounding *No.*

He loosened his hold upon her and took a step back.

The color that had infused her cheeks moments before drained away, leaving her pale. Her eyes were wide and filled with confusion.

He took another step back, at the same time raking the fingers of his right hand through his hair. "I'm sorry. I shouldn't have done that." Yet. He shouldn't have done it yet. And he shouldn't have kissed her in anger. He wanted to cherish her, not brand her as a possession. "Once again, I'm sorry."

She stared at him a short while longer, then without a word she turned and left the room, head high, shoulders stiff. He stepped to the parlor entrance to observe her as she climbed the staircase, listening to her footsteps, knowing she stopped first to look in on Ned before going into her own room and closing the door.

The maid remained silent while she helped Diana out of her evening gown and into her nightclothes. But Liz's silence said more than any words could have. Everyone in the household must have heard Diana's fight with Tyson. Even the servants now knew this was a business arrangement, not a marriage, and it shamed her.

"Thank you, Liz," she said in a soft voice. "That will be all."

"Yes, Mrs. Applegate." The young woman, still avoiding eye contact, dipped a curtsy before leaving the bedroom.

Diana drew a deep breath as she got into bed and pulled the covers up to her neck. Tears threatened and her throat tightened.

They'd fought over Brook, but it wasn't Brook she thought about as she lay there. It wasn't even the quarrel that had ended the evening. It was Tyson and the strength of his arms and the blaze his kiss had set afire inside her.

"Are you in love with Brook Calhoun?"

She wished she could have answered in the affirmative. But she couldn't.

"I'm sorry. I shouldn't have done that."

Fear gripped her. Fear of the future, both the near and the far. Fear because her life had spun out of control. Her carefully made plans were in complete disarray. Tears dampened the pillow, and it took all the willpower she possessed to keep from sobbing aloud. She'd loved Tyson once, and when he'd abandoned her, Diana's world had seemed to end. It had taken time—years—for her heart and emotions to heal. She hadn't wanted to risk feeling like that ever again. With Brook, there would have been safety, though no great passion.

It's what I wanted. It was. It was.

Diana cried herself to sleep.

July 1896

As Diana walked down the hallway, an unfamiliar voice drifted from her father-in-law's study. Unsure why, she stopped and listened.

"Your son's becoming better at covering his tracks, Mr. Applegate. It took us a little longer this time, but we managed to find him again. We've learned Tyson was in India up until about a month ago. Now he's in Italy and has been staying at a villa belonging to . . . to a Mr. Quentin Kingston." The man cleared his throat. "It seems your son's developed a—shall we say—romantic attachment to Mr. Kingston's sister. If you know what I mean, sir."

"I know what you mean," Jeremiah answered, his voice gruff. "Another fortune hunter, I suppose. At least he can't marry her. That's one mistake he can't repeat."

"Miss Kingston is no fortune hunter. She's wealthy in her own right. Not to put too fine a point on it, sir, but she'd make you seem a pauper."

Forcing herself to draw a breath, Diana moved to a nearby bench and sat on it. It surprised her that what she'd overheard could still cause intense pain. Would she die from this hurt? It felt like it.

How she wished she could stop loving Tyson. Why couldn't she? And why couldn't she stop hoping he would return to her?

I've got to leave this place. I'll never stop waiting for Tyson to come back as long as I'm here.

It felt good to make that decision at last. She should have left long ago. If not for her parents' financial troubles and the entreaties of her mother-in-law, she would have.

She would write to her mother and father today to tell them she was coming to stay with them. Nora Applegate had bequeathed a small monthly stipend to Diana in her will, and that money would keep Diana from becoming a burden to her parents. She would go and be set free from the sadness that seemed to fill every moment of every day.

She would go and be set free from Tyson Applegate's hold upon her heart.

SEVENTEEN

"Justice Waverley to see you, sir," Upchurch announced.

Tyson rose from his desk in the library. "Samuel, this is a surprise."

"I hope I haven't come too early."

"Of course not." After shaking hands with the judge, Tyson motioned to a nearby chair. "Have a seat."

Samuel shook his head. "I can't stay but a moment. I have an appointment I must keep. But I promised my wife I would come over. She's lost a bracelet that belonged to her mother. A gold chain with diamonds. The clasp broke on our way over last night, and she put it in her purse. But when we got home, it wasn't there. We've searched the carriage to no avail, so we were hoping it might have fallen out somewhere in your house."

"Upchurch?"

The butler appeared in the doorway.

"Would you inquire if a bracelet was found, please? Mrs. Waverley lost it last night. A gold chain with diamonds."

"At once, Mr. Applegate."

Tyson looked at the judge and motioned once again to the chair opposite him. This time Samuel sat down.

"Iris would wish me to tell you how much we both enjoyed the evening, and we are quite taken with your wife. Even more so than before. She's an asset to you, Tyson, and to your career. I've thought so from the first time I met her."

Tyson suspected he heard a question in the judge's tone, one about Brook Calhoun. Or maybe he imagined it. Maybe no one else thought it strange for Brook to have been one of the guests at Tyson's table.

Why had she done it? Why had she invited Brook into their home? Was it really as innocent as a dinner companion for her mother? And if not, what was the real reason? Was it possible Diana loved Brook? She'd refused to answer that last question. She'd said her feelings were none of his business. But that wasn't true. They *were* his business.

He hadn't seen his wife or his mother-in-law today. They'd both eaten breakfast in their bedchambers. Not the first time Diana had done so since moving into this house, and yet this morning her absence at the breakfast table had felt like a personal affront. But could he blame her for wanting to avoid him?

The judge cleared his throat.

"I'm sorry." Tyson looked at the older man. "Did you say something?"

"You seem distracted. A problem with the campaign?"

"No." He shook his head. "But a great deal on my mind."

"Mmm."

Before either could say more, Upchurch returned. "I'm sorry, sir. No one has found a bracelet. I sent Liz to inquire of Mrs. Applegate, and she hasn't seen it either."

The judge sighed. "That is disappointing. My wife will be heartbroken. It had great sentimental value to her."

"Perhaps it fell into the lawn on your way to or from the carriage," Tyson said. "I'll make sure the grounds staff know to keep an eye out for it."

"Thank you." Samuel stood. "I'd best be on my way. I don't want to be late for my appointment."

Tyson walked the judge to the front door. The two men shook hands again, and Tyson watched as Samuel strode down the walk to where his carriage waited on the boulevard. Then he stepped back into the house and turned around.

Diana stood at the bottom of the staircase. She looked pale. Worse, she looked unhappy. Deeply unhappy.

And Tyson was the cause.

"Good morning," he said.

"Has the judge gone already?"

"Yes. Just now."

"I'm sorry I missed him."

"He only stopped by to check on the bracelet."

"It wasn't found?"

Tyson shook his head.

Diana glanced down the hall behind her. "Is Mother up?"

"I haven't seen her this morning." He took two steps toward her. "Diana, I'm sorry. About last night. I shouldn't have . . . behaved the way I did. Please forgive me."

He saw her shoulders rise and fall. When she looked at him, he thought there might be tears in her eyes, though she didn't let them fall.

"I was in the wrong, Tyson. Not you. I shouldn't have invited Brook without speaking to you first, and I never should have let you be surprised by his arrival. This is your home."

It's your home too.

"I promised I would do my best to get along with you and to not lose my temper during these six months."

"And I promised to do my best not to make you angry or hurt your feelings."

Her hands clenched at her sides. "I shouldn't have expected there wouldn't be disagreements between us."

With sudden insight, he realized that's what he'd expected. He'd expected her to move into his home and to immediately see he was a changed man. He'd expected her to forgive him completely for his past transgressions—the ones she knew about and the ones she didn't. He'd expected her to forget whatever Brook Calhoun had been in her life and cleave to her husband instead.

Unreasonable expectations, all of them.

"You're right, Diana. But will you give me another chance to do things better?"

She didn't answer him at once. Simply looked at him, sadness written on her face. Sadness and confusion. Because of him.

Finally, she said, "We'll both try to do better."

Seated in the shade of her favorite tree that afternoon, Gloria closed the book she'd been reading and studied her daughter. Diana sat on a blanket spread on the lawn, holding Tiger and scratching the cat behind its ears. Ned and Trouble were nearby. Though improving, the dog wasn't fully recovered from whatever ailed it. Ned, on the other hand, showed no sign of his former injury.

It didn't surprise Gloria that her adopted daughter had collected the boy and those two strays in a few short weeks. Diana had a soft spot for the lonely and rejected. Perhaps because she'd felt lonely and rejected herself, first as a child off the orphan train, separated from her mother by death and from her siblings by fate, later as a wife abandoned by the man she'd loved.

How do I help her, Lord?

Gloria had heard Diana and Tyson arguing last night. Her bedroom door had been open, making it impossible for her *not* to hear.

And she didn't blame her son-in-law for being angry about Brook's inclusion at the dinner party. In her opinion, Tyson's anger was justified. It showed the measure of the man that he had apologized despite being in the right.

Gloria was convinced now that Tyson loved Diana. He wanted their marriage to succeed far beyond November. His campaign for the Senate—earnest though it was—was only the excuse he'd used to get Diana into his home so he might prove he was a changed man.

She shook her head, smiling to herself. Tyson wasn't the only one who'd changed. Gloria had changed too. Just a few short weeks ago, she'd been afraid of what tomorrow might bring. But fear—her constant companion since the death of her husband—had lost its grip on her heart. A miracle of sorts.

Now she needed another miracle. She needed a way to stop her daughter from throwing away happiness with both hands.

Diana set Tiger on the blanket and watched to see what the cat would do with a bit more freedom. After two weeks of good care and plenty of food, Tiger had grown hale and hardy. There wasn't a good reason to keep her shut in Diana's room anymore—with the possible exception of protecting her from Mrs. Cuddy.

Tiger moved cautiously toward the edge of the blanket, but before she could step into the grass, Trouble ambled toward her. The cat hunched her back and hissed. The dog stopped, a bewildered expression on his face.

Diana laughed. "Trouble, you'd better stay back. Tiger's claws are sharp."

Trouble seemed to understand and returned to his young master.

Diana felt a small catch in her chest as she looked at the pair. How long would Ned stay now that his ankle had recovered? Could she make him want to stay, even though he was used to a life without boundaries? But even if she could, she supposed something legal would have to be done. Which meant not only would Ned have to agree to it, Tyson would have to agree to it too. Why should he do so? To please her? After what she'd done last night . . .

She lay back on the blanket and stared upward. Beyond leafy tree limbs that danced in the soft breeze, fluffy clouds dotted an azure sky. So pretty. So right. And it frightened her, the rightness of it all. She felt at home here, with Mother and Ned and Trouble and Tiger.

And with Tyson.

She'd agreed to six months.

He'd said he wanted forever.

Was that true or only what he'd needed to say to get her cooperation?

She closed her eyes.

"Diana?"

"Yes, Mother."

"Don't hold your heart so tightly. You cannot protect it from getting hurt in life, no matter how hard you try."

"I know."

A period of silence followed before her mother said, "And yet still you try."

Yes, still I try.

Sorrow pressed against her chest, a keen longing for all that had been lost to her. Her ma in Chicago. Hugh and Felicia. The father who'd adopted and raised her. And the ability to love without holding back a part of herself.

Ned's and her mother's joint laughter found its way through the haze of Diana's self-pity. She sat up, curious to see what caused their mirth. A quick glance revealed the answer. Trouble lay on his back in a pose of complete submission while Tiger sat on his chest, appearing for all the world as if the dog were her personal throne.

"Well, I'll be," came Tyson's voice from behind Diana. "Will you look at that?"

As if Tyson's words had broken a magician's spell, Tiger meowed and launched herself away from Trouble. The dog jumped to his feet and started barking as the cat disappeared up the nearby tree.

Diana twisted toward her husband. "I didn't expect you back from town this soon."

"Writing a speech didn't seem all that urgent today."

For a moment, she thought he might settle onto the blanket beside her. Instead he joined her mother on the stone bench.

Was it possible to be disappointed and relieved at the same time?

"I was wondering," Tyson said, "if you'd all like to go down to the river for a picnic after church tomorrow. The weather is fine for it."

"Can Trouble go with us?" Ned asked.

"I don't see any reason why not."

The boy shrugged. "Okay. I'll go."

Tyson looked at Diana again, his gaze repeating the question.

He's forgiven me for including Brook last night. He's forgiven me completely.

Rather than relief, she felt ashamed. For even when she'd admitted to him that she shouldn't have done it, she hadn't asked him to forgive her. Instead he'd asked for *her* forgiveness. All the more surprising since the old Tyson, the one she'd married, the one who'd left her, had never admitted he was in the wrong, even when he obviously was. When had she switched places with him? When had she become the one so determined to be right?

She pictured herself as a girl of no more than ten or eleven. In the memory, her adopted father was leaning down to her, a patient, loving expression on his face. *"Diana, do you want to be right . . . or would you rather be righteous?"*

Perhaps the desire to be right wasn't a newly acquired trait after all.

November 1896

Tyson's mother was dead. She'd been dead over six months, and he hadn't known it. A son should know when his mother was sick and dying. A good son *would* know.

He wasn't a good son.

Hadn't been a good son.

Never would be a good son.

The letter from Tyson's father had caught up with him in London. It contained few details. Only that his mother's illness had been long, her death slow in coming, and that Diana had been her constant companion throughout but was now living with her parents in Nampa, Idaho, where her father worked for the railroad. Odd, the way that last news affected him. It felt as if she'd left him rather than the other way around.

He let the letter slip through his fingers and drift to the floor as he walked to the window of his hotel room. He could go out for the evening. He could join up with friends. Friends? Not truly. When a man was young and rich, he could have all of the companions—male or female—he wanted, any time he wanted, but that didn't make them his friends.

No, Tyson preferred to be alone tonight. He needed to think.

He closed his eyes and wondered how he'd allowed his life to become such a mess, all in the name of defying his father.

EIGHTEEN

At the close of the service on Sunday, Tyson stood to one side and watched as the others moved out of the pew: first his wife, followed by his mother-in-law, and finally Ned.

It was the boy's presence that had surprised him this morning. How was it Diana had persuaded Ned to come to church with the family and when exactly had she bought him that suit?

He offered his elbow to Diana and smiled to himself, realizing how easily she could prevail upon him to do something he hadn't considered doing before. Ned had obviously fallen under the spell of her charms as Tyson had.

When they reached the sidewalk, they were greeted by a familiar voice.

"Mr. Applegate. Mrs. Applegate. How good to see you again."

Tyson met Kendall Michaels' gaze and offered a tight smile. He had yet to forgive the newspaperman for his behavior at the judge's dinner party.

"Are you a member of this congregation?" Kendall asked.

"Not yet." Tyson glanced at Diana. "But my wife and mother-in-law are. And you?"

"Just visiting."

Why? Are you following me? Tyson swallowed the question.

Kendall turned his gaze on Ned. "And who is this young man? Your son?" His eyes held excitement—no doubt hoping for a scandal to report.

"I ain't his son," Ned answered, scowling.

Tyson wanted to ignore the newspaperman's question and hurry his family toward the carriage, but instinct told him doing so would be a mistake. The best way was to be honest without saying too much. A tricky balance to manage, but he would try. "Ned is a guest in our home."

"And if you'll excuse us," Diana said, her tone deceptively polite, "we have promised our young guest a picnic lunch on this beautiful Lord's Day. We must hurry or our cook will not be happy with our tardiness. Good day, Mr. Michaels."

Tyson wanted to kiss her.

Kendall tipped his hat. "Good day, Mrs. Applegate. Mr. Applegate."

"Excellent job," Tyson whispered as they moved toward the carriage awaiting them at the curb on Seventh Street.

"He's an insufferable man," she replied in an equally soft voice. She stopped, looked up at Tyson. "We need to have a better answer about Ned before someone else asks the same question."

She was right, of course. They did need a better answer. At the very least, they should make certain Ned was an orphan, as he claimed. What if he'd run away from home instead? It wouldn't do Tyson's campaign any good if it was discovered Ned's parents were alive and searching for him.

"You're right. We need a better answer."

Her hand tightened on his arm. "I don't want Ned to leave us."

She doesn't want him to leave us . . .

Us.

The small word felt huge in his heart.

"I'll do everything I can to see that he stays, Diana. I promise."
Her smile seemed brighter than the sun.

"Are you two coming?" Gloria asked from inside the carriage.
"It's terribly stuffy in here."

"Yes, Mother." Diana released her hold on Tyson's arm. "We're
coming."

The spot beside the Boise River was ideal for a picnic. Tall cot-
tonwoods provided ample shade where Diana and Tyson spread
blankets on the ground. The water rushing past them cooled the
midday air.

"Don't get too close to the river," Diana called to Ned as he and
Trouble explored the area.

Tyson must have sensed her concern, for he walked toward
where the boy and dog played, keeping himself between them and
the river.

Liz and her sister Joan, the Applegate maids, had accompanied
the family to the river, and they busied themselves now, setting out
the bill of fare. Mrs. Cuddy had prepared a veritable feast: cold roast
chicken, sandwiches of potted rabbit, bewitched veal, cold baked
ham, egg salad, buttered rolls, hard-boiled eggs, pickles, orange mar-
malade, sugared strawberries, almond cake, and coconut jumbles.
Lemonade and tea were their beverage choices, both of them iced.

Diana's mother marveled aloud over the abundance of food.
"I simply cannot help adding up the cost in my head." She gave a
small shrug. "Too many years of minding every penny, I suppose."

Diana leaned over and touched her mother's arm. "You won't
have to count pennies ever again."

"Spoken with the assurance of the young." Gloria stared
toward the river, her expression wistful. "Your father provided well

for us for many years. He never imagined a national financial crisis could wipe out our savings. He was a careful man with money. He believed in saving for a rainy day and did so religiously, but it all vanished in an instant." Her gaze returned to Diana. "The rain falls on the just and unjust, my dear. We cannot know what tomorrow will bring."

Diana had no reply.

"Mrs. Applegate," Joan said into the ensuing silence. "We are ready to serve the meal."

Grateful for the interruption, Diana looked toward the river. "Tyson. Ned. It's time to eat."

In short order, man, boy, and dog reached the picnic area. When commanded by Ned, Trouble lay in the grass a few feet away from one of the blankets, but his dark eyes remained locked on the platters and bowls.

Tyson chuckled. "That is one hopeful dog."

"He can have something, can't he?" Ned asked.

"Yes, when we're done he can have some of the scraps. But you'll need to make sure he doesn't get any chicken bones or anything else he can choke on."

"I know that."

"Good." Tyson sank onto the blanket next to Diana. "Let's thank God for this food Mrs. Cuddy prepared."

His prayer was brief, though earnest, and afterward they filled their plates. The family dined while seated on the blankets, and the maids and coachman had their own picnic not far removed.

Diana took a bite of chicken and thought, *I'm going to wish my corset wasn't laced so tight.*

"Ned," Tyson said, "do you remember who took you to the orphanage after your mother died?"

The question, so unexpected, caused Diana to stop chewing.

"I d'know." The boy shrugged, failing to display his usual testiness when asked personal questions. "Maybe."

"Do you suppose you could show me where you lived back then?"

Now the familiar scowl furrowed Ned's forehead. "Why?"

Dread trickled down Diana's spine. What if Tyson's questions made the boy want to leave, as he'd threatened to do ever since the first day?

"That man outside of church this morning," Tyson continued, his tone serious, his gaze unwavering on Ned. "He's a reporter for the newspaper. He likes to ask questions and look into the affairs of people in the community. In fact, I believe he's the kind of man who likes to make trouble for others whenever possible."

Diana's gaze moved back and forth between Tyson and Ned. *Stop. Don't say anymore. He's too young to understand.*

"You mean he'd like to make trouble for you and Miss Diana," Ned said.

Obviously she was wrong. He wasn't too young.

"Yes," Tyson answered.

"Because of me."

"Yes. If he can."

"So you want to know more about me before he does."

Tyson set aside his plate and leaned toward the boy. "Ned, Mrs. Applegate and I want you to continue to live with us. We hope that's what you want too. But we cannot do so without going through proper channels. The more we know about you, the more likely it will be you can remain in our home and Mr. Michaels or his like can't use it to cause trouble for any of us."

Varying emotions flitted across the boy's face—uncertainty, distrust, hope, fear, relief.

"Please help us," Diana said.

Ned looked at her. "How long? How long do you want me to stay with you?"

A memory flashed in her head. A little girl on a stage, afraid, everything and everyone strangers to her, all that was familiar gone, feeling cut adrift, feeling unwanted. Tears welled but she fought them back.

"For as long as you want to stay," she answered at last. *Forever,* her heart added.

To love a woman, Tyson was discovering, meant a man became more sensitive to her emotions. He felt Diana's fear in his own heart, the fear that Ned might leave them. He was determined not to let it happen. If keeping the boy in their home was required to make her happy, then he would move heaven and earth to make certain Ned stayed.

But before Tyson could ask another question in an effort to bring about the right result, the boy spoke up.

"It was Mrs. Kennedy who took me to the orphanage after Ma died."

"Mrs. Kennedy? Was she a friend of your mother's?"

Ned shrugged. "I guess. She lived downstairs from us."

"Do you remember where that was?"

"Yeah. I remember. I wasn't a baby."

"Will you show me sometime?"

"I suppose."

Tyson decided this was a good time to let the matter drop. "Thanks."

He picked up his plate and resumed eating. Ned watched him awhile before doing the same.

"Tyson."

He looked at his wife.

Thank you, she mouthed.

Something loosened inside Tyson, a fear that it would take weeks for things to be right between them again after the fiasco of Friday night. He'd apologized but he'd still been afraid. He'd hoped but he hadn't been confident.

Lord, help me find out more about Ned. It's important to Diana that he stay, so it's important to me too.

Like a breeze through the leaves of a tree, words whispered in Tyson's heart: *And because it's important to you, My son, it does not escape My notice.*

He felt God's pleasure wash over him. Not because he did everything right. Not because he'd made no mistakes. But because he listened for the Shepherd's voice. Because he yearned to please the Father by his actions—including by loving his wife.

An easy thing to do, as it turned out.

Brook poured whiskey into two glasses. "And who did they say the boy is?" he asked as he handed one of them to Kendall Michaels.

"Applegate called him Ned. Said he was a guest. That's all I know."

"Interesting."

Tyson Applegate had no siblings, and Diana had lost track of her own brother and sister while still a child. The boy couldn't be a relative to either of them. Unless . . . unless he was Tyson's by-blow. The possibility was delightful, to say the least.

"You should look into it further, Kendall." Brook settled into his favorite chair. "How old do you suppose him to be?"

"Not sure. Nine, maybe ten. Could be another year either way."

Nine or ten? Too old to have been born after Tyson wed Diana.

Too bad. That would have been better. Still, an illegitimate child, even one conceived before Tyson took a wife, wouldn't do a political candidate any favors. So, if the boy *was* his son, where was it Tyson had sown his wild oats? While at college? Or in one of the mining towns up north?

As if reading his mind, Kendall said, "Kid told me straight out he isn't Applegate's son. Made him kind of mad when I suggested it."

"Perhaps the boy doesn't know the truth. There must be some good reason he's staying with them. People of good society don't take in a child for no reason. I want to know who he is and why he's with the Applegates."

"I'll see what I can find out."

"Be quick about it. Time is running out."

Panic roiled in his gut. If he didn't find some way to get his hands on money—lots of money—he would be ruined. This boy could be the answer. If he was Tyson's son out of wedlock, it could be worth a small fortune to keep the story quiet. And even if it wasn't true, it might be worth just as much.

He would get his pound of flesh from Tyson one way or another. By heaven, he would!

Their picnic finished, Ned and Trouble went back to exploring the terrain while the adults—stomachs full and feeling sleepy— reclined on the blankets. Still, Diana kept a vigilant eye on the boy.

"You were about the same age as he was, weren't you?" Tyson asked. "When you lost your family."

She nodded. "I was six when Mum died."

"You never talk about them."

"No, I don't. I suppose because I was given a new mother and father who loved me and provided well for me. It seemed ungrateful somehow. And I was so young. I can't even recall their faces any-more. I think sometimes I can, but then—" She sat up. "In those first months after I arrived in Montana, I dreamed about Hugh coming to fetch me and take me home. I wasn't unhappy with the Fishers, but I missed Hugh and Felicia so much. And our mum."

"What was your last name? I don't think I've ever asked that."

You never cared enough to ask. She pushed the thought away. "Brennan. Diana Brennan. The youngest child of Sweeney and Elethea Brennan of Chicago, Illinois."

Tyson was silent for a spell, before saying, "Maybe that's why God brought Ned to our house. Because you can understand him in a way no one else could."

Diana felt a flush of pleasure at his words.

"He's lucky to have found you, Diana . . . and so am I."

February 1897

Diana put an arm around her mother's shoulders and together they walked away from the gravesite. Hard-packed snow covered the pathway between grave and carriage, and the two women moved slowly along the slick surface.

What are we to do now?

In the days after her father fell ill, Diana had been forced to acquaint herself with the family finances. Circumstances were much worse than she'd anticipated. After paying for the funeral, she and her mother would be left with little besides the small sti-pend she received because of Nora Applegate's will. How could two women manage on that sum alone?

She thought of Tyson—traveling the globe, living in opulence, sparing never a thought for her—and for the first time, she hated him.

NINETEEN

"Dear?"

Seated on a stool in the garden, Diana glanced up from the canvas she was painting upon.

Her mother held out a pair of spectacles. "Have you seen the gold chain for my eyeglasses? The one with the glass stones. I thought I left it on my dresser, but it isn't there."

"The chain Father gave you? No, I'm sorry. I haven't seen it. Did you ask Liz?"

"Yes, I've asked her already. And Joan, Mrs. Cuddy, Mrs. Brown, and Upchurch. None of them recall seeing it anywhere."

Diana stood. "Perhaps it fell behind the dresser. I'll go look for you."

"Don't trouble yourself, dear. Liz already did that. She crawled around on her hands and knees and looked behind everything in my bedchamber." Her mother took a deep breath and released it slowly. "Maybe I lost it on our picnic yesterday. I hope not."

"I can ask Tyson to go there to look when he returns."

"He wouldn't be likely to find it. It's such a delicate chain and the grass was so long."

"He could still try. The chain is dear to you."

Her mother walked closer. "I'm glad to see you painting again. It seems a long while since you picked up a brush."

"It has been." Diana turned toward the canvas on the easel. The rich colors—splashes of greens, blues, reds, purples, and yellows—made her feel happy. Or perhaps they merely reflected the happiness she already felt. "There was something about the flowers this morning that called for me to try to capture them."

"I believe I'm a little jealous. Your father had a head for business. You have an eye for beauty. I've never seemed to excel at anything."

Diana leaned near, holding palette and brush to one side, and kissed her mother's cheek. "You excelled at loving us both."

"Yes." Her mother smiled. "But that was entirely too easy to count."

Diana considered reminding her mother of the times, especially as a teenager, when she'd been determined to have her own way. Headstrong. Opinionated. Willful. But she let it go. Her mother beheld the past through the proverbial rose-colored glasses. There was no point arguing with her.

"Well, I will leave you to your colorful creation." Gloria turned and followed the stone pathway back to the house.

Alone again, Diana recalled the reason she hadn't picked up her paintbrushes in so long.

Brook had come to call upon her, early in their acquaintance, before either of them would have considered it a courtship. He had seen her easel, set up in the parlor of the house she and her mother rented, and had moved to look at her work. *It's good for a woman to have something to occupy her hands, whether or not she has any talent for it.*

She frowned at the memory. The words had stung at the time. She'd put away her art supplies that day and had left them to gather dust for the past couple of years. Brook hadn't meant to hurt her feelings, she'd thought at the time. Even now, she wanted to believe he hadn't meant to hurt her. Except other instances of Brook's cutting comments began to come to her, one after another, until she could deny the truth no longer.

Why had she chosen to ignore the unkindness of his words? It wasn't as if she'd been a stranger to such things. Her father-in-law had been quite gifted in that regard. So why hadn't she spoken up for herself? Why hadn't she demanded caring treatment from the man she planned to wed?

Frowning, she wrestled with the questions until she came upon what she thought might be the reason: she hadn't thought herself worthy of his kindness. Why should she? She hadn't been able to keep Tyson from leaving her. Her husband had been willing to get himself killed in a war rather than be with her. Why should she have expected better treatment from Brook or any other man?

At the root of it, self-pity. It wasn't a flattering truth.

From close behind her, Tyson said, "I was told there's a talented artist in the garden."

A small gasp of surprise escaped Diana's throat as she twisted on the stool.

"I see your mother didn't exaggerate."

She drew a quick breath and strove to make her reply sound light and amused. "Of course she exaggerated. She *is* my mother."

"And I'm your husband, and I say she's correct." He gestured toward the painting. "Look at the way you've created depth with those brushstrokes there. And see how you've used light and shadows there. I may not be an expert, but I recognize a talented artist's work when I see it."

Heat rose in her cheeks, and she couldn't decide if it was caused by embarrassment or pleasure. More confusion. It seemed she lived in a confused state much of the time. Especially when it came to Tyson. She'd lost her grip on the anger, and without it, she felt more vulnerable than ever before. How could she remain aloof to his charms? How could she keep him from meaning more to her than he ought? She must be resolved to keep him at arm's length. She must—

He spoke again, intruding on her thoughts. "I'm taking Ned to look for Mrs. Kennedy. Would you like to come along?"

Her resolve went right out the window. "Yes, I would."

For Ned. She would go along for the sake of the boy and for no other reason. She didn't want to lose Ned, and she might be needed if they found Mrs. Kennedy. Although why, she couldn't say.

She glanced down at the cotton coat she wore over her gown. "I will need to put my paints away and tidy up before we leave."

"I could put these things away for you. If you'll trust me with them."

I think I can trust you with art supplies, Tyson. It's trusting you with my heart that frightens me. She looked up again—and was grateful his eyes were on the canvas.

"I shan't be long." She offered him the pallet smeared with oil paint.

He took it from her and she hurried down the path.

Tyson watched his wife's departure, encouraged because she didn't seem to be fleeing his presence, as had been the case so often over the past month.

Maybe we're making progress again. Maybe she's forgiven me.

Let it be so, Lord.

It took three trips to move the easel, canvas, stool, and paint supplies from the garden into the house. Rather than ask one of the servants to put the items away, Tyson decided one of the empty bed-chambers should be designated as Diana's art studio. He selected the blue bedroom because of the sunlight that spilled through the windows in the mornings and hoped the idea would please her. By the time he came down the staircase for the third time, Diana and Ned were awaiting him in the entry hall.

The fineness of the day allowed the use of the open carriage, which also made it easier for Ned to direct the coachman. The boy called for a few turns that later had to be corrected. Tyson wasn't surprised. Much had changed in the four years since Ned was orphaned. New homes had been built. New streets had been created.

"Stop!" Ned cried, pointing. "That's it. That's where we lived."

The two-story house had an outside stairway to its second level. The paint looked new, and the yard was groomed. Flowers bloomed in profusion from public sidewalk to front door.

"Are you certain?" Tyson asked. For some reason, he'd believed Ned's mother had come from the working poor. This house was nicer than anticipated. Not in a wealthy part of the city but well built and well kept.

"'Course I'm sure."

Tyson looked at Diana. "Perhaps you two should wait in the carriage while I inquire."

She nodded her agreement.

Tyson stepped to the ground and strode up the walkway where he rapped three times on the door. He was about to try again when he heard a sound from inside. Then the door opened.

The woman who looked out at him was bowed at the shoulders, as if she were folding in upon herself. Her hair was a mass of white curls, her face deeply etched by time. "Yes?"

"I'm sorry to disturb you, madam, but I'm looking for a Mrs. Kennedy."

Wariness filled her pale blue eyes, and Tyson suspected she rarely had anyone come to her door.

"Are you she?"

"I'm Mrs. Kennedy," she answered at last. "What do you want?"

He glanced toward the second-story window, then back at the woman. "Did a boy named Ned live in this house with his mother about four years ago?"

"Why?" Her eyes narrowed even more. "Who are you?"

"Mrs. Kennedy, my name is Applegate. Tyson Applegate. A boy known as Ned has come under my protection. My wife and I wish to learn whatever we can about his mother in case we might locate other members of his family. He remembers this as the house where they lived before his mother died. He said a woman named Mrs. Kennedy took him to the orphanage." He glanced over his shoulder toward the carriage and stepped to one side. "That's him, there, with my wife."

"Well, I'll be," the woman said softly, suspicion gone. "Even with my old eyes I recognize him. It's Aileen's boy, all right. I'm sure of it."

"Aileen what, may I ask?"

"Macartan. Odd name, I always thought. Aileen and Ned Macartan."

"Was there a Mr. Macartan?"

She shook her head. "Someone did that poor girl very wrong, though she never told me who it was. She worked as a live-in housemaid, and the son of the household got her in the family way. She thought he'd marry her like he promised, but the family tossed her out on the street as soon as she began to show."

An old and all too familiar story.

"Would you like to come in and set a spell? It'd be good to see a mite closer how the boy's grown up."

Tyson nodded, then motioned for Diana and Ned to join him. When they reached the stoop, Tyson introduced his wife. Ned tucked himself slightly behind Diana, as if suddenly unsure. Then the three of them followed the older woman inside.

The front parlor of the house was small and packed with aging furniture, leaving little room to move about. Knickknacks filled the mantle and table tops. The air was stuffy. A thick layer of dust covered every surface.

Mrs. Kennedy sat on a rocking chair and waved Ned closer. "Come here, boy, and let me have a look at you." Her eyes moved up and down the length of him. "Do you remember me?"

Ned's familiar bravado returned. "'Course I do."

"Little on the thin side, aren't you?"

He shrugged.

The woman looked at Diana, seated on the small sofa. "Near broke my heart to have to take him to the orphanage after his ma died. I'd've liked to keep him here with me, but I've got little enough to live on. And I'm no family to him."

"I understand," Diana replied.

Tyson, standing next to the sofa, placed a hand on her shoulder and lightly squeezed it.

Mrs. Kennedy's gaze returned to Ned. "How is it you came to be with this fine gentleman and lady?"

"I fell off a crate."

"Pardon me?"

Tyson smiled. "It's somewhat of a convoluted tale."

"Sounds like."

Diana leaned forward. "Mrs. Kennedy, is there anything still here in your home that once belonged to Ned's mother? Something you couldn't entrust to a six-year-old's care? Something that might help us discover any family?"

The woman's face crinkled as she gave the question some thought. At last, her eyes widened. "Saints alive! There were some things. Several books. A couple of photographs. A few clothes and hair doodads. I put them all in a trunk and stored them in the attic when the orphanage didn't ever come for them. Forgot all about it."

With hope evident in his voice, Ned asked, "Is there a picture of my ma?"

"Not sure. I think so but it's been a long time since I closed that trunk, and my heart was right sore at the time." She rocked the chair forward and pushed herself up. "If you'll follow me, Mr. Applegate, we'll find that trunk and you can take it with you. Belongs to Ned, the trunk and whatever's in it."

During the drive home, Diana surreptitiously watched Ned, but she needn't have been careful. The boy kept his gaze fastened on his knees the entire way home, his mouth pressed into a thin line. Anxiety, no doubt, over what he would find in that trunk.

She suffered her own bout of nerves. What if there was something in there that would cause Ned to leave their home, to go away, to be *taken* away? It made her wish they'd never gone looking for Mrs. Kennedy. Maybe they didn't need answers about Ned's family. Maybe they'd overreacted to Mr. Michaels' questions outside the church.

Releasing a breath, she gave her head a slow shake before turning her eyes toward the houses that lined the street. No, they hadn't overreacted. Hiding from the truth helped no one. Least of all Ned.

The carriage rolled to a stop in front of the Applegate home. Tyson stepped to the ground, then helped Diana do the same. After Ned hopped out, Tyson grabbed the trunk and carried it up the walk, not waiting for one of the servants to do it for him. Diana followed behind while Ned ran ahead.

"Want the trunk in the parlor?" Tyson asked, glancing back at Diana.

"No. Take it up to Ned's room." Whatever they were about to discover, she preferred they discovered it away from the eyes of the servants.

He nodded.

Upchurch had the door open before they reached the front porch. He nodded to Tyson, but he wore the hint of a smile when he looked at Diana. "It seems your expedition was successful, Mrs. Applegate."

"It would seem so, Upchurch." Although she wasn't convinced yet that it was cause to celebrate.

With some reluctance, she climbed the stairs and stepped through the doorway into Ned's room. Ned's room. Odd, wasn't it, how quickly this small bedchamber with the white walls and simple decor had become this boy's.

Tyson had set the trunk in the middle of the room. The battered-looking black chest had two brown leather straps holding the top closed, and Ned was undoing them, slowly but steadily. Diana held her breath as she waited. Was Ned doing the same? Was Tyson?

The hinges squeaked their complaint as Ned pushed the lid upright. After a moment, he knelt down on the rug, reached inside, and withdrew something. A framed photograph.

"It's my ma," Ned said in a whisper.

Tears sprang to Diana's eyes.

"I forgot how pretty she was." Ned wiped his nose with his right forearm while holding up the frame with his left hand. "See?"

The young woman in the photograph had thick, dark hair swept back from her face and piled atop her head. A high velvet collar encircled her throat. The bodice was light in color, decorated with lace and ribbons. She was turned to one side, not quite full profile, and she wore the hint of a smile.

"She was very pretty, Ned," Diana answered.

"Wish I'd had this with me all the time, but I suppose it might've gotten lost, all the movin' around I've done."

Diana held out a hand. "May I?"

After a slight hesitation, Ned gave her the photo and frame.

She walked to the tall chest of drawers and set it on the top. "There. Now you can see it first thing in the morning. All right?"

"Yeah. I like it up there."

Tyson stepped closer to the trunk. "Let's see what else is inside, shall we?"

Over the next few minutes, Ned withdrew one item after another, looked at it, inspected it, laid it out on the floor for Tyson and Diana to see too. There were two more photos, but without frames—one of Aileen holding Ned when he was a toddler of perhaps two years and another of her as a girl of about fourteen with a boy perhaps two years older, the two of them standing in front of a stone cottage. The young man bore a striking resemblance to Aileen. He had to be her brother.

Diana said, "I'll get you frames so you can put them beside the other photograph, if you like."

"But I don't know who he is," Ned answered, pointing at the photograph of his mother and the young man.

"He's your family. We know that much. Probably your uncle. He looks like both you and your mother."

"I guess. Still don't know his name or nothin'."

Next in the trunk were some clothes: two dresses, one black and one gray, complete with white cuffs and collar; two white aprons; one pair of black shoes; and one white cap. A parlor maid's wardrobe. Diana assumed the woman had been laid to rest wearing her best dress. Perhaps the one in the portrait on the dresser.

Finally, there were nearly a dozen books—all of them novels—lining the bottom of the trunk. Treasured items, Diana was certain, for a woman who had been poor. But for Aileen's son, who hadn't yet learned to read, they were of little interest.

"May I look at them?" Diana asked.

He shrugged. "If you want."

She picked them up one at a time, looking at the covers and the spines, opening each one to see that Aileen had written her name on the inside covers. The young woman's favorite author seemed to have been Henry James; there were four of his novels. There were two Mark Twain novels. Diana remembered Tyson favored Twain; perhaps Tyson might read to Ned from one of them. The remainder of the novels were by Lew Wallace, Thomas Hardy, and Robert Lewis Stevenson.

Aileen Macartan had been from the working class, most likely without much formal education, but she had not been illiterate.

Diana's gaze lifted from the books to the photograph on the dresser. *I will make certain Ned learns to read,* she silently promised the woman. *I will teach him to treasure these books because you treasured them. And I will treasure him as if he were my own son. I promise.*

Late that evening, after the house had grown quiet, Tyson walked down the hall from his bedroom and knocked on Diana's door.

"Yes?"

"It's Tyson. May I come in?"

There was a pause, then, "Just a moment."

He heard her moving around inside.

"All right. You may come in."

He opened the door.

Diana was seated on the stool in front of the small vanity. Over a cream-colored nightgown she wore a soft green dressing gown. Her hair fell loose about her shoulders and down her back. The reason for his visit to her room was forgotten. All he could think was how beautiful she was and how much he wanted to take her into his arms and kiss her and make love to her. Real love. Not with the selfishness of the past.

She rose from the stool. "What did you want, Tyson?"

He swallowed, hard, fighting the desire. If she saw what he felt, it might frighten her. It might destroy any trust she'd begun to feel with him. He couldn't risk that.

He cleared his throat. "About Ned."

"What about him?"

"I'll need to hire someone to look into his mother's family. We have her last name and we believe she had a brother. That's a good start."

Her eyes grew misty. "What if we find his family and they want to take him away?"

"It would be their right."

"I know." She walked to the open window. A night breeze lifted strands of her hair.

"We have to try, Diana. It's the right thing to do."

"I know," she repeated softly.

He longed to go to her, to hold her, to comfort her. Instead he reached for the door.

"We might have had a son. You and I."

He froze, his hand on the doorknob, and glanced over his shoulder.

"I was pregnant when you left me."

Shock made him forget to breathe.

She turned to look at him. "I lost the baby."

"Diana, I . . . I never knew."

"Of course you didn't know. How could you know? You weren't there with me, were you? You didn't write to me."

Her words cut with the precision of a scalpel.

"I wanted your baby, Tyson. I still loved you then, and I loved that baby we made together. But I guess he didn't want me either."

"Diana, don't say—"

"Why shouldn't I say it? It's the truth."

He saw it then, more clearly than before. He saw the depth of the hurt he'd caused her, and he hated himself for it. A baby. Perhaps a son. And he'd never known. She'd had to face the loss alone.

And now she's afraid she'll lose Ned. Because of me.

He shortened the distance between them, drawing close but not close enough to touch her. He didn't trust himself that much. If he got too close, he would take her into his arms, and he sensed that would be a mistake.

"Diana, I may not know much about such things, but I know you didn't lose the baby because he didn't want you."

Her shoulders rose and fell on a shuddered breath.

"And you were never at fault for the things I did or didn't do either. You were an innocent victim of my anger at my father, my resentment toward the life he wanted for me, my complete selfishness. I've said I'm sorry, but I know words don't mean much in a situation like ours. Especially when the hurt goes as deep as yours. Especially with the loss you've known. I would undo it all if I could. I would wish you married to a man you could respect and love and trust. A man who never would hurt you as I have."

There seemed to be a question in her eyes as she looked at him. He waited for her to ask it, but she remained silent.

"But I can't undo it. Not any of it. No matter how hard I try, I can't change the past."

"I know," she whispered.

He reached out, still wanting to touch her, then lowered his arm again. "We could change our future. If we both try, we could make it better."

"Could we?"

"Yes. If we want to. If we both want to."

"I suppose we could." She turned toward the window again. "If we wanted to."

He opened his mouth, but instinct warned him she'd heard all she could handle for now. He swallowed more words of apology, more attempts to make amends, another try to plead his case, to beg her forgiveness. Finally, he said, "Good night, Diana."

"Good night, Tyson."

Strangely enough, her simple farewell made him hopeful as he left her room.

September 1897

Tyson sat in a pew and stared at the magnificent stained-glass window at the far end of the sanctuary. Something stirred inside of him. Something that had been stirring inside of him for a long while.

He'd left behind the last of his friends and acquaintances and had been traveling alone through Europe for many weeks. And wherever he'd found a cathedral, he'd stopped and spent time sitting in shadowy silence, waiting for something, though he knew not what.

Empty. He was so empty. And useless. He was thirty years old but had accomplished nothing of any merit. For the past four years, he'd wandered aimlessly from country to country. Why? Nothing he saw satisfied him anymore. No one he met amused him anymore. He was empty. He was lost at sea, a ship without a rudder.

Pressing his forehead against the back of the pew in front of him, he whispered, "God, help me."

But he had no reason to believe God would hear and answer his prayer.

TWENTY

As the days of June rushed into July, heat blanketed the river valley, baking the foothills of the Boise Front beneath a relentless sun, turning the hillsides a toasted shade of brown. Like the temperature, the campaign for the Senate heated up as well. Tyson, usually with Diana by his side, made several appearances and gave several speeches each week, traveling to towns around the southern part of the state. Articles appeared in newspapers about Tyson Applegate and his beautiful wife. Most of them were fair to the write-in candidate, and all of the reporters seemed enamored with Diana.

Tyson couldn't blame them. He was completely besotted with her himself, and he tried in countless ways, large and small, to show her that he loved her and that she could trust him.

Diana began teaching Ned to read. The boy was bright but unused to the disciplines of a schoolroom. If Ned's restive nature frustrated Diana, she didn't let on to the boy or anyone else.

Tyson hired a private investigator and gave him two assignments. The first he kept a secret from Diana: He asked Lawrence Crawley to learn, if possible, the whereabouts of his wife's brother and sister. The second task for the investigator was to discover if Ned had any living relatives. While he waited for the man to report his findings, Tyson contacted the authorities about necessary legalities related to taking a child off the streets and into their home. The woman he spoke with seemed simply relieved that he wasn't dropping off another orphan at the children's home and waved away his question about any necessary paperwork.

Diana continued to make use of the room that had become her art studio, although she preferred to take her supplies out to the garden when it wasn't too hot. Tyson loved to see the pictures she created, but he enjoyed even more the expression on her face when she painted but didn't know he watched her.

Best of all, there was a new peace between Tyson and his wife. More than peace. He thought a bond was forming, albeit a fragile one. There were many times when Tyson longed to hold Diana, when his love for her wanted to be expressed in more ways than a smile or simple touch, but he didn't give in to those desires. He would be patient. He would be careful. He wouldn't tell her he loved her with words. He would tell her with actions. That was the only way she would ever believe it of him.

Tyson's father returned to Boise on the second of July. Unlike a month earlier, Jeremiah let him know in advance that he was coming. "I want to be there for the Independence Day speechmaking," he told Tyson over the telephone. "Important day for you."

Diana accompanied Tyson to the train depot on the afternoon of her father-in-law's arrival. Despite the stifling heat of the afternoon, she looked remarkably cool and composed in a greenish-blue frock. A matching parasol rested on her right shoulder, shading her face from the relentless sun.

Jeremiah was the first to exit the passenger car. A flicker of surprise showed in his eyes when he saw Tyson and Diana waiting on the platform.

"I expected to hire a cab." He shook Tyson's hand. Then he looked at Diana. "Good of you both to come." His voice was warm, earnest.

It still surprised Tyson, this more courteous version of Jeremiah Applegate. In some ways, Tyson wished he could dismiss the changes he'd observed during his father's last visit, but he couldn't. They appeared genuine and consistent. Besides, Tyson wanted Diana to believe him to be a changed man. How could he do less than believe it was possible for his father?

The threesome moved off the platform and walked to the waiting carriage. Tyson handed Diana up to the seat, then waited for his father to get in before doing the same.

Jeremiah, seated opposite of Tyson and Diana, patted his forehead with a handkerchief. "Mighty hot. Been like this long?"

"Not until recently," Tyson answered.

"I see from the newspapers that you've been busy."

"Yes."

"And doing a fine job of stating your positions, I might add." Jeremiah's gaze moved to Diana. "You seem to have made a great impression on everyone, my dear. Perhaps you were born to be a politician's wife."

Diana gave Jeremiah a tight smile. "I don't believe that's true, but I'm trying to help Tyson as much as I am able."

"How is your mother?"

"She is well."

"Good. I look forward to renewing our acquaintance."

Tyson realized he was witnessing an answer to his prayers. Long before he returned to Idaho, he'd prayed he and his father could forge a new relationship. He'd asked God to help him honor the older Applegate. But he'd expected he would be the one who had to change, who had to give and forgive. He'd thought he would have to shield Diana from her father-in-law's sharp criticisms. But that hadn't happened. Not a month ago. Not now.

It seemed God's answer to Tyson's prayers included softening Jeremiah's heart too. Which was nothing short of a miracle.

"What about Ned?" Jeremiah asked, drawing Tyson's attention.

Diana answered, "He's well too. I've been working with him on his reading skills."

"Indeed?"

"He's come a long way in a short period of time. Eventually he may need a tutor, but—"

"Eventually?" Jeremiah's eyebrows rose in question. "Sounds like you intend for the boy to remain with you."

Diana's chin tilted, as if she was preparing to do battle over the boy she'd come to love.

But Tyson's father surprised them both. "I like the lad. He's lucky to have you, Diana. I hope he's able to stay."

Diana turned her gaze toward Tyson, and without speaking, he reached over and took her hand in his, giving it a reassuring squeeze. And as if Tyson didn't have enough to marvel over already, she didn't pull away.

Jeremiah felt an unexpected pleasure warm his chest. He liked that he'd surprised them. Surprised them in a good way.

The soul-searching that had begun well before his son's return to the living had continued during the past month. Whatever the cause of it—perhaps God Himself—he'd been changed by it. Changed in ways he didn't yet fully understand. Still, he had to admit it was exhausting, gauging his words all the time. It was a new experience. He'd always said what he thought and meant what he'd said, and anyone who hadn't liked it could go hang himself. But lately, as he'd looked back over his life, he'd seen that way of living, of speaking, wasn't the best way.

He'd made his wife unhappy throughout much of their marriage.

His only son had gone to the other side of the world to escape him.

He'd made his daughter-in-law's life miserable when they might have been some solace to each other instead.

Jeremiah hoped to God it wasn't too late for his last years to be kinder than his former years. He was sixty years old. He might meet his Maker tomorrow—though he truly hoped not—or he might live another twenty years or more. But no matter how much time he had left, it would be gone in the twinkling of an eye.

The carriage arrived at Tyson's home, and the small party moved up the walk to the front entrance in the silence that had accompanied them the last part of their journey. The butler opened the door as they came up the steps.

"Welcome back, Mr. Applegate," Upchurch said to Jeremiah. "The green bedchamber has been prepared for you."

"Thank you, Upchurch."

Diana asked if he needed anything to eat to tide him over until the evening meal. He declined.

"I must return to my office in town," Tyson said. "Would you like to go with me, Father?"

Jeremiah was about to accept the invitation, but that was the moment Gloria Fisher came walking down the hall.

"Mr. Applegate," she said with a bright smile. "What a pleasure to see you again."

"And you, Mrs. Fisher." He meant it too. It was a pleasure to see her. More so than expected.

"It's much hotter now than when you were last here."

"Indeed it is."

"I have missed our visits in the garden."

"Likewise."

He realized then that he'd thought about her a great deal during the past month. Almost as often as he'd thought of his son and Diana. It amazed him, for he'd always been more comfortable in smoky board rooms and private men's clubs than spending time with the fairer sex.

A slight flush appeared in Gloria's cheeks, and he realized he'd been staring at the woman while his thoughts wandered. Clearing his throat, he glanced toward his son and daughter-in-law, then back at Gloria. "Perhaps we could take a stroll about the garden now. It would do me good to stretch my legs after the long train ride."

"Of course, Mr. Applegate. It would be my pleasure."

Diana watched as her mother and her father-in-law walked down the hallway to the back of the house. After they disappeared through the doorway, she turned toward Tyson. "What on earth has gotten into your father?"

"I haven't a clue."

Together, they smiled, as if sharing a private joke, and Diana felt happiness flow through her.

"I do have to go into the office, but I'll return as soon as I can."

She thought he might step closer and kiss her. She almost wished he would.

"We could change our future. If we both try, we could make it better." She remembered those words of his almost daily. She'd been changed by them in a way she couldn't yet understand.

But Tyson didn't kiss her. He simply gave her a tender smile before heading out the door to where the carriage awaited.

Raucous noises—a yowl, a crash, a thump, a yell—from upstairs drew Diana around. Crazed barking reached her ears a moment before she saw Tiger come flying down the staircase, ears flat against her head. On the cat's heels was Trouble, and behind them both came Ned.

"No, Trouble! No!" the boy shouted.

The cat sailed around the banister, raced across the entry hall, and disappeared into the dining room. When the dog hit the main floor, his paws scrambled for a foothold on the polished wood, giving the cat more of a lead. His barking increased in pitch.

There was another crash, this one from the kitchen. Then came a shriek.

Mrs. Cuddy!

"Oh, good heavens!" Diana rushed toward the kitchen but was almost knocked off her feet by Trouble as he tried to run past her. She nearly fell a second time as she grabbed for his collar. "No, Trouble!"

Too late. The dog pushed through the swinging door into the kitchen.

Mrs. Cuddy screamed again.

Diana stopped in the doorway, surveying the scene.

The front of the cook's apron was covered in flour and some sort of berry juice. Perhaps raspberries. More flour and berries were on the floor, along with what appeared to be softened butter, a rolling pin, and a shattered mixing bowl. The woman's face was redder than the berries and her eyes were filled with fury. Cat and dog were nowhere in sight, Trouble's barking already grown faint.

"I'm so terribly sorry, Mrs. Cuddy."

Ned arrived at Diana's side, and she put her hand on his shoulder to keep him from racing through the kitchen.

"It's unacceptable, Mrs. Applegate," the cook sputtered. "I can't have a proper kitchen with animals about. Look at the mess they've made."

"Ned and I will help clean it up."

Mrs. Cuddy looked even more upset than before. "You'll do no such thing."

"Truly. It's our fault. They're our pets."

"Mrs. Applegate." The cook drew herself up to her full height and pushed out her ample bosom. "This is your home, madam, but the kitchen is mine. Now I ask you to please go so I might put it in order again. I assure you, Joan and I can manage this without the lady of the house's assistance."

Properly chastised, Diana nodded. Then she realized the barking had ceased. She glanced down at Ned. "We'd better find Tiger and Trouble before they get into more mischief."

In unison, they took a step backward and Diana allowed the door to swing closed.

"I'm sorry," Ned said softly. "I'm not sure what got 'em started but I reckon it was my doin'." He looked at his feet. "They broke somethin' in the hall upstairs."

"Let's worry about that later. Come on. We need to find them."

From behind them came the housekeeper's voice. "The dog and cat are outside, Mrs. Applegate."

Diana turned around.

"I was coming in, and they ran past me before I scarcely realized it."

"Thank you, Mrs. Brown." Although it would have been shorter to cut through the kitchen, Diana would rather swallow a full bottle of castor oil than face Mrs. Cuddy again. Not until her temper cooled. "Come with me, Ned." She steered him out of the dining room and down the hall.

"What if they've run off?"

"I don't think they'll go far. They've both been with us awhile now. They know where home is and they know who feeds them."

He looked at her. "You sure?"

She nodded, hoping she was right.

As it turned out, Diana was more than right. Instead of having to spend a lot of time searching for the pets who'd caused such havoc in the house, they found them within moments of going outside—in her mother's favorite spot in the backyard. Tiger lay on Gloria's lap, bathing herself with her tongue, looking peaceful and serene. Trouble sat on the ground next to Jeremiah, eyes closed as he enjoyed a scratch behind his ears.

When Diana's mother saw her, she smiled. "My goodness, dear. You missed all the excitement. Trouble chased Tiger up the tree." She pointed at the branches overhead. "Fortunately, she didn't go very high and Jeremiah was able to coax her down once Trouble stopped barking." She shook her finger at the dog. "And you'll not do that again. Understand?"

Jeremiah said, "Didn't know you'd added a dog to the menagerie while I was gone." He scratched Trouble again, now looking at Ned. "Mrs. Fisher tells me he was a sick pup when he was found and that you've taken excellent care of him. It's an important thing for a boy to learn, to take care of those who are unable to take care of themselves."

Ned moved away from Diana and knelt on the ground beside the dog. "His name's Trouble."

Jeremiah chuckled. "An apt description, from what I saw a short while ago."

"I used to call him Dog."

"Well, it is probably better that he have a more suitable name than that. Don't you think?"

"Guess so."

Jeremiah looked at Diana. "Would you like to join us?" He stood and motioned to the bench. "It's pleasant in the shade."

Nearly two months had passed since the morning when she'd faced her estranged husband and agreed to this six-month arrangement. She had expected some things would change over the course of time, but never in her wildest dreams could she have imagined this day. She was beginning to believe God had a sense of humor—and she was rather glad He did.

April 1898

Word was the First United States Volunteer Cavalry, commonly called the Rough Riders, would soon leave San Antonio, Texas, and head to Florida before shipping out to Cuba.

Like most of the other young men in the camps, Tyson was ready. Eager even. He'd wasted too much of his life on pointless amusements or doing what others thought he should do. Now he was about to do something that mattered—fight for his country.

Men from all walks of life had come to Texas to train and serve under Lieutenant-Colonel Theodore Roosevelt. The men of the regiment were in perfect health, were skilled with horses, and were crack shots. They were able to learn their duties quickly and to obey their superiors. Tyson was proud to be in their ranks.

"Woolgathering, Applegate?" his friend, Arthur Jenkins, asked from behind him.

Tyson resumed brushing his horse.

"A woman, I'll bet," Arthur continued. "I've been thinking of my girl myself. Wish I could see her one more time before we leave for Florida. Doesn't look like that will happen."

Tyson and Arthur had met on the ship to America back in

February, soon after the sinking of the *Maine*. They'd become fast friends in the past two months. More than that, Arthur had become a mentor in Tyson's newfound Christian faith.

His prayer, once this war was over, was that God would change him into the same kind of man as Arthur, a man whom other people would respect and want to emulate. He didn't know where the future would take him, but he knew he wanted to go there as a man of faith and integrity.

TWENTY-ONE

The route of the Independence Day parade followed Main Street to Fifth Street, turned left, proceeded down to Jefferson Street, and then turned left again. In the parade were decorated floats and marching bands, clowns and jugglers and men on stilts, prancing horses and girls waving American flags.

The Applegate family viewed the festivities, along with other men of government and industry, from an expansive raised platform on the lawn opposite the capitol building. Diana and Tyson sat in the front row of chairs. Behind them were her mother, his father, and their ward, as the newspaper would later refer to Ned.

After the parade and after the speechifying—from far too many politicians puffed up by their own self-importance, in Diana's opinion—the merrymaking continued at the city park, where a band played in the white gazebo while people participated in games and ate food purchased from booths set up around the perimeter.

Ned's excitement was palpable. He'd confessed to Diana that—as a kid without a home, family, or money—he hadn't been welcome in such public gatherings before. And the risk had been, if he snuck in and tried to steal some food, he would be caught and returned to the dreaded orphanage. But on this hot, hazy, late afternoon, he was welcomed at every booth, thanks to Diana's coin purse and his tidy appearance. And it seemed he planned to sample all the food being offered and try his luck at most of the games too.

At the moment Ned had his eye on a large slice of bright pink watermelon. Diana paid the woman in the booth, then guided her charge to a less congested place so he could eat the juicy fruit and spit out the seeds without bothering others.

"Try not to get it all over the front of your shirt," she told him, holding in the laughter.

"I'll try."

She glanced around for a glimpse of Tyson. She'd left him deep in conversation with some supporters, and although she agreed with her husband's stand on most issues, she was tired of listening to people talk about the same things over and over again. As for her mother and Jeremiah, she had no idea where the two of them were. They'd said something about finding a park bench in the shade away from the crowd.

"You oughta have some of this, Miss Diana," Ned said, drawing her attention back to him. The boy's mouth was pink with watermelon juice, and before she could stop him, he wiped his shirtsleeve across it.

"Hello, Diana." Brook Calhoun's voice drew her around a second time. "It's good to see you."

She inclined her head. "Brook." It surprised her, how uncomfortable she felt. What would Tyson think if he saw them together?

"I've missed talking to you. Did you receive my note of thanks for the dinner invitation? And the others I've sent. It's been nearly a month and not a word from you."

"Yes, I got them. But we've been so busy with Tyson's campaign."

"So I've seen from the newspapers. But surely you must have enough time to dine with a friend on occasion."

What could she say to him? The truth was she didn't want to dine with Brook. It wasn't fair to Tyson and . . . and if she needed a friend, she was starting to believe she'd found one in her husband.

"Miss Diana," Ned said, "can I try the fishing booth now?"

She looked at the boy, thankful for the interruption. "Of course. Wait just a moment." She turned toward Brook again. "You must excuse us."

"So it's true about the boy," Brook said, frowning. "Who is he?"

"An orphan we've taken into our home."

"You sure? Maybe he's your husband's by-blow. Ever thought of that? Plenty of men have made room for their—"

"That's enough, Brook." Anger, sudden and hot, made her voice hard.

"I just don't want you—"

"Don't say anything more." She shook her head as she held out her hand to Ned, not caring that his fingers were sticky with watermelon juice. "It's none of your concern."

But before she could move away, Brook looked down. "What's your name, lad?"

"Ned. Ned Macartan."

Brook took a step backward. "I'm keeping you both from the festivities." Then he turned and strode away, disappearing into the crowd.

How glad she was to see him go. It was as if the sun had grown brighter, the air had grown sweeter.

"Can I go fish now?"

She smiled. "Yes, Ned. Let's both go fish."

Off they went toward the chosen booth.

Brook stood in the shadows, his gaze following Diana, his hands clenched at his sides. The rage he felt was white hot, all-consuming. Every day it became more and more difficult to control the fury from bursting forth and scorching those around him.

His prize, the promise of prestige and fortune, had slipped away from him. He'd known it even before today. Even though he and Diana hadn't spoken in several weeks—not since the night of the dinner party—he'd known she wouldn't turn to him again. Not even in friendship. He'd seen it in her eyes when she watched her husband giving his speeches, several of which Brook had attended, always keeping to the background. She'd hated Tyson Applegate because he'd been unkind to her. And yet there she was, loving him again.

Curse her. Curse her husband. By what right were they blessed with good looks, happiness, and great wealth while he was left to live by his wits? They didn't deserve what they had. Not any of it.

It took some finesse, but Tyson finally broke free from those who wanted to talk politics. As he searched for his wife, he did his best not to make eye contact with anyone else, lest another unwanted conversation begin. All he needed now was to catch a glimpse of that butter-yellow dress Diana had donned that morning. It should be easy to see in a sea of women wearing white blouses and white skirts.

But even before he saw her yellow gown, he caught the melody of her laughter. It drew him through the crowd like a bee to a flower. At last he saw them, Diana and Ned. She was leaning down to see something in the boy's hand, and both of them were laughing.

Tyson had seen many wonderful things in his thirty-three

years. He'd climbed tall mountains and swum in warm oceans and hunted exotic animals. He'd sat in majestic cathedrals and dined at the tables of lords and ladies. But he'd never seen anything that stirred his heart more than this woman, his wife.

"There you are," he said as he approached them. "I've been looking for you two all over the park."

Diana straightened. "We wondered if you'd ever tire of talking politics. Are you ready to go fishing?"

"Fishing?"

She held out a stuffed doll with yellow yarn for hair and blue buttons for eyes. But one button had been sewn on lower and closer to the painted nose than the other, giving the doll a comical expression. "You might win yourself a beautiful blonde like this one." She turned the doll slightly to one side, as if to try to straighten her crooked eyes.

What would I want with a blonde when I'm already married to the most beautiful redhead in the world?

Diana's smile didn't change, and yet it seemed warmer and more personal. As if she'd heard his thoughts and welcomed them.

He cleared his throat as he looked at Ned. "What did you win?"

"I got a yo-yo, but I'm not very good with it."

"Hmm. I think I'd rather have a yo-yo than a doll." His gaze returned to Diana. "If that's all right with you."

She shrugged, mischief in her eyes. "I don't understand why you would prefer that small toy to this doll. But if that's what you hope for, so be it."

He didn't care what toy came out from behind the curtain in the fishing booth. What he truly wanted to reel in before this day was over, more than anything else, was a kiss from his lovely wife. That's what would make the entire day perfect.

6

It was just the three of them—Tyson, Diana, and Ned—who stayed to watch the fireworks display. Jeremiah and Gloria declared they'd had more than enough excitement for one day and walked home well before the sun set. Like people all around them, Tyson spread a blanket on the ground and the threesome sat on it. Finally, dusk crept across the park, and the heat of the day loosened its grip.

Diana breathed out a long sigh. "We'll all sleep like the dead tonight." Happiness wrapped itself around her. It really had been the most perfect of days. Seated there with Tyson and with Ned, she could almost believe this could be her future as well as her present. She could almost believe—

"Tyson Applegate!" a woman exclaimed from somewhere behind Diana. "As I live and breathe, we have found you at last."

Diana saw Tyson's eyes widen with surprise. Then he rose to his feet.

"We heard you were killed in the war. I was heartbroken. You know I was."

Diana shifted her position on the blanket.

The woman continued, scarcely drawing a breath, "And then Quentin read that you were running for Congress or some such office in Idaho, of all places. I did not believe him. You always said you would never return to the state of your birth. I made him leave San Francisco and bring me here to prove him mistaken. But here you are." She embraced Tyson and kissed him on the mouth.

Something cold curled in Diana's stomach.

Looking flustered, Tyson took hold of the woman's upper arms and held her away from him. "I never thought to see you again,

Pauline." He gazed beyond her right shoulder and scanned the crowd. "You say Quentin's with you?"

The woman, Pauline, waved her hand dismissively. "He's off trying to help me find you in this crowd."

"What brought you to America?"

"Business. Quentin has invested in shipping in San Francisco. Can you believe it?"

"What I can't believe is that you're here. How long has it been?"

"Four years." She paused. "But you were never out of my thoughts."

Tyson offered his hand to Diana. "Pauline, I'd like you to meet my wife." He drew Diana to her feet. "My dear, Pauline Kingston. She and her brother are . . . friends of mine."

Even in the fading light of day, Diana could see that Pauline was pretty and exotic looking—black hair, olive skin, almond-shaped brown eyes—and her husky voice was tinged with an accent men undoubtedly found inviting.

If Diana wasn't mistaken, that cold sensation in her stomach was jealousy.

"What a surprise to meet you," Pauline said. "Tyson hardly told us anything about his family when we were together. For a time we thought he had no family at all." She glanced away from Diana, looked as if she would say something to Tyson, but instead placed her left hand on his arm while she waved at another man weaving his way toward them. "Here's Quentin now."

When we were together.

Pauline's brother looked a great deal like her—handsome, dusky, with the same brown eyes—although he was a good six inches taller and quite broad in the shoulders.

Tyson performed the introductions.

When we were together.

Quentin bowed over Diana's hand. "How extraordinarily beautiful you are, Mrs. Applegate." Again like his sister, his voice was husky and flavored with a foreign accent. "It's a pleasure to meet you at last."

"When we were together."

The band, which had been silent for the last hour, struck up a new melody, announcing the fireworks display was about to begin.

Without waiting for an invitation, Pauline sank onto the blanket. She tapped Ned on the shoulder. "And who are you?"

"I'm Ned."

Pauline glanced toward Diana, then toward Tyson. Before she could ask the obvious question, the first rocket was fired into the sky and burst into a display of color. Judging by the *oohs* and *aahs* from the audience, the fireworks that followed were a great success, but Diana hardly noticed.

"When we were together."

Her day, one that had seemed filled with much promise, was ruined.

"Blast," Tyson muttered as he lay in bed that night, sleepless. "Blast, blast, blast."

Why did the Kingston twins have to show up tonight of all nights? They'd never been to the United States before. They'd traveled the world after coming into their fortunes, which was how he'd become acquainted with them.

He got out of bed and walked to the window, wishing for a cool breeze but not finding one. Closing his eyes, he remembered the tight expression on Diana's face when he'd bid her good night. The fragile progress they'd made over the past weeks. Gone. Again. This time because of Pauline.

No, because of him. Because of his own choices, his own actions. Because he'd indulged his selfish wants and desires for years.

"God, don't let me lose her now. I love her too much."

July 1898

War was nothing like Tyson had expected. It was made up of disaster after disaster, chaos upon chaos. Terrible food. Shortages of supplies. The sun in Cuba was fierce, and the men's uniforms were meant for winter campaigns. Everyone suffered. Some got the fever and died without ever going into battle.

In the days since the Rough Riders landed, Tyson had more than once wished he'd drowned like Roosevelt's horse before coming ashore. But he hadn't drowned, and so far he'd lived through every battle and skirmish with nary a scratch.

Something told him this day would be different. Word was combined forces of fifteen thousand American troops were to take Santiago today.

Take it or die trying.

TWENTY-TWO

"Diana," Gloria said tersely, "please sit down. Your pacing is giving me a frightful headache."

With a sigh, her daughter obeyed, sinking onto the empty chair near Gloria's bedroom window.

"Now tell me again who it is we're expecting to visit today and why you're so upset."

"Pauline and Quentin Kingston. Friends of Tyson's. He met them during his travels overseas. In Europe or Egypt or someplace like that. They're not from America."

"A married couple?"

Diana shook her head. "No. Brother and sister. Twins." She closed her eyes and groaned softly. "Mother, you should have seen the way Miss Kingston acted around Tyson. When she saw him in the park last night, she kissed him. On the mouth."

"On the mouth! What did you do?"

"What could I do?"

Gloria drew herself up. "Since you're his wife, it would seem to me you could have expressed your displeasure, at the very least."

Diana opened her eyes. "I suppose I could have."

"Does Tyson seem . . . interested in this woman?"

"No." Diana shook her head. "Yes." She nodded. "I don't know.

Possibly. I think . . . I think they may have been . . . lovers. What if . . . What if he . . . What if they . . ." Her words drifted into silence.

Gloria saw her daughter was in real distress. But she recognized something more important than that. Diana was in pain because she cared for Tyson, because she feared losing her husband to this Miss Kingston, because maybe she'd even learned to love him again.

"Well, my dear," she said, leaning toward Diana, "I believe the first thing you should do, the next time you see her, is to remind her that Tyson is *your* husband."

Tyson didn't have an opportunity to talk to Diana before their guests arrived, and he knew it was intentional on her part. She was avoiding him. But she arrived to stand by his side as Upchurch opened the front door to admit the Kingstons.

"How good of you to let us come before luncheon," Pauline said as she clasped Diana's hand and leaned in to kiss her cheek, as if they were the best of friends. "Americans are so much more relaxed about the timing of social calls than the British. Thank goodness, I say. My brother and I never have been very good when it comes to adhering to proper etiquette. All those rules are so dreadfully confining. Don't you think?"

When Pauline turned her attention to Tyson, he hoped she would settle for a handshake. She wouldn't. She rose on tiptoe to kiss him too. But though he was helpless to do anything but allow it, lest he be rude, he did turn his head so she couldn't kiss him on the mouth as she'd done the previous evening.

"Mrs. Applegate," Quentin said as he bowed over Diana's hand, "you have a lovely home. We are grateful for the invitation to spend the day with you and Tyson."

"We're happy to have you both," Diana answered. "And please, call me Diana. No need for formality when you are such good friends of my husband's."

Tyson doubted the others could see behind her smile to the tension coiled inside of her, but he knew her well enough to see it, to feel it. Perhaps even to take some comfort in it.

Pauline moved into the parlor. "Quentin's right. It is a beautiful home. I shouldn't be surprised, I know, but whenever I think of Tyson, I always imagine him living in a tent."

"Why a tent?" Diana followed Pauline into the parlor.

The two men joined them, Tyson moving to his wife's side.

Pauline sent a smile in his direction, even though it was Diana she answered. "Because that was his humble abode when we first became acquainted. Remember, Tyson? We were in India where the nights are sultry and the air smells of spices."

Tyson didn't respond.

Over the past few weeks, he and Diana had spoken little about the places he'd traveled. She'd seemed curious to know more, while at the same time reluctant to hear anything in great detail. Certainly he hadn't told her about the other women whose company he'd shared. Especially not Pauline Kingston. He wasn't proud of the way he'd lived, and the last thing he wanted to do was to hurt her more. It was a delicate balancing act, telling the truth in love.

Pauline wandered over to the window that looked out upon the front lawn. After a moment she turned to look at Diana again. "I suppose you didn't travel with Tyson because you didn't want to leave your home. I can't say as I blame you. But you did miss some grand adventures."

Tyson was tempted to wring Pauline's neck.

Into the silence Quentin said, "I would love to see your stables,

Tyson. I know how much you admire good horseflesh. Is there time before luncheon for me to have a look?"

Tyson didn't want to leave the women here alone, but good manners demanded he agree to Quentin's request. "Of course. Come with me."

"I want to see your horses too," Pauline said.

Relieved, Tyson offered his elbow to Diana. "Then I suppose we'll all go."

Diana took his arm but kept her eyes averted, her expression guarded.

When the small party exited the house through the back door, Tyson saw his father and Diana's mother seated on the stone bench, his mother-in-law's favorite place. It seemed his father's favorite place was wherever Gloria Fisher was.

He frowned. Was that true or had he imagined it?

Jeremiah rose from the bench when he saw the foursome's approach.

"Father, may I introduce Pauline Kingston and her brother, Quentin." He looked at his guests. "This is my father, Jeremiah Applegate. And this is my mother-in-law, Mrs. Byron Fisher."

Quentin stepped forward to shake hands with Jeremiah. "A great pleasure to meet you, sir. And you, Mrs. Fisher."

"The pleasure is mine, Mr. Kingston," Jeremiah returned. "Miss Kingston."

"Tyson told us you own several silver mines."

"Yes. And I understand my son made your acquaintance in India. Or was it Africa?"

"India was where we first met," Quentin answered.

Tyson cleared his throat. "We are taking our guests down to the stables, Father. Would you and Mrs. Fisher care to join us?" He shifted his gaze to his mother-in-law.

Gloria shook her head. "Thank you. No. Your father and I have decided to eat our lunch out here in the shade."

Jeremiah sat beside her again.

Looking at them, Tyson thought they looked like a . . . a . . . couple. But that was absurd. Perhaps they'd formed a cordial friendship. But more than that? Preposterous. Why, his father was sixty and his mother-in-law fifty-one. And even if their ages didn't put them beyond the age of romantic attachments, his father's temperament would prohibit it. No, he had to be imagining things.

As the small party continued their walk to the stables and paddocks, Quentin asked Tyson about his decision to run for public office. He was grateful for something to take his mind off the two older people they'd left behind on the stone bench.

Diana was certain Quentin Kingston, when asking about the Senate campaign, hadn't expected Tyson to share first about his faith in Christ. In fact, when she glanced over her shoulder at the brother and sister, she thought both of their expressions were a bit shocked. Seeing their reaction lifted some of the tension she'd felt.

Tyson reached the end of his story at the same time they reached the wide entry into the stables.

"Never would've guessed you'd become the religious type," Quentin said after a lengthy silence.

"No reason you would, based upon what you knew of me. But I can tell you that now my faith is central to all I am and all I do."

"Mercy me!" Pauline rolled her eyes. "Could this conversation become any more tiresome? Show us your horses, Tyson. That's why we are here in your barn."

Before Tyson could respond, Claude Romano approached. "Pardon me, Mr. Applegate. May I speak with you, sir?"

"Yes."

"The new carriage stock have arrived, but I'm concerned about one of them. Would you have a look?"

"Of course." To the others, he said, "Please excuse me." Then he walked with the head groom toward the rear entrance of the stables. Not waiting for an invitation, Quentin followed right behind.

"Men," Pauline muttered under her breath. "I suppose it is up to you to show me the horses, Diana."

Old feelings of inadequacy and unworthiness rose up, leaving Diana close to tears. And she would rather die than let this cosmopolitan, world-traveling, sophisticated woman—who had obvious designs on Tyson—see those feelings. Drawing a quick breath, she turned away, saying, "I'll show you my mare first."

The two women moved to the stall, and Diana motioned for Pauline to look over the door into the enclosure.

Pauline released a sound of delight. "She is magnificent. How does she go?"

The mare thrust her head over the half door, and Diana stroked the horse's neck affectionately. "As smooth as a child's rocking horse."

"A gift from Tyson?"

"Yes."

"Thought so. It is exactly the sort of horse he would give a woman. He knows how to please the fairer sex." Pauline faced Diana, her head tipped slightly to one side, her eyes narrowed. "Why *did* you let Tyson go traipsing around the world without you? If he were my husband, I wouldn't let him out of my sight." She laughed softly. Suggestively. "Or out of my bed."

A gasp escaped Diana's throat, and she felt her heart skip a beat, then another.

Pauline laughed again. "Yes. I know. Scandalous, aren't I? My brother is forever telling me I need to mind what I say, but I don't find that very enjoyable. Do you? I'm afraid I shall never be considered conventional."

Diana turned away from Pauline and pressed her cheek against the mare's sleek neck, needing to compose herself, to quiet her thoughts.

After a brief silence, Pauline said, "I believe I shall see what is keeping the men so long."

"If he were my husband, I wouldn't let him out of my sight. Or out of my bed." The words stung Diana's heart a second time. There was no room for doubt now. Pauline and Tyson had been lovers. Did he care for her still?

Memories from recent weeks flitted through Diana's mind. Kind moments. Tender moments. Her heart told her Tyson wouldn't betray her with Pauline or any other woman again. He was, indeed, a changed man. A good man. But that truth didn't guarantee he would learn to love her.

And what did that matter? She didn't love him either. In four months, Idaho voters would choose their new senator. If Tyson was elected, he would go to Washington, DC. If not, he would find another occupation. Either way, Diana and her mother would move to a place of their own and she would start building a new life. That was their agreement, hers and Tyson's. She meant to hold him to it.

Tyson and Quentin were returning to the barn when Pauline stepped into the sunlight. She stopped and shaded her eyes with one hand, smiling when she saw the two men approach. He knew that look. Self-satisfied. Smug. Like the cat that swallowed the canary, if he understood what the adage meant.

"Tyson, dear boy, that mare of Diana's is truly magnificent. I really must take you with me next time I'm looking to buy a horse."

"I could only do that if you were looking for a horse near Boise."

She lifted an eyebrow. "Surely you don't mean to remain in this small city year round."

"No. God willing, Diana and I will spend a great deal of time in Washington, DC." He didn't smile as he moved past her. His gaze swept the inside of the barn for his wife. She wasn't in sight. He spun about on his heel. "What did you say to her, Pauline?"

"Say? Nothing much at all. I told Diana the horse was beautiful and asked if it was a gift from you. She said it was and that the mare's gait was like a rocking horse." Pauline gave a small shrug. "Then I decided to come outside to see what was keeping you two. I thought she would follow."

He didn't believe her. There was more that had been said. He was sure of it. And whatever it was, it had made Diana run away from him rather than to him.

August 1898

Diana saw the headline on the second page of the newspaper and felt her body grow cold: "SON OF IDAHO SILVER MAGNATE JEREMIAH APPLEGATE BELIEVED DEAD IN CUBA."

"Diana," her mother said, "is something wrong?"

She looked up. "It's Tyson. He's dead."

"*What*? When? How?"

Her gaze returned to the brief article. "He was fighting in Cuba. His body is missing."

"They must be mistaken, dear. Tyson wasn't in the army."

Odd, that pinched feeling in Diana's chest. She'd learned to hate the very sound of Tyson's name. She'd hated him with every fiber of her being. But eventually hate had cooled into indifference. Complete indifference. He didn't matter to her any longer. She didn't care if he was in Europe or Africa or the South Seas. She didn't care where he went or who he went with. He simply did not matter to her.

But dead? Had she wished him dead?

She pictured the two of them on the evening they'd first met. She, a girl of not yet eighteen. Him, a man of twenty-five. She was such an innocent. He seemed so sophisticated. She remembered the sound of his laughter as they sat on the dock in the dark, splashing their bare feet in the water. She'd learned to love him that night. She'd loved him for a long, long time. Far longer than she'd hated him. Far longer than she'd been indifferent to him.

Tyson was dead.

TWENTY-THREE

Diana stood beside Tyson on the front porch and watched as the Kingston twins followed the walkway to the waiting carriage. Once there, the sister and brother turned and waved, then Quentin assisted Pauline into the carriage and they drove away.

Never in her life had Diana been so grateful to see the back of a vehicle as she was this one.

"I'm sorry," Tyson said.

"For what?"

"For whatever Miss Kingston said that upset you earlier. In the barn."

"I wasn't upset," she lied.

He saw through it. "Won't you tell me what she said?"

"Nothing of any importance." Another lie. She turned and walked into the house.

Tyson followed right behind. "Pauline Kingston isn't always tactful."

Oh, really?

"I appreciate that you made them feel welcome, despite her carelessness. I doubt either of them knew you were upset."

Suddenly angry, she stopped and turned at the bottom of

the staircase. "I told you I wasn't upset. Nothing Miss Kingston could say to me would matter in the least. She is your friend and not mine."

"That's all she is, Diana. A friend. And not a close one."

"Does *she* know that?"

A frown drew his brows together. "Of course she knows."

"Did she know when the two of you were together in India? Did she know it when she was in your bed?"

Guilt tightened his features. "That's in the past, Diana. It's behind me. I'd like it to be behind us. Can't we—"

"I'm tired of pretending. Doesn't it wear you out too? Acting as if our marriage is real when we know it's only temporary. Pretending we feel more than we do."

Guilt was replaced by a look of sadness in his eyes. "Perhaps it *would* make me tired, if I were pretending." He gave her the slightest of bows. "If you'll excuse me, I believe I shall go into town for a few hours. I've neglected my work lately. Don't wait supper for me. I'll dine at the club."

He was in the wrong. So why did *she* feel responsible for their quarrel?

"Upchurch?"

The butler appeared seconds later. "Yes, Mr. Applegate."

"I'm walking to town." He moved toward the front door, opening it before Upchurch could do it for him. "Send Gibson to my office for me at eight."

"Yes, sir."

Tyson didn't glance Diana's way before he went out. The sound of the door closing caused her to wince.

"Mrs. Applegate," the butler said into the silence, "is there anything you need, madam?"

"No, thank you, Upchurch." Then she spun about and hurried up the stairs to her room.

Tyson had planned to walk straight to his office, but his feet carried him to the entrance of the church instead. When he entered the sanctuary—empty of people on this Thursday afternoon—sunlight filtered through the west-side stained-glass windows, the colors dancing upon dust motes that drifted in the air. He slipped into the third pew from the back on the right side of the aisle and stared at the gold cross on the altar.

Why did Pauline have to come to Idaho now, just when he thought there was hope for him and Diana? He hadn't seen or talked to the Kingstons in four years, and when he'd left Italy he'd made it clear to Pauline that he wouldn't be coming back. So what had possessed her to come to Idaho when she'd learned he was alive and well and running for the Senate?

But he knew the answer to that. It was a game to her. She'd lost his interest and was determined to win it back. Not because she cared about him. No, it was because she liked to win.

What had Pauline said to Diana? He didn't know, but he could imagine. And whatever she'd said or done, Tyson couldn't blame her for Diana's unhappiness or the state of his marriage—as much as he would like to. He let out a slow breath, slipped off the pew seat and onto his knees, and bowed his head. Praying by his posture more than the words in his head and heart.

Perhaps it had been wrong of him to ask Diana to live with him again until he'd tried to earn her forgiveness. He'd wanted a chance to prove he could love her as Christ loved the church. Proving his love, earning her forgiveness seemed good and righteous desires.

But maybe they were selfish ones as well. They were what he wanted. What he thought was right.

What about Diana? What did she think was right? What would make her truly happy?

Nearly a month ago, on their picnic by the river, Tyson had realized that what mattered to Diana mattered to him. He'd felt God speaking to him, and he'd listened. But maybe he hadn't listened long enough or hard enough. To God or to Diana.

I can't force her to love me.

There. That was a cold, hard truth: he couldn't force his wife to love him. No matter how much he'd changed already, no matter how much he might change in the future, no matter how much he wanted his marriage to thrive, he couldn't make Diana want or feel the same things he wanted and felt.

I've got to let go of her.

He shook his head. Let go? How could he let go? He loved her. He wanted to grow old with her. He wouldn't divorce her. God hated divorce. Society hated divorce. He would hate divorce.

Will I trust God, even if the worst I fear happens?

His breath caught, and he lifted his eyes once more to the altar cross.

Conditional trust isn't trust, is it, Lord?

His eyes and throat burned. His lungs felt starved for air. Now that he knew what he wanted, now that he loved his wife with his whole heart, could he let go of her if God asked him to?

A rap sounded on the bedroom door. "Mrs. Applegate?"

Diana sat up on her bed and dried her eyes. "Yes, Liz?"

The door opened enough for the maid to stick her head through the opening. "That woman is here again."

"What woman?"

"That Miss Kingston. She asked for Mr. Applegate, but when she was told he isn't here, she asked to see you."

"Did she say what she wanted?"

"No, ma'am, but she said it's important."

"Tell her I'll be down in a moment."

Diana waited until Liz closed the door again before she went to her dressing table and sat on the stool. Her reflection in the mirror told the truth. Her eyes were red and puffy. No amount of powder could hide that she'd been crying. Still she tried her best before heading downstairs to face Pauline.

The woman waited for Diana in the parlor, pacing back and forth near the front windows.

"Miss Kingston? What brings you back so soon?"

Pauline faced Diana, and there was fury in her eyes. "One of your employees is a thief."

"What?" This was not what she'd expected to hear when she came down the stairs. Not even close.

"Someone stole my diamond and ruby ring. I removed it because it is uncomfortable with the gloves I wore. I left my purse there—" She pointed to the table in the entry hall. "—while we were down at the barn. That's when someone must have taken the ring."

Diana shook her head. "I assure you, every member of our household staff is honest and trustworthy. They would never steal from you or anyone else."

"Don't be naive! Of course they would steal if they had the chance. The servant class learns to steal while still in the cradle. I demand you call them out here so we can find the culprit."

Diana couldn't describe what she felt in that moment. It wasn't exactly anger. It wasn't truly courage. But whatever the feeling, it allowed her to forget her tears and uncertainty. She stiffened her spine and lifted her chin. "I will not allow you to interrogate my staff, Miss Kingston. But if you'll describe the ring thoroughly, we will search the house and grounds to see if we can find it."

"You're refusing me the right to question them?"

"I'm afraid you have no such right in this home."

"Tyson shall hear how you've treated me."

"Yes, he shall. I will tell him as soon as he returns."

"Ooooh." Pauline headed for the entry hall. "I despise this country. I have no idea why my brother wanted to do business with you Americans." She disappeared from view, and a few seconds later the door slammed closed.

Diana had only a moment to feel satisfied before uncertainty rushed in. Iris Waverley had lost a bracelet the night of the supper party, and her mother still hadn't found the chain for her glasses. And now a ring. Was it possible someone—

"Bravo, Mrs. Applegate."

At the butler's words, Diana spun about. "You heard?"

"I heard, madam. Might I thank you on behalf of the entire staff for your trust in us."

"You're welcome." She sat on the nearby chair, hoping her sudden doubts weren't evidenced in her tone.

Upchurch waited a short while, then bowed and excused himself.

Surely no one on their staff would have stolen the missing items. Still, it was a concern. Iris's bracelet and Pauline's ring were valuable, without question. Her mother's eyeglass chain had only sentimental value, but perhaps a thief wouldn't know that at first glance. It did glitter in the light.

Frowning, she rubbed the crease between her brows. Tyson must be told. Would he side with his wife or a former lover? A sigh escaped her. She was tired. So very, very tired.

Tyson's words whispered in her memory: *"Perhaps it would*

make me tired, if I were pretending." Wasn't he pretending? Weren't they *both* pretending?

Her head ached. Hoping a cup of tea would help, she rose and walked toward the kitchen. When she pushed open the door from the butler's pantry, the sight before her made her forget why she'd come. There was Mrs. Cuddy, leaning down, stroking Tiger's back while the cat lapped milk from a bowl.

Mrs. Cuddy feeding the cat? Mrs. Cuddy petting the cat? Impossible!

Another woman's voice said Diana's name, intruding on her stunned silence. Only then did she see others were present. In a line near the other doorway stood Upchurch, Liz, Joan, and Mrs. Brown. It was the housekeeper who'd spoken to her.

Now Mrs. Brown asked, "Was there something you need, ma'am?"

When Diana still didn't reply, an uncomfortable silence engulfed the room, and she realized whatever had been said before she entered the kitchen, it had been about her.

"Ma'am?" Mrs. Brown looked worried now.

"I'm sorry." She gave herself a mental shake. "Yes. Yes, there *is* something. I . . . I would like a cup of tea."

Mrs. Cuddy straightened and seemed to be pretending the cat wasn't in the room. "I'll have it ready for you in no time, Mrs. Applegate."

Mrs. Brown gave Liz and Joan a quick glance, and the maids made hasty departures, followed soon after by the butler. Diana sat at the table in the center of the kitchen, aware that she'd surprised these two women a second time by staying in the room.

Tiger finished the milk in the bowl, then made a circle around Mrs. Cuddy's skirts before meandering over to where her mistress sat. Diana leaned down and lifted the cat onto her lap. "Aren't you rather pleased with yourself?" she whispered. "I guess Mrs. Cuddy doesn't think you have fleas anymore."

Mrs. Brown looked her way. "I'm sorry. What was that, Mrs. Applegate?"

"Nothing." Diana shook her head. "I was . . . talking to myself."

Mrs. Cuddy turned away from the stove. "It's no wonder, Mrs. Applegate. That Miss Kingston would make me talk to myself too. And I want to thank you for giving her a piece of your mind."

But what if I'm wrong about one of you? The headache worsened. *What if Pauline Kingston is right?*

Tyson paid little heed to the passage of time as he sat in the church sanctuary, praying, wrestling with his feelings, struggling with what he believed God spoke to his heart versus what he wanted on his own. But eventually he noticed the change in the light filtering through the windows. Hours must have escaped him in this quiet, holy place. He left the church and hurried through town to his campaign office, arriving just as the Applegate carriage came into view.

Gibson saw Tyson standing near the curb, and a look of concern crossed the coachman's face. "I hope you haven't been waiting long, sir."

"No, Gibson. You're right on time." He motioned with his hand when the driver moved to get down, then opened the door for himself and stepped into the carriage.

On the drive home he tried not to think what might await him when he got there, what he needed to say to Diana and when he needed to say it. He feared making a mistake, making things worse. Which meant, of course, he still wasn't trusting God to see him through.

Upchurch was watching for his arrival and opened the door before Tyson reached it.

"Where is my wife?" he asked the butler as he entered.

"She retired early, sir. She had a headache."

Not a good sign. Should he go up and try to speak to her now? Wouldn't that be inconsiderate if she was asleep? Perhaps if he—

"Mr. Applegate, I believe you should know what happened while you were out."

His gaze flicked toward the staircase. "Yes?"

"Miss Kingston returned, sir, to speak to Mrs. Applegate."

He looked at the butler. "She did?"

"She claims someone on the staff stole something from her purse earlier today. A valuable ring."

"Whom did she accuse?"

Upchurch drew himself up, his expression grim. "No one in particular. All the staff in general."

"What did Mrs. Applegate say?"

The butler revealed the hint of a smile. "You would have been proud of her, sir."

Tyson waited, assuming there was more to come.

"Miss Kingston demanded to confront the staff and accuse them to their faces, but Mrs. Applegate refused her. When Mrs. Applegate wouldn't change her mind, Miss Kingston left. In a huff, I might add."

"I can imagine."

"May I say, sir, that I am confident no one working in this house has stolen anything from anyone. Mrs. Brown has done an excellent job hiring the household servants, and we all have great respect for you and Mrs. Applegate. None of us would abuse your trust in such a way."

"Thank you, Upchurch." Tyson drew in a deep breath. "What

about my father and Mrs. Fisher? Were they present when Miss Kingston came to speak with my wife?"

"They were still outside in the garden, sir. But when they learned what happened, they helped in searching for the lost ring." Anticipating Tyson's next question, the butler added, "It wasn't found."

"And where are they now? My father and Mrs. Fisher."

"They went for a walk after Mrs. Applegate retired."

He glanced toward the stairs. "I'd better go up and speak with my wife."

"Yes, sir."

Diana stood at her bedroom window, watching as gloaming fell over the valley. She'd seen Tyson's return from town, and by now Upchurch would have told him about Pauline and the missing ring. Any moment now Diana expected to hear her husband's footsteps in the hall outside her bedroom.

What would he say to her? What would she say to him? Would he believe Pauline or believe his wife? Might it be better to talk in the morning or get it over with now? Or maybe it would be worse if he didn't come to see her, if he didn't want to talk to her. About anything.

But he did come. She heard the anticipated footfall as he drew near her room. A rap sounded moments later.

"Come in, Tyson."

The door opened before him. She saw a hesitancy in his eyes that she hadn't seen before.

"Upchurch told me about Pauline's accusation."

Diana nodded.

A small frown creased his forehead. "That's the second item to go missing."

"The third."

"Third?"

"Mother's eyeglass chain has disappeared. You've seen it in the past. Gold with glass beads. When she wasn't using it, she kept it in the same place in her room. It's been gone almost a month now."

He shook his head. "Why didn't you tell me?"

"It didn't seem important. It isn't valuable. And, Tyson, I'm *sure* no one on our household staff could have taken the jewelry."

"I don't want to believe it either, Diana, but three missing items seems more than a coincidence. Don't you think so?"

She drew in a deep breath and let it out on a sigh. "I suppose you're right."

"I'll make certain Pauline doesn't bother you or anyone else in this house again. Still, we'll have to get to the bottom of this."

Diana nodded, then glanced out the open window. Daylight was gone, although full night had yet to arrive. She felt the air cooling as it brushed the skin on her arms.

"Diana?" He spoke her name softly, and there was sadness in his voice.

She looked at him again.

"I did a lot of thinking and praying while I was out."

Dread nearly stopped her heart.

"I've been unfair to you. I shouldn't have asked you to pretend to feel more for me than you do."

"You didn't."

"Yes, I did. I asked you to stand beside me and smile and look like a wife who loves her husband. I believe God wants me to run for the Senate. I believe I'm running for the right reasons. But what I want and what I believe is right shouldn't be forced onto you. Not after the way I treated you. Not after the ways I hurt and betrayed you. You have little reason to trust me or believe me."

Pauline's image returned to taunt Diana. "What are you saying, Tyson? That you don't want me here after all?"

"No." He moved to stand before her. "That's not what I'm saying. I want you here. More than you know. But I don't want it to be because I forced you or because we made a bargain you're unhappy with. If you *want* to stay, I'll be glad of it. I want to honor the vows of marriage I took. But if you don't want to stay, I'll make certain you and your mother and Ned have a nice home to live in and all else that you need to be comfortable. I promise you. You won't lack for anything, and I won't interfere in your life." He took a long breath. "I don't want you to be tired from pretending any longer."

A lump formed in her throat and tears pooled in her eyes. Unable to answer with words, she nodded.

Tyson leaned in and brushed her cheek with his lips before whispering, "I'm sorry for all the times I've made you cry. Truly, truly sorry." Then he turned and left the room, closing the door behind him.

And only then, as her heart began to break, did she realize she wasn't pretending to love him. Hadn't been pretending, though for how long she didn't know. She loved Tyson and could only hope she hadn't discovered it too late.

October 1898

The nurse stuck another pillow behind Tyson's back. "There you go, Mr. Brown. How are you feeling? Is your head hurting still?"

"I'm better today. Thanks."

He *was* better, and in more ways than the nurses or doctors knew. His memory was returning. Slowly, but enough so he knew his name wasn't Brown. And enough so he believed this might be the best thing to ever happen to him.

"Call me if you need me," the nurse said before leaving the room.

Pretending to be asking about a friend, he'd learned Tyson Applegate was believed killed on the battlefield. That meant he could be anybody he wanted to be. He could remain Mr. Brown— the name they had given him when he arrived at the first hospital stateside. If he did so, he would never again enjoy the wealth and privileges of the former Mr. Applegate, but neither again would he have to war with his domineering father. Never again would he have to live a life he didn't want. It seemed the perfect solution to let Tyson Applegate remain dead.

"Are you awake, Brown?" Martin North, another patient, wheeled himself into Tyson's room, not waiting for an answer. "Feeling up to some company?"

"Sure."

Tyson didn't know why Martin had attached himself to the fellow with no memory and no name. But he was glad he had. He was a pleasant young man whose father was a minister at a church here in Washington, DC. Martin, who'd lost his right leg in Cuba, was intelligent and well read, not to mention being a master storyteller. He was also grounded in the Scriptures, and on days when Tyson's head didn't hurt as much, he liked to ask Martin questions about the Bible and Jesus and the Christian faith.

This was going to be one of those days.

TWENTY-FOUR

"I want you here. More than you know. But I don't want it to be because I forced you or because we made a bargain you're unhappy with."

Diana tossed aside the light bed coverings. After slipping into a dressing gown, she ran a brush through her hair, although it did little to tame its morning unruliness. But she cared not a whit what her reflection said and left her room, hurrying down the hallway to her husband's bedchamber.

She rapped softly on the door. "Tyson? I know it's early, but I wish to speak with you?"

No answer.

"Tyson? May I come in?" Another rap.

Still no answer.

Holding her breath, she opened the door a few inches and peered in. The bed was empty, still made.

Abandoned. Again. That's what it felt like.

The sound of a throat being cleared behind her caused her to turn, hope leaping in her chest. But it was Tyson's valet who stood at the top of the servants' staircase. Hope died a quick death.

"May I help you, Mrs. Applegate?" Robert asked.

"I . . . I was looking for my husband." She felt heat rise in her cheeks, embarrassed because of her disheveled appearance and because the staff knew her marriage to Tyson was a sham—and the fault was hers.

"He left for his office before daylight, madam."

But his bed was never slept in. "Thank you, Robert." She hugged herself as she returned to her room. Tears threatened, but she refused to let them fall. Crying wouldn't help. It never had. What was needed instead was action. Tyson *was* a different man than he'd been when he left her. He'd told her so, but more important, he'd shown her so. Now it was her turn to show the same thing. *She* was different too. She wasn't going to let circumstances sweep her along and then settle for whatever happened.

He's never said he loves you. He might not truly want you.

"Go away," she told that ancient voice of doubt and insecurity. "I won't listen to you anymore."

Weariness tugged at Tyson's eyelids, and he set aside the newspaper he'd been looking at without comprehension for the past hour. He hadn't slept a wink last night. Hadn't even gone to bed. He'd sat in the library with the doors closed, reading his Bible, praying, worrying, wondering, debating until he'd thought his head might explode. That's when he'd left the house and walked into town, hoping work would give him relief from his own thoughts.

It didn't.

He looked at the framed photograph on his desk. It had appeared in the newspaper the day after he announced his candidacy. He'd sent an assistant to buy a copy for his office because he'd liked the way he and Diana looked together. Like a married couple. A happy couple. In the photograph, his arm was around Diana, and both of them were smiling. She'd looked lovely in a hat of straw wrapped in chiffon. Of course, the photograph was black and white, but he remembered the exact bluish-green color of her dress, the way the gown had complemented the color of her eyes and the pale tone of her skin.

From the doorway, Herbert Eastman cleared his throat. "A letter came for you, Mr. Applegate. It's marked important." He stepped forward and placed the envelope on Tyson's desk.

"Thank you."

His assistant withdrew from the room.

Tyson picked up the envelope. The handwriting looked like a woman's. Diana's, perhaps? Hopeful, he opened the envelope. His eyes scanned the note inside. It wasn't from Diana. It was from Pauline. She asked to see him again. He shouldn't be surprised. Pauline never had been sensitive to the feelings of others. She could be very single-minded when she wanted something. He would write to her at once. He would tell her it would be best for all concerned if they didn't see each other again. He would—

"Excuse me, sir," Herbert interrupted once again. "There is a man here to see you. A Mr. Crawley."

Lawrence Crawley was the investigator Tyson had hired to search for Ned's and Diana's families. He must have news of some kind. Would it be about Ned or about Diana's brother and sister? Pauline's note was forgotten.

"Show him in, Mr. Eastman." He stood, suddenly anxious, afraid the news would not be good.

Lawrence Crawley—a smallish man who sported a large mustache—stepped into Tyson's office, hat in hand. But he wasn't alone. Another man followed him into the room. The second fellow wore a white shirt with a frayed collar and wool trousers that had seen better days. A laborer, judging by the calluses on his hands. He seemed nervous, and there was something about his eyes—

· "Mr. Applegate," Lawrence Crawley said, "this here is Dillon Macartan."

"Macartan?" Tyson only knew one person with that last name. Ned.

"Yes, sir. The boy's uncle."

"Aileen was me sister," Dillon said, voice thick with an Irish accent.

But Tyson had already surmised that. He'd seen the photograph in Ned's room, and there was no doubt in his mind this fellow was related to the boy. The family likeness was uncanny.

"Please." He motioned to the chairs opposite him. "Be seated."

Diana would grieve if Ned was taken from their home. She loved that boy with all her heart. Loved him like her own flesh and blood.

Dillon leaned forward on the chair. "Mr. Applegate, sir. I'd given up thinkin' I might find the lad. I feared he might even be dead like his poor mum. So you can imagine me surprise when Mr. Crawley found me."

"Tell me how this all came about. There was no mention of family in this country when your sister died and Ned went to the orphanage."

"Me sister came to America to better her lot in life. I was being against her coming alone, but I couldn't go meself, needed as I was on our da's farm in Ireland. When she got herself in the family way, she wrote to me. Ashamed, she was, but she said she was all right. She was still believin' the gentleman might marry her after all. Foolish girl."

Tyson nodded to show he listened.

"When Aileen knew she was ill and could be dyin', she wrote to me again. This time she begged me to come for Ned, but I—" Dillon Macartan glanced toward the window, and when he

continued his voice was lower. "I'd got meself in a bit of trouble."
He cleared his throat. "Soon as I was out of prison, I worked and
sold what I could to raise the passage to America. Our da had
passed on by then, and the farm was belonging to another family."

"The orphanage made no mention of Ned's uncle looking
for him."

"I'm not easy about givin' out me name. No point draggin' the
past here with me, if you know my meanin'. And I had nothing to
prove I was the lad's relation. I'd lost Aileen's letters, and without
them I didn't know where she'd been livin' when she passed. Then
me money run out. I got work where I could, and I looked about
for the lad, hopin' I'd one day see him walkin' down the street."

"Do you mind telling me why you were in prison, Mr. Macartan?"

"I got into a fight in a pub." Dillon shrugged. "Another man
got hurt and it was by way of bein' me own fault."

"I see."

"Mr. Applegate, I've never raised me hand to a woman or child.
I'm not a violent man. I give you me word. I loved Aileen. I was
good to her and I'd be good to her son. I'm the only blood kin he
has left."

This man was undoubtedly related to Ned, but Tyson had personal wealth and powerful political connections. He could keep
this immigrant from taking Ned. He could keep the boy for Diana.
He could—

He cut the thoughts short. As much as he might want to do
those things, he couldn't. It wouldn't be right. Not even for Diana's
sake.

"Now may I be askin' you a question, Mr. Applegate?"

"Yes."

"How is it the boy is livin' with you? Your Mr. Crawley didn't
tell me that."

"A while back, he tried to steal a pie but stole my wife's heart instead." Tyson smiled as he said it, picturing Diana and Ned together. "He's been with us ever since."

The boy's uncle cocked an eyebrow, a silent request for more details.

Tyson told him the story, ending with, "My wife has come to hope, Mr. Macartan, that Ned would remain with us until he's grown and off to a university."

"University," Dillon echoed.

"Yes. He's a bright boy and learns quickly. He's behind in his schooling but catching up fast. My wife has been giving him instruction."

Silence fell and grew thicker with each tick of the clock on the fireplace mantle in Tyson's office.

At long last, Dillon Macartan spoke again. "I'm a poor man, Mr. Applegate. I'm a good farmer and a hard worker, though I've no employment at present. I'm thinkin' I'll never have much money. Not even here in this good country. I could never be sending Ned to university." He sighed. "But I promised me sister I'd come for him."

"Thank you, Gibson." Diana held the coachman's hand as she stepped to the ground.

At nine o'clock on a Friday morning, the sidewalks on this street in downtown Boise City were mostly empty, save for a few men in suits, hurrying to and from offices.

"Shall I wait for you, ma'am?"

"Yes, please do." She had no idea how long she would be inside. A couple of minutes? A couple of hours? It all depended upon Tyson.

She lifted the hem of her skirt and stepped from the street onto the sidewalk. A deep breath for courage, then she gave her chin a stubborn tilt and moved with a confidence she didn't feel toward the door of the "Tyson Applegate for Senate" campaign office. Before she could give her name to the young woman at the first desk, Owen Hanson, the campaign manager, recognized her.

"Mrs. Applegate, what a pleasure to see you."

"And you, Mr. Hanson. I need a moment with my husband. May I go back to his office?"

It was Tyson's young assistant, Herbert Eastman, who answered her question from several desks away. "He's with someone, Mrs. Applegate, but I don't think he'd mind being interrupted." He motioned her forward.

"If you're certain."

"I am."

Herbert led the way through the desks in the front office, then slowed to walk beside her as they traversed the hall. Through the open doorway to Tyson's office, Diana heard her husband's voice. Nerves jangled in her stomach. She should have waited until whoever was with him had finished their business.

But it was too late to change her mind.

Arriving at the doorway, Tyson's assistant said, "Pardon me, Mr. Applegate. Your wife is here."

"Diana?"

Drawing a quick breath, she stepped into view. Tyson's expression was difficult to read as he rose from the chair behind his desk. Then he glanced at the two men seated opposite him and back to her again.

"Come in, Diana. And Mr. Eastman, if you would close the door please."

"Yes, sir."

Tyson rounded his desk and went to stand beside her. Nerves were replaced by dread. Something was amiss. She'd come to tell

her husband she loved him and wanted to make amends, but her
reasons were forgotten as the two strangers stood and faced her.

"Mr. Crawley. Mr. Macartan. May I introduce my wife, Diana
Applegate."

Macartan? She felt the blood drain from her head.

Tyson took hold of her arm, as if knowing she needed steadying.
"Mr. Macartan is Ned's uncle. Ned's mother's brother."

The explanation wasn't necessary, of course. She saw the
resemblance.

"'Tis good to meet you, Mrs. Applegate. Sure, and it is."

Try as she might, she couldn't say the same.

"Diana, is Gibson waiting with the carriage?" Tyson asked.

"Yes. Yes, he is. I didn't know how long I'd . . . we'd be."

"Then perhaps we should take Mr. Macartan to the house with
us and introduce him to his nephew."

*Don't let him take Ned. Ned belongs with us. I love him too much
to lose him.*

Her husband looked at her with a mixture of sadness and com-
passion in his eyes, and she realized this was hard for him too. But
he'd become an honest man, a man of integrity. He couldn't keep
Ned from his uncle, no matter how difficult it would be for either
of them.

Was it possible to admire and despise him at the same time for
those qualities?

Tyson glanced at Dillon. "Mr. Macartan, you'll understand
that after several years of fending for himself, Ned doesn't give his
trust or affections easily. It took time for us to earn both. I should
imagine it will take time for you to do the same."

"Aye. I should imagine."

"Then I have a proposition for you. You say you're a hard
worker and a good farmer. We don't have a farm, but we do have an

extensive garden. Since you aren't employed elsewhere at present, come to work for me as one of the gardeners. Give Ned a chance to get to know you before you decide what to do. You can stay in a room over the stables and take your meals with the rest of our staff."

Diana wanted to kiss him. He'd given her a little more time with Ned. Not forever, but a little more time.

Brook's office was stifling hot. Sweat trickled down the sides of his face, but he resisted wiping the moisture away with a handkerchief. Not while that burly thug stood opposite him, threatening him with ruin—financial for certain, physical if required.

"You're out of time, Calhoun. Your creditors want their money, and they sent me to collect."

"I'll have it soon. I only need another two weeks. I'll have payment for you in full. With interest." That was a lie. He had no way of repaying those loans. He *would* have been able to pay them if Tyson Applegate hadn't shown up in May. If Brook could have married Diana and got his hands on—

"One week," the man said. "That's all you'll get. One week and then I'll be back. Have that money or pay the price." He left, closing the door behind him.

Fear gelled in Brook's gut. Fear and rage. He grabbed a ledger off his desk and threw it at the wall. It missed its mark, hitting the window in the door instead. Shards of shattered glass flew everywhere.

His secretary ran into the room, but before he could say anything, Brook told him to get out. The fellow wisely did as he was told.

Brook cursed as he paced the length of his office. He had to get his hands on that money. A large sum of money. Without it he would be ruined.

This was *Diana's* fault too. As much as it was her husband's fault for being alive. She'd led Brook on. She'd made him think she would marry him. She *owed* him, and he needed to collect.

May 1899

Diana stood near the window and watched Brook Calhoun get into his buggy and drive away.

"Did you have a pleasant evening, dear?" her mother asked from a chair in the parlor.

Diana turned. "Yes, we did."

"Will you accept if he asks for your hand in marriage?"

"Good heavens, Mother. I have no expectation he will ask me to marry him." She sat on the sofa. "Besides, I'm not free to marry, and Mr. Calhoun knows that."

"Tyson isn't coming home, Diana. He's dead."

"Presumed dead is not legally dead."

Her mother sighed as she set aside her yarn and knitting needles. "Could you be happy with Mr. Calhoun?"

Diana pondered the question. She had no strong emotions for Brook, good or bad. He was pleasant enough company. He was a merchant with a growing business in a growing city. He would be able to provide for a wife and family. They could have a comfortable life together.

I would never love him.

Perhaps that was what attracted her the most to Brook Calhoun. She didn't love him and didn't believe she ever would. Which meant he wouldn't be able to hurt her.

At last she answered her mother, "I would be happy enough."

TWENTY-FIVE

The closer the carriage got to the house, the more confident Tyson became he was doing the right thing, taking Dillon Macartan home to meet his nephew. But his chest hurt when he glanced at Diana. Her heart would be broken when Ned left them.

His gaze shifted from his wife, seated on his left side, to Dillon Macartan, seated opposite him. Tyson considered himself a fair judge of character, and his gut told him Ned's uncle was exactly who and what he said he was. A hard worker and a man who kept his promises, even when it took longer than expected.

When they arrived at the house, the party descended from the carriage and made their way to the front door. Upchurch was there to meet them, as usual.

"Where might we find Ned?" Tyson inquired.

"I believe the boy is down at the stables, sir. The new horse arrived a short while ago, and he heard about it."

Diana said, "New horse?"

He shrugged. "I thought Ned should have a horse of his own."

Oh, she mouthed without a sound.

Tyson wanted to gather her close and kiss away the sadness in her eyes. Instead he looked at Dillon. "We'll go down to the stables to meet Ned, and then I'll introduce you to the head gardener."

"Mr. Applegate, I—" Dillon stopped, shook his head, and then nodded.

"Come with me."

Tyson had expected to see his mother-in-law and father seated in the shade, but the bench was empty for a change. He discovered why as they drew near the stable entrance.

"By heaven!" His father's voice. "That's a fine horse you have there, my boy. Very fine horse."

"My boy."

A rare pleasant memory from Tyson's boyhood flashed in his mind. He'd been a year or two younger than Ned, and his father had lavished praise on him as he'd ridden his horse in the arena on the Applegate estate.

"My boy."

They stopped in the doorway. There was Ned in the center of the barn, holding the gelding by its lead rope, while Jeremiah Applegate walked a slow circle around horse and boy. Standing near one of the stalls was Claude Romano with Gloria Fisher, Trouble's leash in her right hand. Tyson was about to speak when Ned saw them.

"Miss Diana! Come look. Did you know I was gettin' a horse of my own?"

She released her hold on Tyson's arm and moved toward Ned. "No, I didn't know. It's a wonderful surprise, isn't it? It was Mr. Tyson's idea."

"Thanks, Mr. Tyson!" But Ned's gaze was back on the chestnut gelding.

"Mr. Applegate," Dillon said softly, "How long has the boy been staying with you."

"Almost two months."

"Should we not delay telling him who I am?"

Tyson wanted to agree but knew he couldn't. It wouldn't be the truth and he'd learned the value of telling the truth. Besides, Ned was a smart kid. Even if he wasn't told Dillon's last name, he would see the family resemblance.

When Diana reached Ned, the boy turned and hugged her.

The sight made Tyson remember the baby she'd lost more than six years ago. He hurt for his wife even more than when she'd first told him about it. He hurt for himself, too. His selfish acts of long ago kept rippling through the years. Would they always do so? Would they never stop hurting the innocent?

"Come along, Mr. Macartan," he said, his voice gruff with emotion.

The two men walked toward the center of the barn. Tyson stopped at Diana's right, and he was soon the recipient of Ned's enthusiastic appreciation, hugged tightly around the waist by little boy arms.

The weeks in the Applegate home had changed Ned. Good food had put meat on his bones. Kindness had removed distrust from his eyes. Love had given him new confidence and the ability to express his emotions.

God, don't let it all be undone.

"Thanks, Mr. Tyson," the boy said as he released his hold and took a step back.

"You're welcome." He cleared his throat. "Ned, we have another surprise for you."

"Yeah? What?"

Tyson put his hand on Ned's shoulder. "This man is your uncle, Dillon Macartan. Your mother's brother. He came from Ireland to find you. He's been looking for you for some time without success."

Ned's eyes widened, then promptly narrowed as he turned toward his uncle.

"Sure and you're the spittin' image of your ma when she was a girl." Dillon held out his hand to Ned.

The boy didn't take it.

"'Tis sorry I am it took so long for me to find you. I never would if not for these good folk. 'Tis even more sorry I am that I wasn't here when your ma needed me. Sure and she was dear to me."

Tyson glanced toward where the groom stood with Gloria Fisher. With a jerk of his head, he indicated Claude should come and take the horse. To Diana, Tyson said, "Let's all go back to the house to talk."

"Yes. We should."

But Ned stopped them. "Is he gonna take me away?" The stubborn expression on his face was familiar, though it had been absent for a while.

The three adults exchanged looks. *God, give us wisdom.*

Ned stuck out his chin. "I ain't gonna go. I'm stayin' here."

It was all Diana could do not to drop to her knees, pull Ned into a tight embrace, and declare neither one of them were leaving. Not ever. They belonged together, Tyson and Diana and Ned. They were a family. They should stay a family.

But circumstances demanded a different response. "Ned." She held out her hand to him. "Please. Your uncle has come a long way. Your mother would wish for you to talk to him."

She supposed it was unfair to use the memory of his mother to manipulate his behavior, but it was the only thing she was certain would work. And it did. Ned took hold of her hand and walked with her toward the house.

Diana thought back to a month before, to that picnic by the river with Tyson, her mother, Ned, and Trouble. The memory seemed warm and alight with hope and joy. She'd been happy, although she hadn't had the good sense to realize how happy at the time. She'd been falling in love with Tyson for the second time in her life, although she hadn't had the good sense to realize that either.

I saw through a glass darkly.

Or perhaps she was simply a fool.

They went to the veranda. Diana's mother and Jeremiah had made themselves scarce, taking the dog with them, so it was just the four of them. While the others were seated, Tyson opened the door to the kitchen and asked Mrs. Cuddy for coffee for the adults. Then he went to stand behind Diana, placing a hand on her right shoulder. She was thankful for it. When Tyson had kissed her cheek last night and told her he was sorry, she'd wondered if she would ever feel his touch again.

"Ned"—Dillon leaned toward the boy—"may I be telling you something about the Macartans?"

Several heartbeats passed before Ned acquiesced with a nod.

Dillon returned it. "Your granda owned a farm in County Tipperary in Ireland. That's where your ma and me and our baby brother were born, and where our brother and ma died before either of us was grown. 'Twas a hard life but a good one, but your ma wanted something more. She thought a better life was to be found in America. A chance to make somethin' more of herself than to be a poor farmer's wife. There were things I was wanting too, but there was only enough money for one passage so I had to wait."

"Took you long enough," Ned said.

"Aye, it did at that. But not for lack of tryin', lad."

The boy grunted.

"Your ma, prettiest girl in the county, she was. Eyes that sparkled with laughter. She was smart, too, and determined. Fearless, our da said, and 'twas true. Aileen never let anything stop her from what she wanted to do. I'm thinking, from what Mr. Applegate's told me about you, that you must be like your ma in that."

Diana closed her eyes, hating the story because it was taking Ned away from her, loving the story because these were things Ned should know. The same way she sometimes wished she could know more about her own father, Sweeney Brennan, and how and why he'd come to America from Ireland. The same way she wished she could know more about her older brother and sister. She remembered too little of them. Like Ned, much of the past had been taken from her by the death of her mother. How wonderful it would be if someone showed up in her life, to tell her all the things she didn't know about her family.

Dillon's voice intruded on her thoughts. "Mr. Applegate has offered me a job, lad. Will that be all right with you now? To have me workin' here so we might get to know each other."

"Really?" Ned turned toward Diana. "He's not taking me away?"

The best she could do was shake her head and give him the slightest of smiles. *Not today, Ned. Not yet.*

Jeremiah and Gloria sat in the shade on the east side of the barn, both of them looking at the horses grazing in the paddock.

"Will that man take Ned?" Gloria asked softly.

"Perhaps. But I could stop it from happening."

"You?" She glanced his way.

"Yes. Me." Jeremiah had never hesitated to use his wealth to get exactly what he wanted. He would do the same for Tyson and Diana.

"But *should* you stop him from being with his uncle?"

He drew a deep breath and released it. "I don't know." The words felt odd on his tongue. Uncertainty was a stranger to him.

Gloria twisted on the bench to face him. Her expression was tender, yet serious. "Jeremiah, I'm asking you not to interfere."

"Interfere? But—"

"Our children love each other. I'm sure of it. But there are still hurts and mistakes that must be overcome, and they need to overcome them on their own, as a couple. Without *help* from either of us."

She made "help" sound like a foul word.

"Only God knows for sure if Ned is to be part of the family they make together. We must allow your son and my daughter to listen for God's direction."

Jeremiah leaned his back against the wall of the barn. "I've never been good at watching from the sidelines. I like to be in control of events."

"'Pride goeth before a fall.'"

"Pride? What has pride to do with it?"

"When we think we have control, it means we aren't trusting God to take care of us. That's pride."

Jeremiah stroked his beard. He'd never considered it that way before. But then he'd never given much thought to his Maker either. Not until he'd come to Boise and heard his son speak openly about his faith. Not until he'd found himself changing, little by little, because of this woman by his side.

"'Thou hast beset me behind and before,'" she said, "'and laid thine hand upon me. Such knowledge is too wonderful for me; it is high, I cannot attain unto it.'"

"I guess that must be from the Psalms."

Gloria smiled gently. "Yes. Psalm 139. You should read it, Jeremiah."

"I will." And he would, although it surprised him to realize he was willing to do so.

To Tyson, the day felt laden with traps for him to fall into, and by the time the household settled in for the night, he was mentally and physically exhausted.

Dillon Macartan had been introduced to the head gardener and advised of his new duties. He'd been given a room above the stables, which seemed to suit him well. And although it had felt awkward, Ned's uncle—both stranger and employee—had been invited to join the family for supper that night. The meal had passed without misstep, but the strain had shown on everyone's faces.

In his room, the house quiet, Tyson dismissed his valet for the night and sank onto the edge of the bed.

"Thy will be done, Father," he whispered. "Thy will be done."

It was a prayer he'd repeated in his mind throughout this day. It was the best thing he could pray for Ned and the future. Tyson knew what the boy said he wanted—to stay with the Applegates. He knew what Diana hoped for—to become Ned's adoptive mother. He knew what he envisioned—to raise the boy in a home where everyone served the Lord. But he couldn't be sure what God's plans were, even though he knew whatever they were would be for Ned's best.

God's will be done.

A soft rap drew Tyson's gaze to the door. "Yes."

"It's me," Diana answered. "May I come in?"

"Yes." He stood as the door opened.

She wore a yellow-gold dressing gown that would look at home in a ballroom. Her hair fell artfully over her shoulders and down her back. She was incredibly beautiful. So beautiful, inside and out, he wondered how he'd left her so long ago, even to spite his father. A memory of the two of them, husband and wife, holding onto one another amid rumpled sheets flashed in his mind. Desire surged, strong and white hot.

"Tyson, we . . . I . . . I never was able to . . . I didn't get to tell you why I came to your office this morning."

He swallowed hard. "No, you never did."

Her eyes seemed darker than usual in the dim light of the bed-chamber, her complexion even more pale, her lips ever more kissable.

"Why don't you tell me now?" He wondered if she could understand the effort it took for him to stand in one place, keeping all that distance between them.

She folded her hands before her waist and drew a breath. "You aren't forcing me to stay with you. I'm not . . . I'm not staying because we made a bargain."

He caught the glitter of tears in her eyes now.

"Tyson . . . could you give me another chance?"

"Chance for what?"

"To make our marriage work. To learn to be your wife."

"Are you certain, Diana?" Tyson couldn't stop himself from moving closer now. "Absolutely certain?"

She nodded.

Though what he wanted was to crush her against him, instead he folded her into a tender embrace. He wanted to declare his love but was afraid it might frighten her off. Yet he would not be denied the taste of her lips.

Not again.

Not now.

I love you, Tyson.

As the kiss deepened, wild sensations shot through Diana, leaving her limp and unresisting in his arms. She wished he would sweep her off her feet and carry her to his bed—and the desire to be joined with him again surprised her more than anything. She'd thought such passion had been the headstrong recklessness of youth. Apparently it was not.

I've been a fool... A fool... A fool...

At last Tyson broke the kiss. "I'd better walk you back to your room."

In the past she would have taken his words as a rejection, as a sign he didn't want her, but she sensed his protection. He was giving her time to be sure. He did it because he cherished her, something he'd promised to do on their wedding day.

A little more of her hurt from the past fell away.

February 1900

God was a relentless God. He pursued those who belonged to Him in unfathomable ways. His lordship demanded obedience, not out of fear but out of love.

These things and many more Tyson had learned during his months of convalescence, during the time he had hidden his identity from everyone, even those whom he now called friends.

But God knew who he was and God would not allow the lies to continue. The Lord had work for Tyson to do, and that work would require honesty, integrity, and humility. It would require hard choices, perhaps painful choices. It would require he do whatever was necessary to heal those he'd harmed. And cleaning up the mess he'd made of his life had to start within his own family.

Beginning with his wife.

God help him. He would need a miracle to make things right with Diana.

TWENTY-SIX

The sweltering sun of July beat down upon the Applegate home two Sundays later. The heat was relentless. Not a whisper of a breeze stirred the tree limbs.

After a light luncheon following the family's return from church, both Diana and her mother went to their rooms to lie down. But Ned—being a ten-year-old boy who was crazy about a horse he'd named Wild Bill—seemed unfazed by the triple-digit temperature; once out of his Sunday best, he hightailed it down to the stables. Tyson followed at a slower pace half an hour later.

Life was good—very good, indeed—and he couldn't help counting his blessings.

His write-in campaign for the Senate was going strong, and he had gained backing from several newspapers and quite a few men of influence around the state.

His father had been surprisingly accommodating. Never in Tyson's memory could he recall Jeremiah Applegate being so genial.

The arrival of Dillon Macartan hadn't turned everything upside down as he and Diana had feared. In truth, the Irishman had begun to feel like one more member of their extended family. Dillon was a hard worker, as promised, and his affection for his nephew was real.

As for Ned, he was a different child from the urchin who'd fallen through a crate outside their kitchen window. The boy trusted Tyson and Diana and was beginning to trust his uncle too. Ned knew he was safe, and it showed in what he said and did.

And then there was Diana. Tyson grinned to himself. All he could say about her was she drove him to distraction . . . in the very best of ways. It wouldn't be long now until she was ready to hear how much he loved her. He could feel it. The time was almost here.

Laughter drifted to him through the open doorway of the barn. He moved inside and stopped, thankful for the cooler air of the shady interior. After his eyes adjusted, he saw Dillon and Ned outside a stall off to his left. Dillon was settling a saddle onto Wild Bill's back while Ned held the lead rope with both hands.

"'Tis a lucky boy, you are, Ned. I'm hopin' you know it."

"I do. Wild Bill's a perfect horse."

Dillon stopped adjusting the cinch and looked at the boy. "'Twasn't the horse I was meaning. Sure and you'll be listening to me, lad. The Macartans never had much money or land, but we were a good family, good people. You've got no reason to be ashamed your family was poor or Irish. Still, there's no way your ma or any of your kin could've given you a life like this."

"Yeah." Ned sounded properly chastised.

Dillon stepped closer to the boy and put a hand on his shoulder. "More than anything else I'd be meaning to say, I want you to hear this. Mrs. Applegate, she loves you like your own ma loved you. I saw it in her eyes the first day I met her. She don't pay no mind to how you came into this world. She loves you and is proud of you, she is."

"Yeah."

"And you'll be loving her too. And Mr. Applegate himself."

Ned stared at his uncle for a few moments before nodding. "Yeah."

There was a lump the size of a baseball in Tyson's throat, and he was thankful the pair hadn't noticed him yet. Dillon leaned down, bringing himself to eye level with Ned, their noses mere inches apart. Though his voice was low, it still carried to Tyson.

"The day we met, Ned, you said you didn't want me to take you away, but I thought you'd be changing your mind in time, once you got to know me. Only 'twas me who was havin' his mind changed. You belong with the Applegates. 'Twould be wrong of me to take you away. But I'm askin' something of you. Let me go on bein' your uncle. Will you do that? Whether I keep working for Mr. Applegate or not, I don't plan on going anywhere too far from you. Sure and I made a promise to your ma that I mean to keep."

Tyson took several steps backward, back into the sunshine and out of view of the man and boy inside. Hastily, he wiped unaccustomed tears from his eyes and fought to clear his throat. The emotions roiling inside of him were foreign, the discovery unexpected—he loved Ned every bit as much as Diana did.

He'd become a father in his heart and didn't even know when it happened.

Too hot to feel rested, even after a nap, Diana opened the door to her bedroom just as Tiger came flying up the stairs, a blur of gray fur, Trouble hard on her heels. The cat yowled and the dog barked as they disappeared into Ned's bedroom. Something crashed to the floor. Another yowl and more barking.

Diana hurried into the boy's room. Marbles were strewn everywhere, the box that had held them overturned on the floor. "Trouble, sit," she commanded in her sternest voice.

The dog obeyed and fell silent, although he kept his eyes pinned to the spot where the bedspread met the floor.

"Poor Tiger," Diana whispered. "I thought you two were learning to get along."

Trouble whimpered as he pressed his muzzle against the floor, still staring toward the bed.

Diana got on her knees. Lifting the bedspread, she peered into the dark space beneath. Two green-gold eyes peered back at her from the farthest corner.

"Come on, kitty. It's all right. I won't let the bad dog get you. Come on."

She recalled the last time Tiger sought refuge under this bed. Tyson had pulled the cat out, suffering scratches and bites in the process.

"But you wouldn't scratch me, would you, pet? You sweet girl." She shimmied forward on her stomach and reached out with her hand. "Come here, kitty. It's okay."

Tiger hissed.

The tight space made Diana feel claustrophobic. If Tiger didn't want her help, so be it. "You're on your own, kitty. Ungrateful beast."

As she drew back her hand, she discovered what felt like a large piece of cloth wrapped around something. Several somethings, actually. She supposed she should be glad it wasn't alive and slimy, since this was a boy's room. Smiling at the thought, she worked her way out from under the bed, bringing the hobolike bindle with her.

She got to her feet and dropped the cloth sack onto the bedspread before brushing imaginary dust from the front of her dress with both hands. Then curiosity got the better of her. She wanted to know what a boy of ten tied up in a handkerchief.

It took a moment to loosen the knot, but at last it came free. She placed the bindle onto the bed again and unfolded the corners of the square cloth. What on earth? Her breath caught as she pressed the palm of one hand over her breastbone. A silver teaspoon. A woman's ivory comb. Some buttons. A few coins. A fountain pen. And amongst those items, Mrs. Waverley's diamond bracelet, her mother's eyeglass chain, and what had to be Pauline's diamond and ruby ring.

"Oh, Ned." She sank onto the edge of the bed.

He'd been stealing. All this time she'd thought he was adjusting well, and he'd been stealing. Not just from those within the household but from guests too.

Tyson took the stairs two at a time. "Diana?"

"I'm in here. In Ned's room."

He followed her voice, eager to tell her what he'd overheard, that Dillon had decided to leave Ned with them, to let them be the boy's parents. But the look on Diana's face caused the words to die in his throat.

She took something off the bed. "Look." She held whatever it was out to him.

He moved forward, unsure what to expect.

"Ned took Pauline's ring. And Mother's chain and Iris Waverley's bracelet." She dropped the items, one by one, into his palm. "Among other things."

The diamonds and glass beads sparkled in the light from the window.

"What do we do, Tyson?"

The question rolled around in his head for a few moments. "We have to act like parents."

"If we discipline him, he might—" She broke off abruptly.

But he understood what she hadn't said. "Run away? Choose his uncle over us and leave with him?"

She nodded.

"That doesn't change the need for us to do the right thing." He sat beside her. "We took him into our home. We must do whatever is best for him. Not what's easiest for us."

Diana stared at her hands, folded in her lap. "Perhaps I don't make a very good mother after all."

"You make a wonderful mother." He set aside the stolen jewelry, then cupped the side of her face with his hand. "And Ned adores you." *So do I.*

She drew a deep breath. "I never realized before how I've let fear determine my actions. Even when I've acted calmly and with care, even when I've thought things through to their rational end, deep down, fear has determined my course." She met his gaze. "Why didn't I realize that before?"

You don't need to fear me, Diana.

Her gaze lowered to his mouth. It was invitation enough. He leaned close and kissed her, slow, deep.

She broke the connection and drew back. "We shouldn't put this off, Tyson." A small smile tipped the corners of her mouth. "Not even in such a pleasant way."

He wanted to kiss her again. After all, she thought it pleasant.

"We must talk to Ned now."

He nodded. "Yes. I guess we must."

They gathered the evidence and went downstairs. Tyson asked Joan to fetch Ned and his uncle from the barn, and then he and Diana waited for the boy in the library. His wife sat. Tyson paced as he prayed for wisdom. The minutes dragged by.

Cheerful voices entered the library just before Ned and Dillon came into view.

"Miss Diana," Ned said, grinning, "you shoulda see Wild Bill. He—" He broke off as his gaze landed on top of the desk, the open bindle and contents in full view.

Tyson looked at Dillon. "Close the door, if you would, please."

Dillon nodded, a question in his eyes.

"Ned, could you tell us about these items we found in your room?"

There was that stubborn expression the boy had worn so often in his first weeks in the Applegate home.

"Ned," Diana said softly, "please tell us why you took them?"

"I dunno."

"It isn't right to steal from others."

He shrugged.

Tyson pictured himself at the same age, standing before his father, waiting for some kind of discipline to be visited upon him, and for a change he felt a shred of sympathy—and empathy—for any father of a decidedly headstrong boy.

Eyes narrowed, Ned waited. Suspicious. Fearful despite his bravado.

Tyson sat at his desk. "You're going to have to return these things to their rightful owners."

"Don't know where I got some of them," came the sullen reply.

"We'll figure that out together."

A tense silence filled the room. Tyson wished he could glance at Diana and Dillon, wished he could guess what they thought of his approach, but he dared not look away from the boy.

At long last Ned said, "You ain't sendin' me away for it?"

"No."

The boy looked over his shoulder at his uncle. "And you ain't takin' me away either? Like you said before. I can still stay."

Dillon answered with a nod.

"All right, then." Ned shrugged, feigning nonchalance. "I guess I can take them back."

April 1900

Diana listened intently, Brook Calhoun by her side—where he had been more and more over the last year—as the attorney explained what she should expect when her husband of the past seven years was declared dead.

"And when it is finished, Mrs. Applegate, you will be a very wealthy woman. The firm has ascertained where in Europe your husband kept his fortune. We cannot access full information about it until Mr. Applegate is declared dead, of course, but it is no small amount."

Diana didn't care about the fortune she would inherit from Tyson. Well, that wasn't true. It would be nice not to have to count every penny she and her mother spent, but she didn't care about being rich. A wealthy widow, that's what the newspapers would call her.

But she wouldn't be a widow for long. Brook had finally asked her to marry him. Although their engagement wouldn't become official until after Tyson was pronounced dead, her future with Brook was assured.

TWENTY-SEVEN

Diana stepped from the carriage into the street outside of the hotel, Ned following right behind. "We won't be long, Gibson," she told the driver.

Good moments and bad alike had filled the last six days since the discovery of the stolen items. Ned had been required to face each person he'd taken something from and apologize. This final confrontation had been delayed—much to Diana's temporary relief—because the Kingston twins had been visiting Yellowstone National Park. They'd returned to their hotel yesterday.

Diana reached for Ned's hand, wishing she hadn't insisted she and the boy come without Tyson. Two weeks ago she'd stood up to Pauline on behalf of their household staff and had been right to do so. But in the end, someone in her home had stolen the ring. She must face the woman and admit it, and she needed to do it without Tyson at her side.

It was part of the new Diana. The woman who would take courage from God even when afraid in her spirit and flesh. It was enough to propel her forward into the lobby of the hotel, Ned in tow. A short while later, they were shown into the suite of Pauline and Quentin Kingston.

Pauline stood near the fireplace, a look of dislike in her dark eyes. "Mrs. Applegate." Her gaze flicked to Ned, then back again. "What a surprise."

"Thank you for seeing us."

"Tyson isn't with you?"

"No. Ned and I came alone. It . . . it's about your ring."

Triumph flashed across Pauline's face. "I was right. Who took it? Your butler. Or was it that silly kitchen maid who helped at lunch? Has the culprit been arrested?"

Diana released Ned's hand and gave the boy a nod.

He took a few steps toward Pauline. "I took it, Miss Kingston. I'm sorry." His gaze locked on the carpet, he held out one hand, palm up, revealing the ring.

"The orphan boy." Pauline plucked the jewelry from his hand. "I should have known."

Ned returned to stand beside Diana.

Pauline tipped her head slightly to one side. "You are not who I thought you would be before I met you, Mrs. Applegate. And I gather you are not who Tyson thought you were when he left you alone all those years."

Diana knew the woman hadn't meant it as a compliment, but she took it as one, all the same. "Perhaps none of us are who people think we are."

"You were afraid of me when we first met."

"Yes, I was."

"You thought I might take Tyson away."

Yes.

"But you aren't afraid of me now."

"No." Diana smiled, realizing how true it was.

"I suppose you have won."

Yes!

"Then this is good-bye, I suppose. My brother and I aren't likely to return to this horrible little town again."

Diana grabbed Ned's hand and they hurried out of the suite. Her heart felt lighter than it had in days. But when they exited through the lobby doorways a short while later, the carriage wasn't waiting near the curb. She looked up and down the street. Where had Gibson gone?

"One of those horrid motorcars frightened the horses."

She turned at Brook Calhoun's words.

He tipped his hat. "It's good to see you again, Diana." His gaze lowered to Ned. "And you, young man."

Brook had lost weight since she'd seen him in the park on Independence Day. Dark shadows underscored his eyes, and his skin had ghostly pallor. An uneasiness shivered through her.

"I saw what happened with your carriage horses and told your driver to wait for you around the block on Idaho Street. There's less traffic there at this time of day." Brook offered the crook of his arm. "And I promised him I would escort you."

"There's no need of inconveniencing you. Ned and I can find him." To prove it, she turned and moved along the sidewalk.

"No inconvenience, my dear. I'm headed in that direction myself." He matched his stride to hers.

She tried to tell herself it was silly, this uneasiness. Still, there was something in the way Brook glanced at her, a particular light in his eyes that seemed . . . different.

They turned the corner. She looked up and down the street, but there was no sign of Gibson and the Applegate carriage.

"I wonder where he is," Brook said. "Not a cab in sight either. Come with me to my office, and I'll call for one."

"That isn't necessary. Really. Ned and I will walk home. It's a pleasant morning, and it isn't all that far."

His hand closed around her upper arm. "Please, Diana. I insist. I feel as if this is my fault. Allow me to make it up to you."

From the window in the library, Tyson saw the return of the carriage. He waited for Diana and Ned to come into the house, anxious to know how things had gone with Pauline, hoping nothing had gone awry to shake the foundations of his marriage once again. He wasn't really afraid of that happening, but Pauline could be unpredictable.

Tired of waiting, he headed toward the back of the house, guessing Diana had stopped to talk to her mother and his father in the garden before coming inside. But she wasn't there. Nor were their parents.

Peculiar.

He strode down the path toward the carriage shed. When he arrived, he saw Gibson and Fernando leading the team toward one of the paddocks.

"Gibson!"

The coachman stopped and turned.

"Where are Mrs. Applegate and Ned?"

"At the hotel, sir."

Tyson frowned. "You left her there?"

"She sent down a hotel message boy to tell me they were staying for lunch with Miss Kingston and I was to return home as they would hire a cab when finished."

Lunch with Pauline? That seemed unlikely. Didn't it? Pauline Kingston wasn't the forgive-and-forget sort. He couldn't see her issuing such an invitation, no matter what Diana said to her.

Maybe he should go into town. Then again, Diana hadn't wanted him along. She'd felt the responsibility was hers and had been determined to see it through on her own. She wouldn't welcome his interference now.

Turning on his heel, he started back toward the house at a slower pace. He rubbed the back of his neck, wishing he knew why this bothered him so much. It shouldn't, but it did.

Upchurch opened the back porch door as Tyson started up the steps. "I was coming for you, sir. There are some gentlemen to see you. I showed them into the parlor."

"Did they give their names?"

"Yes, sir. A Mr. Crawley. I didn't catch the other gentleman's name."

Crawley, calling at his home. And it could only be about the second matter he'd asked the investigator to look into. Diana's family. Finding Dillon Macartan had turned out well. Tyson could only hope the same would hold true again.

When he reached the parlor entrance, he stopped. Lawrence Crawley stood near the front windows while another man looked at photographs lining a table near the far wall. The stranger was tall with the build of a working man, something attested to by his attire—cotton shirt, Levi's, and boots. He held a hat by its wide brim in his left hand.

Tyson cleared his throat.

Both men turned.

Crawley grinned. "Mr. Applegate, I have more good news." He motioned for the other man to come forward. "This gentleman is Hugh Brennan. Turns out while I was looking into his whereabouts he was doing the same about your missus. Mr. Brennan, this is Tyson Applegate, your sister's husband."

They shook hands.

Afterward, Hugh pulled a piece of paper from his shirt pocket. A clipping from a newspaper, it looked like. When he unfolded it,

Tyson saw it was a photograph. A photograph of him and Diana from a recent campaign event. "Diana looks like our mother, even in this grainy photograph."

"Where did Mr. Crawley find you? How far have you come?"

"Not far. My wife and I live on a ranch along the Boise River. Our other sister and her family live in Frenchman's Bluff."

"Both of you, here? So close to Boise? All these years?"

"No." Hugh shook his head. "Not long. I didn't come west from Illinois until just over a year ago. Felicia grew up in Wyoming and moved to Frenchman's Bluff to teach school in '97. I found her last year, but locating Diana was more difficult."

"Excuse me a moment." Tyson went to the doorway and called for Upchurch. "Send Gibson into town at once. Tell him Mrs. Applegate is required at the house immediately."

Concern filled Upchurch's eyes. "Is something amiss, sir?"

"No, Upchurch. It's good news. The very best kind."

May 1900

When Tyson learned about the impending announcement of Diana's engagement, the earth seemed to shift beneath his feet.

For several months, he'd planned for his return to Idaho. Not to the home of his father but to the capital city—where, it so happened, his wife resided with her mother. How perfect was that? Detail after detail had fallen into place, concerning his new residence in Boise, concerning his run for the Senate seat, concerning his money that had been carefully kept out of his father's control.

It had all been so easy. Tyson had assumed it was a sign of God's blessing. Perhaps that's why the news of Diana's plans to marry another man hadn't alarmed him at first. He'd assumed even that would go away with little inconvenience to himself.

But he hadn't expected her to announce her engagement the night prior to the anticipated proclamation of his demise. Tomorrow had been the day he'd planned for her to learn she wasn't a widow.

He couldn't wait until tomorrow. He didn't want her to be subject to public ridicule. He would have to stop her tonight. It wasn't the way he'd imagined their first meeting after so many years apart, but it couldn't be helped.

TWENTY-EIGHT

Brook's second-floor office was empty of secretary and clerks on this Saturday morning, and the silence inside the brick building felt almost eerie to Diana as she waited for the cab he'd promised would come soon. Or maybe it was the way Brook stood before the closed door, almost as if he were barring it.

Oh, dear. Her imagination was running away with her. This was Brook Calhoun, a man steeped in convention. She'd spent a great deal of time with him over the better part of two years. He was the least confrontational person she knew. One thing that had drawn her to him was that she'd known what to expect from him—the ordinary, the regular, the simple, the anticipated. Never once had he surprised her. At least, not that she could recall.

"Brook, I feel as if we are inconveniencing you. We truly could walk home."

"No, Diana. I insist you stay."

There was that nervous shiver up her spine again.

"I'm curious," Brook said. "Why take in this boy? He's nothing to you. He's a nobody. Have you no plans to start your own family that you must take in an orphan?"

It was almost funny. She'd been thinking how Brook never

surprised her—and now he did. The question seemed out of character . . . and highly inappropriate.

He continued, "Your husband must have some reason for it. Don't you think so?"

"Other than to try to give Ned a good home, no. That's the only reason." *Unless perhaps to please me.*

"I don't believe that's the only reason. Have you ever considered who his father might be?"

Her unsettled feelings grew stronger. "Come along, Ned. It's time for us to leave." She stood and reached for the boy's hand.

"Diana, sit down." The words came out soft and cool, more threatening than a shout, and the look in his eyes was unnatural . . . Unhinged.

Seeing it, she became afraid. *Oh, God. Help us.*

Instinct caused her to step away from her chair and move to the opposite side of the room, drawing Ned with her. She hoped Brook would follow her. He did. In fact, he closed the distance between them and grabbed hold of her wrists. Diana prayed Ned, the little street urchin who used to know how to protect himself, was paying attention and would guess what she wanted him to do.

"You ruined me, Diana." Brook's grip tightened. "You and that husband of yours. Ruined me. And you must pay."

Now, Ned. Go now.

As if Diana had shouted the words instead of thought them, Ned shot away from her and reached the door in a heartbeat. She saw him yank it open and disappear through the opening.

Run, Ned. Run!

Brook's hands released her wrists, then grabbed her upper arms. He shook her. Hard. "Where does he think he's going? The little brat." With a shouted curse, he struck her with the back of his hand. Pain exploded inside her head and a scream was torn from her throat. Only his grip on her arm with his other hand kept her from falling to the floor.

Oh, God. Help me. Ned, hurry. Run. Run.

Tyson couldn't recall a time, not even on the day the coachman was hired to work for the Applegates, when Gibson had stood in the entry hall of the house. His appearance there now, hat in hand, brought Tyson to his feet. "Gibson?"

"Mrs. Applegate wasn't at the hotel, sir. Miss Kingston denied asking her to stay for lunch. Sir, I don't know what to say. I had no reason not to believe the messenger boy."

"It's all right, Gibson. I'm sure there was simply a misunderstanding. Perhaps Diana took Ned to a restaurant for lunch before returning. Or maybe she is trying on a dress she saw in a shop window."

The coachman said nothing, but his expression spoke clearly of his doubt. And Tyson didn't believe his own suppositions. Hard to put his finger on why. They were plausible. Now he wished Lawrence Crawley hadn't left. Maybe the investigator would have understood the reason for his unsettled feelings.

He turned toward his remaining guest. "Mr. Brennan, it seems Diana is—"

The front door opened—drawing all eyes when it crashed into the wall. Ned tumbled into view, ending up on his stomach at Gibson's feet.

"She's . . . in trouble." The boy pushed himself onto his knees, gasping for breath as he spoke. "Miss Diana's . . . in trouble."

Tyson crossed the room in an instant. "What happened, Ned? Where is she?"

"With that fella. The one you don't like."

"The one I don't like?"

"You know. He come to dinner. Same night I took that brace-let. You were real mad 'cause of him."

There was a moment or two of confused thoughts before Tyson understood. "Brook Calhoun?"

"Yeah, that's him. I got away and come for you."

Got away? Tyson's heart stilled in his chest. "Where, Ned? Where are they?"

"I'll show you. But we gotta hurry. He looked plumb loco."

Tyson thought to go for his horse, but Gibson stopped him. "The carriage is out front, sir. It will be faster."

"Then let's go."

From behind Tyson, Hugh Brennan said, "I'm coming too."

In quick succession, they ran out the door.

Diana sat in the chair Brook had pushed her into, on the far side of the room from the exit. Her jaw throbbed where he'd hit her.

Brook paced the width of the office, never getting too far from her. He continued to mutter unintelligible things beneath his breath, but every so often she caught a word or two. Enough to allow her to piece together what must have pushed him over the edge of sanity.

And he was, without a doubt, insane. This wasn't a man who was angry. This was a man who'd lost reason. There was murder in his eyes. He wanted to kill, and he didn't care who he made his victim. Since she alone was with him—

Dread shivered through her. And sorrow. Sorrow because she might die before she could tell Tyson all he meant to her, how much she loved and adored him. Regret because she might die before she could tell her mother one more time how blessed she was to have been raised by the Fishers. Remorse because she might die before she could see Ned grow to manhood, loved and cared for the way a child deserved.

Fear not! On the heels of that thought came peace. Real peace. If God was for her, who could be against her? She smiled, comforted.

"How dare you laugh?" Brook slapped her again. "How dare you laugh at me?"

She hadn't noticed him come that close again, had stopped watching him pace as those she loved filled her thoughts. She hadn't expected Brook to strike her again. "I wasn't laughing," she answered, tears filling her eyes.

"You were. You were. You did this to me on purpose." He called her a foul name.

Until today, she wouldn't have thought Brook even knew such a word, let alone would speak it to her. She stood. No, it felt as if an unseen hand lifted her. When she spoke, she sounded calm and unafraid. "Brook, when was the last time you slept?"

"Sleep?"

"You look tired. You should sit down and rest. You've been working much too hard."

If she could get a little closer to the door . . . put a little more distance between them . . .

Brook might have lost touch with reality, but he wasn't blind. He saw the small step she took to the side and he reached for her. That was the moment the door burst open. Diana saw Tyson a heartbeat before the crook of Brook's arm pressed against her throat, choking her.

But it was all right. She still wasn't afraid. Tyson had come for her and God was with them both.

Tyson was familiar with the look in Brook's eyes. He'd seen it in the eyes of soldiers who'd broken under the strain of battle. Ned was right. Brook was plumb loco. Crazy enough to do anything.

Crazy enough to kill Diana.

He kept his gaze locked on Brook as he took a few steps to the right. "You don't want to hurt her, Calhoun. Diana's done nothing wrong. She's been a friend to you."

Tyson felt a little crazy himself as he watched Diana grow paler beneath Brook's grip. But he had to be careful not to alarm her assailant. In the meantime, he hoped Hugh Brennan would be ready to act when the time came.

"I'm not letting her go." Brook's eyes narrowed. His voice was filled with petulance. "Not until somebody pays for all the trouble she's made for me."

Tyson took another step to the right. "I completely understand why you're upset, Calhoun. I would be too." He didn't know what had pushed Brook over the edge, but he would say anything if he thought it might defuse the situation. "But this isn't how to settle the matter. These things need to be talked about. You're a smart man, a reasonable man. Anybody can see that. Why involve her?"

If Tyson moved too soon, Brook might break her neck with one swift yank. If Tyson didn't move soon enough, Brook might choke the life from her while they stood talking. He would have to risk it. He would have to—

From the left, something sailed across the room, striking Brook in the head. Tyson vaulted into action, and a moment later, he held Diana in his arms, drawing her away from the crumpled form of Brook Calhoun. A bottle of ink spilled its contents over the floor near Brook's head. Tyson looked behind him.

Hugh shrugged. "We played a lot of baseball as kids in Chicago. I had a pretty good arm back then."

"I'd say you still do."

Tyson felt Diana pull away from him, her attention also on the other man in the room.

Hugh smiled. "Hello, Diana. Your husband thought you might want to see me again after all these years."

She looked up at Tyson, disbelief in her beautiful eyes. He answered the silent question with a nod. Then he drew her close again, pressing her cheek against his chest, kissing the crown of her head again and again.

Her brother would have to wait awhile longer to speak to her. Tyson had no intention of letting go of her just yet. Not until she had no doubts left how much he loved her. Not until he'd kissed her until she was breathless. Not until he'd held her in his arms throughout the night. Not until she confessed she would never stray too far from his embrace.

And maybe not even then.

EPILOGUE

Thanksgiving Day 1900

As Tyson blessed the feast they were about to eat, Diana silently said her own words of thanks to God. She couldn't remember a Thanksgiving when she'd sat down at a table with more than three or four people. Today, including the two infants and one toddler (Diana's nephews and niece) asleep upstairs, there were fifteen of them. Fifteen!

My family. They're all my family.

She opened her eyes to take in the sight of them, and joy flooded her heart. What a beautiful gathering they made—her brother, Hugh, and his wife, Julia, and Julia's mother, Madeline Crane; her sister, Felicia, and her husband, Colin Murphy, and their twelve-year-old daughter, Charity; Diana's father-in-law and her mother, a couple who were preparing for their wedding on New Year's Day; Dillon Macartan; Ned, who would soon legally wear the last name of Applegate; and of course, Tyson. What an abundance of people for her to love and be loved by.

Thank You, God, for each one of them.

A moment after Tyson said, "Amen," the room filled with happy conversations and laughter. It was all slightly chaotic, but Diana loved it for that very reason.

Was it selfish of her to be at least a little thankful Tyson hadn't won the Senate seat in the recent election? If he'd won, they would be preparing to leave for Washington, DC. Now they would be staying in Boise, in their home, and Diana could easily envision many more gatherings with her brother and sister and their families. She could imagine more children sitting at the table as they came of age and more infants sleeping in the upstairs bedrooms, her babies among them. She'd begun to suspect there might be an Applegate heir as early as next Independence Day.

Tyson's gaze caught her attention, and she knew he'd read her thoughts. He smiled, and she felt his contentment in her heart. It amazed her how hard he had worked to be elected, yet how at peace he was after the loss. He'd told her there were other ways for him to serve God and country. All he need do, he'd said, was seek God's will and follow where He led.

Once more she looked around the table, and as her gaze lingered upon the faces of her precious expanded family, she remembered her wedding day—once a memory that brought sorrow but now brought such joy. She recalled the minister saying, *"Dearly beloved . . . "*

And it was true! She *was* Tyson's beloved, as he was hers. What a miracle it was, two hurt, stubborn, rebellious people finding their way into each other's heart. But as she sat there, looking around that table, she heard God whisper those same two words, *Dearly beloved*, and she understood them as she'd never understood before.

When God looked upon her and upon Tyson and upon every person seated around this table, He called them His dearly beloved.

And that was the greatest miracle of all.

READING GROUP GUIDE

1. What would you say is the major theme of *Beloved*? Did the opening surprise you? Could you relate to the main characters in the novel?

2. Like the prodigal son, Tyson Applegate lived a dissolute existence for many years. While he didn't waste his fortune, he did discover a barrenness of his soul. Have you tried to fill an emptiness within that God wanted to fill with His Spirit? How did you finally recognize it?

3. Diana Applegate had been wounded by many losses in her brief life. To protect herself from more hurt, she planned to marry where there was no love. Have you ever avoided love because of the risk that comes with it? What happened because of your choices?

4. Tyson's sins were legion, but he found forgiveness in Christ. Should he have asked or expected the same forgiveness from Diana? Could you have forgiven him?

5. Jeremiah underwent a change of heart during the story, but not in the same way as his son. Is it possible for God to change a person before they belong to Him? Do those changes always lead a person to Him?

6. Tyson and Diana learned to love Ned and wanted the boy to stay with them. But both of them had to become willing to let

go if that was God's will. Have you ever had to let go of something or someone? How easy or hard was it to do?

7. Tyson discovered that "conditional trust" wasn't trust at all. Has God ever asked you to trust Him in what seems an impossible circumstance? What was the outcome?

"Hatcher is a consistent
'must read' author."

—*Romantic Times*, TOP PICK! review of *Betrayal*

 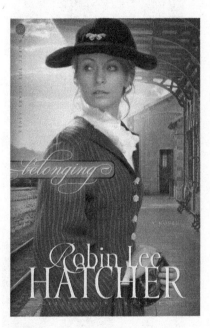

The Where the Heart Lives Series

Available in print and e-book

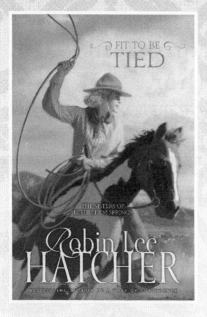

The sisters of
Bethlehem Springs—
smart, confident
women who are
not afraid to defy
convention, live
their own dreams,
and share their
lives . . . if the right
man comes along.

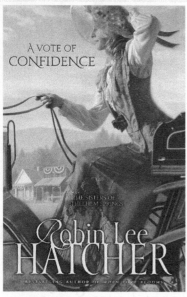

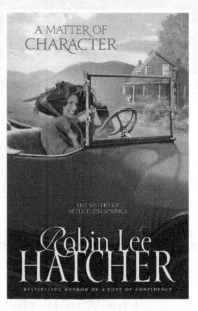

The Sisters of Bethlehem Springs Series

Available in print and e-book

Allison believes God promised
to save her marriage. So why did
He allow it to end in divorce?

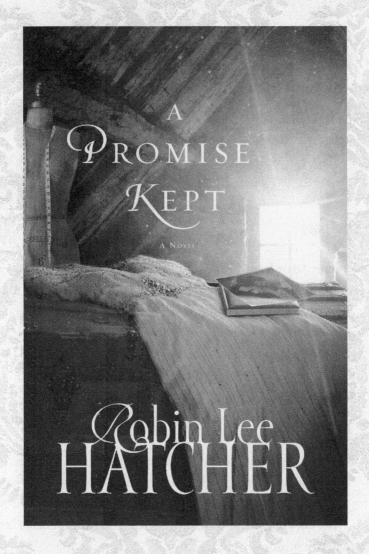

Available January 2014

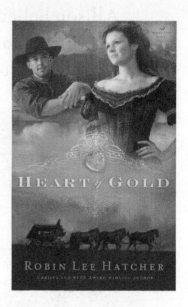

AN EXERPT FROM *HEART OF GOLD*

ROBIN LEE HATCHER

May 1864

Shannon Adair leaned close to the door as the stagecoach slowed, trying to catch her first glimpse of Grand Coeur, wanting it to be more than she had any right to hope it would be. She'd said good-bye to everything and everyone she loved in order to come with her father to the Idaho Territory. She was both scared and excited now that the dirty, bonejarring, difficult, and sometimes treacherous journey was at an end.

The coach jerked to a stop, and the driver called down, "Grand Coeur, folks."

Shannon glanced toward her father, seated across from her.

The good reverend gave her a weary smile. "We are here at last."

"So it would seem."

The door opened, and the driver offered his hand. "Let me help you down, miss."

"Thank you." Shannon placed her gloved fingers in the palm of his hand. "You are ever so kind."

The driver bent the brim of his dust-covered hat with his free hand, acknowledging her comment.

Once out of the coach, she turned a slow circle, taking in her surroundings. Her stomach plummeted. This was Grand Coeur? Merciful heavens! It was not better than she'd hoped. It was *worse* than she'd feared.

The street they were on was lined on both sides by unpainted wooden buildings of various shapes and sizes. The boardwalks in front of the buildings were uneven, sometimes nonexistent. And the hillsides that surrounded the valley had been stripped clean of trees, undoubtedly for the wood used to throw up this ugly, sprawling goldmining town of more than five thousand souls.

"Oh, Father," she whispered. "Whatever shall we do here?"

"Don't look so despairing, Shannon."

She turned to find her father had disembarked from the coach and now stood nearby.

"We knew it would be different from home," he said. "And we are needed here."

More than they'd been needed in the war-torn South, where he'd ministered to his flock and she'd been able to help nurse the injured?

As if he'd heard her unspoken question, he said, "I have always tried to answer God's call, even when I don't understand it completely. Would you have me do differently now?"

"No, Father."

The lie tasted bitter on her tongue. She would have him do differently. She would have him decide to go back to Virginia, to recognize that God wanted him to be there to help rebuild when the war was over. When the South no longer had to fight for its existence, the Confederacy would need men like her father. He was a natural leader with a head for governing and a heart for the kingdom of heaven. He was strong in his faith and able to forgive and show others the grace of God.

What on earth made him believe the Lord wanted him in such a place as this?

"Reverend Adair?" a voice called.

Shannon and her father turned in unison to see a rotund man in a black suit hastening toward them.

"Are you Delaney Adair?"

"Yes, sir. I am."

The man stopped in front of them and thrust out his hand. When her father took it, the man gave it a hearty shake. "We've been watching for you on every stage for the past week. Welcome. Welcome. We're glad you've come. I'm Henry Rutherford."

"It's a pleasure to meet you, Mr. Rutherford. May I introduce my daughter, Miss Shannon Adair."

"How do you do, miss?" Henry bowed in her direction.

She decided a simple smile and nod of her head would need to suffice. If she opened her mouth, she was certain she would say something disparaging about Grand Coeur.

"My wife's got the parsonage all ready for you. 'Course, it probably isn't what you're used to. Kinda small and plain. But we hope you'll be comfortable there, you and your daughter."

"I'm sure we will be," her father replied.

Shannon wasn't at all sure.

"I've got some men with me to help with your luggage." Henry turned and waved his helpers forward. The three men were a roughlooking bunch, with scruffy beards and weathered faces. Their trousers, held up by suspenders, were well-worn, as were the dirt-encrusted boots on their feet. The sleeves of their loose-fitting shirts had been rolled up to their elbows, revealing dark skin on their arms. Miners, she supposed, who spent every hour of daylight panning for gold in the streams and rivers somewhere nearby. At least that's how she'd been told it was done.

Shannon's father identified their trunks and one small crate, then he took hold of her arm at the elbow and the two of them followed Henry Rutherford down a narrow side street.

She saw the church first. Built on the hillside, its steeple piercing the blue sky, the house of worship had white clapboard siding, giving it an air of elegance in comparison to the mostly unpainted buildings in the town. There was even a round stained-glass window over the entrance.

Perhaps Grand Coeur was not completely uncivilized if the citizens had taken the time to build such a church.

Her moment of hope crumbled the instant Mr. Rutherford pointed out the parsonage. It was little more than a shack. Crude, cramped, and completely unsuitable.

Oh, Father. You cannot mean for us to live here.

Matthew Dubois opened the door of the Wells, Fargo & Company express office and stepped inside. At the far end of the spacious room, William Washburn looked up from the open ledger on the desk. The instant he recognized Matthew, he grinned.

"Well, I'll be hanged. Is that you, Matt?"

"It's me, Bill."

"You're not the new agent they sent?"

"I am."

William rose and came to meet him in the center of the office, giving his hand a hearty shake. "You tellin' me you're givin' up drivin' for the company?"

"Only temporarily."

William cocked an eyebrow.

"My sister's ailing and needs a place to stay—Alice and her son—until she's back on her feet. They don't have any family but me. She lost her husband in the first year of the war."

"Sorry to hear that. Right sorry."

Matthew acknowledged William's sympathy with a nod.

"Can't say Grand Coeur is the best place to bring a woman and young boy, but I reckon you already knew that."

Matthew nodded a second time. Over the years, he'd seen the ugly underbelly of more than one mining town between San Francisco and the Canadian border. He'd known Grand Coeur would be no better. But this was where his employer had sent him, so this was where he and his sister and nephew would live.

"Alice with you?"

"No. I don't expect her and the boy until the end of the week."

"The company told me they wanted a house for the new agent. Couldn't figure out why the spare room upstairs wouldn't do, but I guess it's 'cause of the family."

The comment needed no response from Matthew.

"Might as well show you the place." William turned toward the door leading into a back room. "Ray?"

A few moments later, a young clerk appeared in the doorway.

"Yessir?"

"Mind things. I'll be back directly."

"Yessir."

"Come on, Matt. I'll show you where you'll be living."

The two men went outside. The Wells, Fargo coach was no longer in sight. Matthew's replacement driver had already taken it to the station to harness fresh horses for the journey back down to Boise City.

William motioned toward the east. "We'll go thisaway."

Matthew fell into step beside him.

"Your sister and nephew ought to be comfortable. The house is away from the center of the town. Up there on the hillside." He pointed as they turned a corner. "Bit quieter in the evenings, if you know what I mean."

He knew. The saloons did great business at night in a place like Grand Coeur, and the center of town could get rowdy. Better to keep his sister—an attractive widow in ill health—away from the eyes of men starved for female attention.

The street they were on carried them up the steep hillside. Up ahead and to his left, he saw a white church complete with steeple. Off to the right were a half dozen two-story homes. Doubtless the residences of the town's more prosperous citizens. And, surprisingly, it was to one of these houses that William took him.

"Bill, you don't mean this for us."

"I do, indeed." He took a key from his pocket.

"I won't be able to afford the rent."

"Yes, you will. The fellow who built it was killed 'fore he could move in. Company got the house, furnishings and all, for next to nothin'. Not sure how or why. Only know they're rentin' it to you for a song. Now I know who they sent, I reckon I know why they're doin' it. They don't want to lose you when the time comes for you to start drivin' again."

Matthew took pride in the job he did. He was one of the top drivers in the country. Maybe the top driver. If a freight company wanted their stage to get where it was going and get there on time with the cargo safe and secure, Matthew Dubois was their man. He could only hope he wouldn't be gone from the job so long that Wells, Fargo forgot they felt that way about him.

William opened the door and the two men entered the house. It wasn't unusually large. Nothing like the palatial homes of many of those who'd made their fortunes in gold and silver around the West. But it was more spacious than any place he'd lived before.

The downstairs had a front parlor, a small dining room, and a kitchen with cupboards, a butler's pantry, and a large stove. Upstairs there were three bedrooms and an honest-to-goodness plunger closet. He'd heard about such things. Just never thought he'd live to see one.

It ought to please Alice.

It would be nice to please his sister. He hadn't done much of that when they were younger. He'd been too stubborn and selfish back then, too determined to have a life of his own that didn't include watching after his baby sister.

If their mother was looking down from heaven, she had to be mighty disappointed by the choices he'd made in the years since her death. Maybe looking after Alice and her son, Todd, would make up for some of those poor choices.

Besides, he supposed a few months living in this house and working in the Wells, Fargo office wouldn't be too bad. He wasn't much for being in one place for long. He preferred wide-open spaces to towns with people packed in like cookies in a tin. But Alice would be strong and healthy before long. Then he'd be back on a coach, holding the reins of a team of horses racing along a narrow road, dust flying up behind him in a cloud.

The story continues in *Heart of Gold* by Robin Lee Hatcher.